Survivor Lessons

Survivor Lessons

Essays on Communication and Reality Television

Edited by MATTHEW J. SMITH
and ANDREW F. WOOD

McFarland & Company, Inc., Publishers
Jefferson, North Carolina, and London

LIBRARY OF CONGRESS CATALOGUING-IN-PUBLICATION DATA

Survivor lessons : essays on communication and reality television /
   edited by Matthew J. Smith and Andrew F. Wood.
      p.   cm.
   Includes bibliographical references and index.

   ISBN 0-7864-1668-8 (softcover : 50# alkaline paper)

   1. Reality television programs—United States.   I. Smith,
Matthew J., 1971–   II. Wood, Andrew F.
PN1992.8.R43S87   2003
791.45'6—dc21   2003014407

British Library cataloguing data are available

Cover photograph ©2003 PhotoSpin.

Manufactured in the United States of America

*McFarland & Company, Inc., Publishers
   Box 611, Jefferson, North Carolina 28640
      www.mcfarlandpub.com*

Contents

III. LESSONS BEYOND THE LENS

Introduction: Culture, Communication, and Community Revealed in and through Reality Television

Matthew J. Smith and *Andrew F. Wood*

> "From this tiny Malaysian fishing village, these 16 Americans
> are beginning the adventure of a lifetime. They have volunteered
> to be marooned for 39 days on mysterious Borneo. This is their
> story. This is *Survivor*." (*Survivor* host Jeff Probst)

The shows are cheap, cheesy, chock full of clichés, and, as the above quotation suggests, overly melodramatic. Lighting torches, eating bugs, and wearing loincloths hardly seem like the staff of hip TV. But *Survivor* and its many reproductions have offered a bizarre blend of ethnographic exhibit, adventure tale, and family drama that has grabbed the attention of hundreds of millions of people around the world. As we rounded the turn into the twenty-first century, it seemed that every producer was searching for the new wave of reality television and that every viewer was transfixed by each new version of the same basic plot: introduce a diverse group of people, put them into situations bound to induce conflict, and watch them squirm. While numerous permutations of these dynamics vary from series to series, the larger theme—television as a process through which we examine our own interpersonal dynamics—remains. Reality television continues to demand critique because television remains such a reality to many of us.

The genre is hardly new. Television has always striven for "reality"

1

since its inception as a largely live medium. Indeed, in the early days of television broadcasts such as Edward R. Murrow's *See It Now* featured the spectacle of bringing reality into one's living room. For instance, *See It Now* amazed the nation when it broadcast side-by-side images of the Atlantic and Pacific oceans simultaneously. Even as television grew more scripted when situation comedies and dramas came to dominate broadcasting schedules, reality had a powerful way of intruding into the typically polished world of the small screen. One can recall the image of Walter Cronkite removing his glasses and pausing to compose himself before announcing the assassination of John Kennedy in 1963. Cronkite, a trained broadcaster, was nonetheless transformed into a supremely ordinary man facing an extraordinary crisis. His reaction, his tentativeness, his humanity bought the reality of the national tragedy into the living rooms of millions of Americans. Likewise, one may remember multiple camera angles that captured the last moments of the space shuttle *Challenger* as it disintegrated before the world in 1986. However, the singular power of that first glimpse (videotaped or otherwise) as television showed the Challenger crew meeting their fate could be called nothing less than "real." Even more recently, the television broadcast of the O. J. Simpson murder trial called into question the increasingly blurred boundaries between fact and fiction, between news and entertainment, between what was coverage of an event and what was spectacle for our consumption.

What, then, is this genre called "reality television"? Is it live? Not necessarily. Is it completely unscripted? Rarely. As a genre, reality television involves placing "ordinary" people before the camera and deriving some entertainment value from the perception of their activities being unscripted. This genre did not begin with *Survivor*, of course, but *Survivor* introduced an element that neither live-television documentaries (such as the 1970s documentary *An American Family*) or dramas (such as the 1990s' *The Real World*) could boast: competition. Rendered safe through its artifice, the ritualized conflicts of *Survivor* provided a means for a jaded public to experience some vicarious thrills. In response to this cultural phenomenon, pundits and cynics have decried reality programming as pandering to the lowest common denominator without necessarily analyzing what this trend has to teach us about the media or ourselves.

Even this critique, however, seems benign in the wake of the televised terror attacks of September 11, 2001. Surely, we have all seen far too much reality on our televisions since first glimpsing those burning images of passenger jets turned into flying bombs, and naturally we might ask: Can shows such as *Survivor* justifiably be called "reality television"? Even before that horrific day, social observers warned that reality television had slipped off the prime axis of popular consciousness, becoming merely another fad that had overstayed its welcome. But since the attacks, and the reminders of the deadly reality of war and its many human consequences, one might propose this topic to be all too facile. Hardly a barometer of public life, reality television may no longer seem worthy of scholarly analysis.

We disagree. This volume is not an historical account of a dead genre, nor is it merely an outdated response to a failed idea. Rather, these authors have sought to reveal the strategies employed by television producers, directors, and writers (as well as the ordinary "actors" of these performances) to craft an experience that reflects on a larger theme in public life, one that endures even after September 11. *Survivor Lessons: Essays on Communication and Reality Television* reflects the emergence of a "corporate reality" in which self and society becomes mediated through commercial artifacts. Here, a key distinction must be made between traditional commercial television that enables viewers to imagine separate realities between the consumer appeal of advertisements, dramatic narration of the stories between the ads, and interpretation of those stories for individual purposes. Reality television continues to demand our attention because its stories replace our "real ones," becoming more important, more immediate, more "real" than our lived experience.

From this perspective, *Survivor Lessons* adopts a critical perspective on reality programming, one that evaluates what goes on within the text of such artifacts and how these artifacts reflect or affect the larger culture within which they are embedded in order to learn from them. Indeed, *Survivor* and its various imitators have become rich sources for discussion, both within and beyond the academy. Suddenly, the communicative strategies of "castaways," "housemates," and "competitors" have become texts subject to careful analysis. One of the editors of this volume recalls conversations with a first-time viewer of *Survivor* who caught the show upon its first season finale. Previously distant from the rumblings of discussion about the Machiavellian intricacies of its participants, the viewer became obsessed by the show before the first torch was extinguished. Within minutes, a series of magazine articles, news stories, late night television jokes, and workplace conversations assumed rich meaning and personal significance for this viewer. Suddenly, a whole lot of public life made sense. What remains to be analyzed is the ways in which shows like *Survivor* shape and reflect contemporary mechanisms of community, an extension on the ideological labor and personal analysis employed by each viewer of these sorts of shows.

This book is a forum where scholars extend those analyses in thoughtful and rigorous ways, addressing issues of interpersonal and group dynamics that occur within these series and of the larger cultural effects that have been wrought in the wake of their broadcast. Indeed, given the audience's phenomenal response to reality television, the producers' rush to create more and more series of the ilk, and now the scholarly critiques left in their wake, we stand to learn from them a good deal about the media industry, norms of communication, and the impact of media products upon us. Part of this approach emerges from the tradition in media studies holding that audiences actively reshape, re-articulate, and reconstruct the texts provided them by popular media. As much as "producers" imagine themselves empowered to fashion consumer experience through astute selection of scripts, stars, and situations, folks who watch reality television shows often bring radically different expectations to the experience. Watching television is, therefore, not quite as passive as some critics have alleged. The nature and purpose of the act presents opportunities to ask big questions about the nature of reality itself. The scholarly essays collected here help to make sense of what television shows like *Survivor* reflect of our culture, our values, and our interpersonal communication practices.

The underlying themes of "Culture, Communication, and Community Revealed in and through Reality Television" rest upon an important foundation. The authors resist the snobbish divide between "high" and "low" culture, and the corresponding assumption that certain texts are simply worthier of analysis than others. We share the assumption of many pop culture researchers that our topic is more than simply an excuse to watch television. Rather, we seek to understand a series of texts whose value lies in their articulation of values. Students of popular culture generally agree that the mediated intersection of artifacts like television shows, novels, comics strips, top 40 music, and other texts offer a shifting matrix of meaning through which significant themes of a culture may be understood. Certainly, one may reveal stirring insight about life through careful explication of Marcel Duchamp's *Nude Descending a Staircase*. However, one may find more useful insight into the manners in which folks make sense of postmodern life by watching a few episodes of *The Simpsons*. Moreover, the conflicts between various sub-cultures in their desire to articulate their identities, contest alternative interpretations, and shape some "homeland" for their adherents become apparent, or at least accessible, through the texts of popular culture. Therefore, shows such as *Survivor* provide important clues for the ways in which culture has been influenced by reality television programming.

Survivor began to build that sense of community in 2000, when CBS aired its 16 hour-long episodes during the summer. Historically, networks have seen few successful new series launched in the summer. However, by the time *Survivor* reached its finale on August 23, 2000, an audience of nearly 52 million television viewers tuned in, making it one of television's most watched summertime broadcasts (Huff, 2000). Interest in the series and its denouement had become a national obsession by then, having become the focus of much media attention as well as the topic of everyday conversation.

The series was given shape by producer Mark Burnett (2000), who had already produced similar reality programs for European television. Burnett's idea was to take 16 unknown contestants and place them in a hostile environment. The contestants would find themselves challenged by living conditions that deprived them of everyday creature comforts like shelter, by contests of physical and mental endurance, and by the social dynamics of learning to cooperate with complete strangers. The twist on the series was that the number of competitors was whittled down as contestants voted to remove members of the group from the island. This meant that a contestant not only had to play well when it came to relay races and trivia questions, they also had to play well with others, maneuvering themselves through a tricky field of alliances and betrayals on the way to the determining the sole survivor. And what incentive was offered to the participants to endure more than a month of such pressure: a grand prize of one million dollars to the last person sparred in the competition.

Meanwhile, the home viewer could watch the contestants' every titillating comment, every clandestine meeting, and every personal confession from the comfort of an easy chair. The omnipresent camera crews filming the contests captured every moment of the ordeal and then neatly edited it down to the juiciest moments for the home viewer.

Survivor gripped the American psyche that summer, transforming us into a nation of voyeurs who shared a vicarious adventure in the South China Sea. The media machine was quick to seize upon commercial interests in the collective fascination. In short order, Burnett (2000) published his behind the scenes look at the show, million-dollar-winner Richard Hatch (2000) soon followed with his book, and CBS unleashed an array of products ranging from videocassettes with never-before-seen footage to designer wear emblazoned with the show's logo. CBS subsequently launched *Survivor: The Australian Outback* with an impressive premiere slot immediately following the Super Bowl on January 28, 2001, before moving it to its regular time slot on Thursdays at 8 P.M. Eastern Standard Time. Although for well over a decade NBC had ruled Thursday nights with its "Must See TV" line-up of situation comedies (including the perennially popular *Friends*), interest in the new *Survivor* series successfully dethroned NBC, and an average of 28.5 million watched the second series on a regular basis (Kloer, 2001).

The success of both *Survivor* series and the looming threat of a writers' and actors' strike in the summer of 2001 (which would have crippled production on traditional sitcoms and dramas) seemed to inspire network executives to move a whole host of reality programs into production. *Survivor* became such a ratings success for CBS that it spawned not only a succession of spin-offs, including *Survivor: The Australian Outback* and *Survivor: Africa*, but numerous imitators. Indeed, both broadcasting and cable networks responded to *Survivor's* popularity with a wave of reality-based programs, rushing into production series like *The Amazing Race, Bands on the Run, Big Brother, Bootcamp, Cannonball Run, Fear Factor, Lost, Love Cruise, Making the Band, Manhunt, Murder in Small Town X, The Mole, Popstars, Temptation Island,* and *WWF Tough Enough,* among many others. Certainly, the volume of imitators itself provokes questions about the attraction of the genre.

Each of the chapters in this volume tackles issues of reality television from a different angle and reaches some insightful conclusions through an array of critical methods. This is a multi-disciplinary volume of essays, pulling on the talents of scholars in communication studies, political science, psychology, and sociology. At this point, a fair question may be asked: How is such an eclectic collections of voices superior to an assemblage from a single discipline? We respond, joyously, that a little intellectual rough and tumble between such disparate perspectives is long overdue, that our protective cathedrals of words, histories, citations, methods, and privileges hardly reflect the broader currents of popular conversation about shows like *Survivor*. It's about time that edited volumes look more like conversational salons than uniform armies. Of course, even though no two authors in this volume approached the phenomenon in quite the same fashion, concurrent themes have emerged in the wake of their investigations, and we have used those commonalties to organize their contributions into three sections.

The chapters in the first section, "Lessons about Reality," address the larger social contexts into which this resurgence in reality television must be factored. Contributions in this section examine the history and structure of these programs, revealing insight into the social processes that have governed the business of producing programs within this genre. We begin with a contribution by Terri Toles Patkin, who explores the unreality of reality television by critically examining the manner in which these shows construct the individuals and the situation portrayed within them. April L. Roth then frames *Survivor* in terms familiar to public relations specialists, providing us with a view of the series as a purposeful and masterful work of media engineering. Next, we turn to an examination of the publicity rights associated with the contestants in reality shows. Debora Halbert reviews the legal and social ramifications of the contract wouldbe contestants sign. Finally in this section, Sean Baker provides an historical analysis of the medium, reaching back to television's formative years to provide some context for the most recent surge in popularity for reality programming. His essay helps to further an understanding of how television has sought to present, if only to mimic, reality.

In the second section, "Lessons about Playing Social Games," we examine how perennial issues of interpersonal dynamics such as conflict, nonverbal communication, and group decision-making have contributed to the dramatic tension of and ultimately people's interest in watching such series. We open this section with a chapter that studies how conflict among the participants helps to shape the internal reality in a variety of reality television programs, ranging from *Survivor* to *The Real World*. Ellis Godard contends that while the patterns captured on film are parallel to everyday confrontations, reality television may focus on atypical social geometries given the nature of their being edited and packaged for viewers. In the next chapter, R. Thomas Boone investigates how contestants use cues based on nonverbal communication to detect deception among their fellow players. In particular, Boone scrutinizes the behavior of several participants in the first two *Survivor* series to assess how capably certain players were able to strategize based on their reading of deception cues. Kathleen M. Propp approaches the contestants' behavior from another angle, that of decision-making within a group context. Propp analyzes the metaphors that contestants on the original series used to describe the manner in which they went about deciding how to act. Their language choices suggest that they characterized their decisions in terms of metaphors from benign politics to outright war. Finally in this section, Ed Wingenbach considers the contestants' voting behaviors from a political science perspective. He contends that *Survivor* presented an opportunity to observe voting behavior where one of the more popular theories of voter behavior, social choice theory, would dictate rational behaviors from the contestants. However, more often than not, the contestants did not vote in a rational way, and Wingenbach argues that other factors weighed heavily upon the votes—a lesson to be taken to heart in trying to understand voter behavior in larger social contexts as well.

The third section, "Lessons Beyond the Lens," features chapters that consider the impact or potential impact of shows like *Survivor* upon our culture, most especially the community of the workplace, to which the series has been compared to numerous times. For instance, Jennifer Thackaberry reviews how people have talked about *Survivor* in terms of "office politics" and about office politics in terms of *Survivor*. Thackaberry warns that this discourse, carried forward both in the news media and in everyday conversations, can encourage a cynical attitude about the workplace. Steven S. Vrooman also examines the cultural effects of the genre. He turns his focus to *Survivor: The Australian Outback*, paying attention to the way in which this very Western series was cast in the very non–Western Outback. Vrooman takes this latest exploitation of native culture to task, calling into question why the "Other" is still such a popular trope for Westerners to define themselves. Next, the degree to which the *Survivor* series reflects culture's ethical dimension is examined by Marilyn Fuss-Reineck. In her probe, Fuss-Reineck uses the National Communication Association's Credo for Ethical Communication as a framework and consults students in her advanced courses to question how the contestants' decisions measured up to contemporary ethical standards. As educated viewers, Fuss-Reineck's students proved to be capable of identifying ethical lapses displayed by the participants. Fuss-Reineck advocates that the Credo be introduced as a tool to help people with media analysis.

Finally, we conclude this volume with a contribution from Marcy R. Chvasta and Deanna L. Fassett. These co-authors share narratives of their own experiences in coming to the genre as viewers. In due course, they question not only the reality they see projected on the screen but the larger social reality surrounding the consumption of these shows. As they note, reality not only inspires television, but television also shapes our social reality.

It is our hope that the ideas presented in these chapters are valuable, but by no means the final word on reality television or its consequences. Indeed, we hope that they can serve as a starting point for further dialogue about the genre and the specific issues focused upon herein.

This project has provided the opportunity for the editors to get to know an impressive group of scholars who shared their time, talent, and patience as the book evolved. We are grateful to them for their willingness to share their top-flight analyses with us, and with you in this volume. We also wish to thank our respective departments at Wittenberg University and San José State University for the intellectual space and supportive atmosphere upon which we've come to rely when we collaborate. Finally, we thank our wives and best friends, Susan and Jenny. They tolerate our late night writing, provide counsel and clear-headed editing, and inspire us to aim higher. Reality television would be fake, indeed, without them.

References

Burnett, M., and Dugard, M. (2000). *Survivor: The Ultimate Game*. New York: TV Books.

Hatch, R. (2000). *101 Survival secrets: How to Win $1,000,000, Lose 100 Pounds, and Just Plain Live Happily*. New York: Lyons Press.

Huff, R. (2000, August 30). *Survivor* lands on its own special ratings island. *Daily News*, p. 85.

Kloer, P. (2001, May 4). Tennessee mom wins *Survivor*'s $1 million. *Atlanta Journal and Constitution*, p. 1E.

Survivor. (2000, May 31). CBS.

I

Lessons about Reality

1

Individual and Cultural Identity in the World of Reality Television

Terri Toles Patkin

Reality programming isn't about the threat of a writer's strike or inexpensive production or creativity and innovation or ratings and advertising dollars. It's not even about that frisson of illicit pleasure from sneaking a look into the neighbor's window or peering through the bushes in the back garden. The audience isn't watching just for the contrived tests and challenges or for the weekly ritual of eliminating someone we've come to love or hate. We watch because reality shows promise a window to the soul. We symbolically construct our own identities—both as individuals and culturally—through watching these select few compete. Culture, as an intersubjectively produced and publicly held phenomenon, relies on the media to create a false sense of community through vicarious experience instead of a real sense of community through shared experience.

Our need for community has been turned upside down by the mediation of culture, and so we find "virtual" communities, people who share common interests with us (Drucker & Gumpert, 1991; Giddens, 1991; Ellul, 1965; Rheingold, 1993; Stevenson, 1995). We reconstruct a feeling of community—*Gemeinschaft*—while continuing to enjoy the anonymity of urban society—*Gesellschaft*. We create, in short, a pseudo-*Gemeinschaft* that looks superficially like community but whose roots do not go as deep (Tonnies, 1955). Media create a false sense of intimacy by turning public and private inside out, and strengthen the illusion through the ability to read the nuances of every performance with little or no expectation of reciprocal obligation on the part of the audience (Cerulo, Ruane, & Chayko,

1992; Patterson & Wilkins, 1998; Sennett, 1974). Mediated entertainment also shapes identity, both that of participant and of audience member. At its most basic level, identity tells us who we are and where we are placed in time and space. Identity is fluid, constantly being balanced between cultural production and consumption, constantly being regulated and changing. Its symbolic marking simultaneously denotes difference and emphasizes shared characteristics (Woodward, 1997). Reality shows prove their unreal nature through the demographics of the players in this constructed world, the risk-free production environment that presents itself as threatening and dangerous, and the selective editing and deception employed. Identity is mediated first by community, then reconstructed via the media, and finally reconvened through play.

Demographics

Reality shows are cast carefully in order to maintain the illusion of play as well as to make the show entertaining for viewers. Physical and psychological tests not only help the producers avoid embarrassing moments such as that suffered when the first player voted off the Swedish version of *Survivor* committed suicide; they also provide important clues as to compelling plot twists, and ensure high ratings. Typically, the players include an equivalent number of men and women, based on the information offered on network web sites associated with the programs (*Big Brother*, 2003; *Boot Camp*, 2003; *Survivor*, 2003; *Temptation Island*, 2003; *The Mole*, 2001). Players also appear to be conscientiously chosen to represent various ethnic and racial groups in American society. Players are, on the whole, single or divorced. However, other players were described as being in ongoing heterosexual or homosexual committed relationships. The point of *Temptation Island* was, of course, to include only unmarried couples, although the couples were supposed to be in "committed but unmarried" relationships. A small minority of contestants have children, although few primary caregivers of small children are able to spend the amount of time required to play the game away from—and out of contact with—their families (even for a generous cash prize), thus reinforcing the image of the independent fun-loving individual that the games emphasize.

The age of the contestants is relatively young. *Survivor* contestants boasted the highest mean age, at 36.6 years. Each show (with the exception of *Temptation Island*) features one or two "older" players, who sometimes assert they're participating to show the younger ones that their elders can still be competitive. On *Boot Camp*, older players had significantly more difficulty with the physical activities. The older players are often relegated to the role of "lovable curmudgeon" à la *Survivor's* Rudy, whose politically incorrect comments provided some of the best scenes in the program. And of course, on *Survivor: Africa*, younger and older players on one team explicitly expressed their animosity toward one another.

There's a lot of talk about sex but not a lot of actual sex shown, at least in the American versions of the shows. An alleged attempt by the producers to heat up the romance on *Survivor* by sending Jenna and Sean to a private all-night beach party failed (Lance, 2000), and even Jerri's blatant attempt to frame a reward of a day at the beach as equivalent to a honeymoon getaway failed when Colby deliberately ignored the implications of the statement (*Survivor: The Australian Outback*). Perhaps the constant glare of the cameras—or possibly the need to climb Maslow's hierarchy—dampens whatever aphrodisiac there may be in spending nearly six weeks with a potential partner.

All the players are good looking, which seems to be a prerequisite for success. Even the *Survivor* crew liked Gretchen for more than her camping skills. "The desire to see her win was almost unanimous. She was wholesome, she was a survivalist, she looked great in a bathing suit. She was worthy" (Burnett & Dugard, 2000, p. 92). Sexiness is certainly a theme on the shows, most explicitly so on *Temptation Island*, but although it is less blatant on the others, it still plays a significant role. Discussions of masturbation and sexual fantasies are interspersed with the game structure. Colleen and Greg's (*Survivor*) nightly sleepouts alone in the bushes, incipient romantic attachments among cast members, and a late-night rendezvous in *Mole* players' hotel rooms are all presented to us with a nudge and a wink. Sexual orientation is openly discussed on the show, but is revealed according to production needs; the audience never even knew that *Survivor's* Sonja was gay until the reunion show following the final episode, for instance. Jim's (*The Mole*) visit from his partner at the midpoint of the series set us up for some viewable tension with Charlie in the final scenes, most notably in the art gallery when Charlie calls Jim's artwork "fruity," not realizing that Jim is listening.

There is an inherent anti-intellectualism in reality shows. The American ideology of egalitarianism leads us to insist that everyone is more or less equal. George Boswell, the roofing contractor who was playing *Big Brother* in order to send his daughter to college, became a folk hero in a way that he would not have been able to do had it been his own intellectual development he was pursuing. Of course, one doesn't want to appear to be too anti-intellectual, just enough so that you appear "normal." Rudy analyzed the difficulties of the *Survivor: The Australian Outback* players after their shelter (built in a dry stream bed) was washed away during a flash flood: "Some people blame the elements. I blame their stupidness" (*Survivor: The Australian Outback* Final Episode, 2001). Much in the same way that *Millionaire* over-represents "lighter" questions (entertainment, sports, food, leisure activities) in the early part of the game and reserves "heavier" topics (high culture, history, languages, science and mathematics) for the bigger prizes (Hetsroni, 2001), so too do reality shows emphasize the simpler physical challenges at the beginning of the game and place the more sophisticated social and cognitive challenges toward the end. The players only get to prove their higher-level abilities after they've managed to remain in the game on the most basic levels for a period. In an eerie echo of secondary school culture, the social order constructed by the reality shows emphasizes physical prowess and social skills over intellectual capabilities.

Ritual speaks deeply to both the participants and the audience. *Survivor's* tacky tiki torches and fake Stonehenge monoliths give us the aura of ancient practice with the constructed symbolism of snuffing out torches providing just enough background for our imaginations to fill in the gaps. On *The Mole*, the same effect is achieved in a more high-tech manner, using laptops and a large projection screen, but the security of the end-of-show ritual provides comfort. Additionally, the final words of the outcast (from the parking lot or the "confessional") offer closure. The reminiscences of players and the montage of top moments (especially on *The Mole*) function in much the same way as a eulogy.

While there is no official religion on reality shows, religion, particularly Christianity, receives its fair share of comment. Other than Jewish contestant Ethan's refusal to eat a reward of ham (*Survivor: Africa*), other religious beliefs have not been addressed at all, and one suspects that a potential contestant would find strict religious observance that might interfere with the production schedule to be a liability. Many survivors weave their faith into their final words, bring a Bible as their luxury item, or donate their winnings to a church or favorite charity. One of the most gripping scenes in any of the shows occurs when Rodger (*Survivor: The Australian Outback*) intones grace before meals just after Michael is evacuated with serious burns; the prayer offers closure and hope both to the participants and to the audience members. The show does attempt to construct a spiritual ritual just prior to the final tribal council, reflecting perhaps the imminent close of the play frame.

The occupations of the players bear a strong resemblance to the occupations portrayed in the world of television. Television over-represents higher-status occupations, particularly medical, legal, law enforcement, show business and military jobs. Minorities and women, when not entirely invisible, tend to be portrayed in relatively stereotypical and low status ways. The content as a whole reflects dominant, official, consensus, non-controversial viewpoints (McQuail, 1987). The depiction of occupations on reality programs reflect the "program" end far more than the "reality." Twelve of the original sixteen survivors have worked in entertainment or media since the show aired; only seven had worked in media or aspired to do so previously (*Survivor*, 2003). Some player occupations appear to be misrepresented by the production team. *Survivor: The Australian Outback*'s Rodger is described as a farmer and high school shop teacher, while his former position as business owner and CEO of a bank is downplayed. Abstract paper-pushing jobs are downplayed while interesting careers and hobbies and emphasized. It's much more interesting to think of *Boot Camp*'s Recruit Meyer as a snowboarding instructor than an urban planning graduate student or Recruit Yaney as a balloon sculptor than a graphic designer or Recruit Coddington as a nanny (her part-time job) rather than a scholarship coordinator (her day job). The demographic package of the players reinforces our perceptions regarding personal identity as displayed through media.

Risk and Reality

There is a growing cultural preoccupation with risk and the reduction of dangers associated with physical, social and technological factors, resulting in a diminished sense of personal control over everyday life, a sense emphasized by often-sensational media coverage (Furedi, 1997; Grant, 1996; Mulgan, 1996; Perkinson, 1996; Tavener, 2000). Reality shows offer virtual risk that we can watch from the safety of our homes. While the manifest message of reality programs appears to stress risk-taking and independence, little actual risk is shown. The medics just outside camera range are ready to step in at a moment's notice; even the signed waivers do not mitigate the basic fact that killing game show contestants is, at least to date, unacceptable.

Reality programs offer a safe vision of TV-land, *Truman Show*–esque hyperreality. Why else would behind-the-scenes dramas like Gervase, Jenna and Greg's "brush with death" as they sat with crew members in a disabled boat (the *Sea Quest VIII*) be eliminated, only to be discussed in the companion book to the series? (The *Sea Quest* was later swept out to sea in the same storm with two crew members, who were never recovered, on board, but this real risk is never mentioned.) Why not include the alleged scene where Joel, rafting at night, was held at gunpoint by offshore pirates or shots of the Malaysian Navy gunboats stationed off the island to deter uninvited visitors? "One answer might be that the *Survivor* experience was more sanitized Disney Adventureland than gritty *Lord of the Flies*. With all the carefully planned challenges and product placements, the production schedule was very tight and any unanticipated or unscripted outside 'event' might have interfered" (Lance, 2000, p. 126). Even as they appeared starving and malnourished, with Elisabeth's hair falling out in clumps, *Survivor: The Australian Outback*'s players were given vitamins off-screen by the well-fed crew (Dark, 2001).

Reality shows allege to be about independence and risk-taking, but hidden beneath the surface, the latent message of the programs is conformity and subjugation. Players vote out those who do not "fit" in various ways. First to go is "anyone who plain doesn't fit in, no matter what the reason" (Burnett, 2001, p. 153). The next the players eliminate are those who are dispensable, then those whose personalities clash with others, and finally those who threaten to usurp the winning pot from the most powerful player.

The most obvious victims are the weak and elderly. The first to be eliminated are often the oldest: Sonja, BB, Maralyn, and even Debb, who at 45 is by no means elderly, but who shared little with the younger members of the tribe. Often, older players are eliminated because they simply can't keep up with the physical challenges of the games such as the sincere-but-out-of-shape pig farmer, Rebecca Haar, whose *Boot Camp* experience strained her muscles within the first few days.

Weakness also counts against players. With the exception of *Big Brother*, where the challenges were more social and emotional, no player with a physical or mental handicap is included in the population. No one is fat or ugly—not even Richard Hatch, who lost 100 pounds prior to the show (although he was referred to as "Machiabelly" by both cast and crew). Certainly, Colby's streak of immunity and reward challenge wins on *Survivor: The Australian Outback* played an important role in his success—having won a string of food rewards (with, of course, proper product placement), his superior nourishment/health/strength allowed him to gain an advantage over the other players. But strength does not count for everything, as Recruit Wolf discovered during *Boot Camp*'s "The Gauntlet," the final 48 hour physically exhausting trial. Although Wolf (male) nailed six of the seven physical and mental challenges, his slightly more likeable opponent, Whitlow (female), garnered all seven of the other players' votes to win the game.

Now that the winners of reality shows have represented an extraordinarily varied sampling of different social groups, early accusations that the programs favor white men can be discarded. More important than any demographic factor is conformity; there is a tendency to vote out independent thinkers who threaten group solidarity. Kimmi's (*Survivor: The Australian Outback*) vegetarianism set her apart from the Kucha tribe from the start, and the difference is intensified when she refuses to eat meat in the "disgusting food" competition and fights with other tribe members. *Boot Camp* recruit Mark Meyer's phony apology to teammates bought him some time, but several players eyed the staged apology, complete with tears, suspiciously. Even when they are not subject to manipulation by fellow players, the contestants are under the constant control of the production team. *Survivor: The Australian Outback* contestants were lured away from their posts (literally) during an immunity challenge with the offer of food as cameramen tired of the eleven-hour shoot. *Big Brother* contestants at one point talked about staging a "strike" against the production, as producers tried to lure away a "boring" contestant and put in someone more interesting (*Big Brother*, 2003).

Assertiveness is the downfall of many players, especially when it is not supported by action that benefits the group. Rich (*Survivor*) is described by teammates as being a charming Machiavellian, but he also provided food for the group, whereas Debb's take-charge attitude failed to result in successful fire-building. Kel's independent military training made him separate from the group in the Australian Outback, even as he unproductively hunted for food to feed the group. He states "I knew right from day one it would be hard for me to fit in. I'm a military guy, and ... they're entertainers. They're singers, songwriters, actors—even a chef that has his own TV show. It was going to be very hard to fit into that mixture" (*Survivor*, 2003).

It is well known by now that success follows from the formation of alliances with other players (Hatch, 2000). Sometimes, group solidarity is constructed by careful editing when it does not actually exist, and many players have complained that the final footage doesn't provide an authentic representation of their personalities. Despite the "reality" promise, the shows deliver a carefully crafted menu of tightly planned activities. Just as technical reproduction removes the context from a work of art so too can mediated relationships strip the context from a life (Benjamin, 1955; Funkhouser, 1990).

Reality shows provide a safe, nonthreatening—risk free—alternative to everyday life. Unlike a studio-based game show, these productions take place on location, with the cameras and crew hidden, allowing viewers (but probably not contestants) to pretend that it is unscripted. Tourism has for a long time been an increasingly scripted experience, and reality shows now allow us to be virtual tourists, visiting the land of our everyday lives.

Selective Editing and Deception

Reality shows construct artificial identities for the players through selective editing and deception. The games assert that they show reality, but of course the reality the audience sees is highly scripted and carefully edited. Even children in the audience quickly learn that they are being set up to believe certain things, such as the likely candidate to be voted off in that episode. The ultimate reality-as-image came on *Survivor: The Australian Outback*, when Michael had to be evacuated due to a medical emergency. External reality intrudes on the play frame as the helicopter lands and we see the videographers' tent supplied with portable refrigerator and other amenities mere yards from where the players have been roughing it for weeks. Michael's previously-taped statement emphasizing the fun of playing rather than winning is emphasized several times during the show, serving to pull the viewer back into the play frame as quickly as possible.

There is an inherent tension between the play frame and reality, accentuated as viewers search web sites for information about the players and watch them discuss the game on morning news shows. Much is made of the months of secrecy about the winner, and we marvel that the secret is so well kept for so long by so many people, even when the producers stage phony on-scene delivery of the electoral ice bucket to some civilized location for the final episode.

Selective editing appears to have taken place, not only in the depiction of certain personalities (Stacey Stillman was made to appear more confrontational, for example), but in the timing of certain statements and episodes being aired (Devinney, 2001a; Devinney, 2001b). Richard went naked part of each day as did other tribe members, but these were ignored in favor of playing up his difference from the tribe in the "birthday suit" episode (Lance, 2000). We were not shown Tina's picky eating habits on camera, even though she routinely overcooked her portion of rice so that it was extra-crispy (Pappas, 2001).

Interestingly, the *Survivor* production team admits some scenes, especially those involving helicopter shots, which would have shown extraneous video crews and camps, were re-enacted to appear more "authentic."

Ironically, these may even have been performed with stand-in look-alikes for the contestants. The differences largely involved changing camera angles and did not influence the outcome of the contests. Burnett may even have helped the players by putting fish into empty traps set by hungry contestants (Rutenberg, 2001).

Some deception is deliberate. The infamous phony "final four" shot and Rudy's spotlight at the *Survivor* wrap party were disinformation planted by Burnett to ensure secrecy until the end of the show (Burnett, 2001). When Kelly won an evening in an "authentic Malaysian bar" (a reward hastily concocted due to the rising expectations of the castaways; Burnett didn't want to lower morale by offering the original prize of a single Bud Light), the crew quickly redecorated the local bar used by the production staff to resemble the program's mythical image (Burnett & Dugard, 2000, p. 202). She never suspected that it wasn't real. And maybe it doesn't matter, given how real everything else on the show was.

Although one might convincingly argue that the manners and morals of the *Survivor* cast are far from civilized or that the very premise of some of the shows undercuts whatever evolution our culture has achieved, the point remains that the setting for the show seeks to emulate untouched nature. We are shown beautiful scenery, warned of the dangers of crocodiles and poisonous snakes, cringe at the thought of sleeping with rats running over our bodies.

Our constructed presentation of self is altered when that self is paraded publicly in the media. Media alter our parasocial interactions and change the social significance of spatial settings, blurring childhood and adulthood (Goffman, 1959; Meyrowitz, 1985; Postman, 1982). Postmodern production emphasizes style over substance and becomes hyperreality. We satisfy our need to understand the world through the creation of pseudo-heroes, the celebrities of the moment. It is, in fact, increasingly difficult to say what is real any longer; image supersedes reality (Boorstin, 1971; McGuigan, 1999; Mitroff & Bennis, 1989).

The Play Frame

Games and play extend social structures, clarifying cultural forms which have become so familiar that their meaning is lost or obscured as we conduct the familiar routines of everyday life. Play is unique in that it stands apart from ordinary life by virtue of its being "not serious" (i.e., noninstrumental in nature) but at the same time absorbing the player utterly and intensely. The expressive nature of play and games is important on two levels, the structure of the temperament of the individual (psychological structures) and the temper of the society (socio-cultural ones). Indeed, it has even been proposed that culture itself evolved from play (Ball & Loy, 1975; Caillois, 1979; Geertz, 1973; Giddens, 1964; Glenn & Knapp, 1987; Goffman, 1974; Huizinga, 1950; Meltzer, 1964; Sapora & Mitchell, 1961; Sutton-Smith, 1976).

Games are recreational activities characterized by organized play, competition, two or more sides, criteria for determining the winner and agreed-upon rules. Games may model various cultural activities or social interactions: games of strategy related to mastery of the social system, games of physical skill associated with mastery of the self and environment, and games of chance linked with mastery of the supernatural (Roberts, Arth, & Bush, 1959). Reality shows, of course, incorporate all three elements.

No material interest or profit accompanies play, which proceeds within its own boundaries of time and space according to rules fixed in advance. It is often difficult to maintain the play frame over the period of time required for a successful television production (although it is important to note that the viewers see only a few minutes culled from hours of actual experience and that editing can compromise accuracy and authenticity). Kathryn sighs in the series-ending retrospective that the hardest part of being *The Mole* was having to maintain the play frame throughout the entire production. Apparently, even the show's traveling psychologists were not informed of her true identity, so she had to undergo "fictional" therapy in order to maintain her role credibility.

Denying the play frame endangers the entire frame for all participants, who are expected to cooperate in the construction of a consensual reality (Goffman, 1974). On *Temptation Island*, when Billy's relationship with his girlfriend becomes threatened, he holds back the cameramen while snarling about their invasion of his privacy and reminding the crew that "this is people's lives." The audience, of course, watches this unscripted act eagerly, hoping to catch a glimpse of "real" backstage behavior unscripted by the producers.

Emergent play that develops naturally in the absence of commercial pressure both reflects and shapes culture. Reality programming clearly is not naturally emergent, but developed with commercial motivations in the foreground. Still, players are expected to ignore the potential profit outside the play frame in order to preserve the illusion, not just for themselves but to convince the audience of the reality of the show. The contestants who signed up for Fox's *Boot Camp* soon realized the folly to subjecting themselves to the rigors of the program with money as the sole motivation as the drill instructors kept up a litany of high-volume insults in their faces. The player, Jane Katherine, who quit midway through day one, admonishes her fellow players that there are some things more important than money.

We want to believe in the play frame, and feel uncomfortable when players violate it. Play is a fragile activity; at any time reality may rudely reassert its rights either from outside the game context (through some interruption) or from within (by means of an offense against the rules or a collapse of the play spirit). *Survivor: The Australian Outback's* Michael puts it best when he asserts that, for him, the purpose lies in the meeting the game's challenges; the outcome is irrelevant. Colby's choice of Tina as his partner for the "final two" on *Survivor: The Australian Outback* was viewed by many as a miscalculation in the game; what it really represented was Colby's stepping outside the play frame, moving from a finite to an infinite game, as it were (Carse, 1986). It is not just that Colby allowed his personal feelings and external life to overshadow the game strategy; the move represents his conscious decision to throw off the play frame imposed by the television show and situate his actions in the larger context of his own identity.

Marshall McLuhan (1976) once said that North Americans may be the only people in the world who go outside to be alone and inside to be social. With the advent of reality programs, we can invite the 51 million other people who watched the final episode of *Survivor* to join us on the sofa as we allow Rudy, Kelly, Susan, Richard and the others to channel our identities. It's immensely more comfortable to watch *Fear Factor* contestants confront rats crawling over them or to smugly watch "the weakest link" being summarily dismissed that it is to confront our own fears and weaknesses in real life.

The ultimate message of reality programs is that the players are "plain folks," people just like you and me. We are offered the chance of auditioning for future shows, emphasizing the notion that we *could* play if we wanted to. Burnett (2000, 2001) would have us place the host as tribal chief or high priest, but the host's real function is to serve as everyman, representing the rest of us watching from home. The host sits in the power seat, with no need to eat grubs or play political games; his function is to serve as our eyes and ears in the players' camp. He asks the questions we would ask the contestants if we could, he gets to watch the competitions from a front-row seat, he gets first shot at counting the votes at tribal council. Afterward, he gets to retire backstage with the newly voted-off tribe member and find out what that person really thinks—all in the comfort of the production tent. Just as fire represents life at tribal council, the host represents the audience throughout the program.

We argue our awareness of the phoniness of the program even as we tune in weekly to share in the illusion. The identities we construct individually combine to create the stage set on which our culture plays out the "dramality" of everyday life; reality shows merely allow us to reflect on our own identity through observation of the behaviors of the nearly-fictional players on the screen. We are, after all, the tribe that has spoken.

References

Ball, D. W., and Loy, J. W. (1975). *Sport and Social Order*. Reading, MA: Addison-Wesley.

Benjamin, W. (1955). The work of art in the age of mechanical reproduction. In *Illuminations*. New York: Harcourt Brace Jovanovich.

Big brother. (2003). Guests. Retrieved January 10, 2003, from www.cbs.com/primetime/bigbrother

Boorstin, D. (1971). *The Image: A Guide to Pseudo-events in America*. New York: Harper Colophon Books.

Boot camp. (2003). Recruits. Retrieved January 10, 2003, from www.lmnotv.com/news/shows/bc/bc_master.htm

Burnett, M. (2001). *Survivor II: The Field Guide*. New York: TV Books LLC.

Burnett, M, and Dugard, M. (2000). *Survivor: The Ultimate Game*. New York: TV Books LLC.

Callois, R. (1979). *Man, Play and Games*. New York: Schocken Books.

Carse, J. P. (1986). *Finite and Infinite Games*. New York: Ballantine Books.

Cerulo, K. A., Ruane, J. M., and Chayko, M. (1992). Technological ties that bind: Media-generated primary groups. *Communication Research*, 19 (1), 109–129.

Dark, L. (2001, May 6). It's not war, but this game is hell. *New York Times*, p. D16.

Devinney, C. B. (2001a). Burnett vs. Stillman. *3Big Shows.com*. Retrieved February 21, 2001, from www.3bigshows.com/survivorii-burnettstillman.shtml

Devinney, C. Brian. (2001b). Survivor II cast members rebuff Stillman's claim. *3Big Shows.com*. Retrieved February 22, 2001, from www.3bigshows.com/survivorii-s2castrebugg.shtml

Drucker, S., and Gumpert, G. (1991). Public space and communication: The zoning of public interaction. *Communication Theory*, 1 (4), 294–310.

Ellul, J. (1965). *Propaganda: The Formation of Men's Attitudes* (K. Kellen, Trans.). New York: Alfred Knopf.

Funkhouser, G. R., and Shaw, E. F. (1990). How synthetic experience shapes social reality. *Journal of Communication*, 40 (2), 75–87.

Furedi, F. (1997). *Culture of Fear: Risk-taking and the Morality of Low Expectation*. Washington, D.C.: Cassell.

Giddens, A. (1964). Notes on the concepts of play and leisure. *Sociological Review*, 12 (1): 473–89.

Giddens, A. (1991). *Modernity and Self Identity*. Cambridge, UK: Polity Press.

Geertz, C. (1972). Deep play: Notes on the Balinese cockfight. *Daedalus*, 101 (1), 1–37.

Glenn, P. J., and Knapp, M. L. (1987). The interactive framing of play in adult conversations. *Communication Quarterly*, 35(1), 48–66.

Goffman, E. (1959). *The Presentation of Self in Everyday Life*. Garden City, NY: Doubleday Anchor.

Goffman, E. (1974). *Frame Analysis: An Essay on the Organization of Experience*. New York: Harper and Row.

Grant, L. (1996). Violent anxiety. In S. Dunant & R. Porter (Eds.), *The Age of Anxiety* (pp. 21–39). London: Virago.

Hatch, R. (2000). *101 Survival Secrets: How to Make $1,000,000, Lose 100 pounds, and Just Plain Live Happily.* New York: Lyons Press.

Hetsroni, A. (2001). What do you really need to know to be a millionaire? Content analysis of quiz shows in America and in Israel. *Communication Research Reports*, 18 (4), 418–428.

Huizinga, J. (1950). *Homo Ludens*. Boston: Beacon Press.

Lance, P. (2000). *Stingray: Lethal Tactics of the Sole Survivor*. Portland, OR: R.R. Donnelley, Inc.

McGuigan, J. (1999). *Modernity and Postmodern Culture*. Philadelphia: Open University Press.

McLuhan, M. (1974). At the moment of Sputnik the planet became a global theater in which there are no spectators but only actors. *Journal of Communication*, 24 (1), 401–411.

McLuhan, M. (1976). Inside on the outside, or the spaced-out American. *Journal of Communication*, 26 (4), 46–53.

McQuail, D. (1987). *Mass Communication Theory* (2nd ed.). Beverly Hills, CA: Sage Publications.

Meltzer, B. (1964). Mead's social psychology. In Center for Sociological Research, *The Social Psychology of George Herbert Mead* (pp. 10–31). Kalamazoo, MI: Western Michigan University.

Meyrowitz, J. (1985). *No Sense of Place: The Impact of Electronic Media on Social Behavior.* New York: Oxford University Press.

Mitroff, I., and Bennis, W. (1989). *The Unreality Industry: The Deliberate Manufacture of Falsehood and What It Is Doing to Our Lives.* New York: Oxford University Press.

Mole. (2001). Players. Retrieved November 14, 2001, from www.abc.go.com/prime time/mole/index

Mulgan, G. (1996). High tech and high angst. In S. Dunant and R. Porter (Eds.), *The Age of Anxiety* (pp. 1–19). London: Virago.

Pappas, B. (2001, April 30). Who will survive? *Us Weekly*, 324, 30–35.

Patterson, P., and Wilkins, L. (1998). *Media Ethics: Issues and Cases (3rd. ed.).* Boston: McGraw-Hill.

Perkinson, H. J. (1996). *No Safety in Numbers: How the Computer Quantified Everything and Made People Risk-aversive.* Cresskill, NJ: Hampton Press.

Postman, N. (1982). *The Disappearance of Childhood.* New York: Delacorte Press.

Rheingold, H. (1993). *The Virtual Community.* Reading, MA: Addison-Wesley.

Roberts, J. M., Arth, M. J., and Bush, R. R. (1959). Games in culture. *American Anthropologist*, 61 (4), 597–605.

Rutenberg, J. (2001, June 4). *Survivor* suit test of faith for contestant, and viewers. *New York Times*, p. C1.

Sapora, A. V., and Mitchell, E. D. (1961). *The Theory of Play and Recreation.* New York: Ronald Press.

Sennett, R. (1974). *The Fall of Public Man: On the Social Psychology of Capitalism.* New York: Vintage Books.

Stevenson, N. (1995). *Understanding Media Cultures.* Thousand Oaks, CA: Sage.

Survivor. (2003). Survivors. Retrieved January 10, 2003, from www.cbs.com/prime-time/survivor

Survivor: The Australian Outback. (2001, May 3). CBS.

Sutton-Smith, B. (1976). A structural grammar of games and sports. *International Review of Sport Sociology,* 11 (2), 117–138.

Tavener, J. (2000). Media, morality, and madness: The case against sleaze TV. *Critical Studies in Mass Communication,* 17 (1), 63–85.

Temptation Island. (2003). Islanders. Retrieved January 10, 2003, from www.fox.com/temptation

Tonnies, F. (1955). *Community and Association* (C. P. Loomis, Trans.). London: Routledge and Kegan Paul. (Original work published 1955)

Woodward, K. (1997). *Concepts of Identity and Difference.* London: Sage.

2

Contrived Television Reality:
Survivor as a Pseudo-event

April L. Roth

"It is not any -ism, but entertainment that is arguably the most pervasive, powerful and ineluctable force of our time—a force so overwhelming that is has finally metastasized into life" (Gabler, 1998, p. 9).

"We have used our wealth, our literacy, our technology, and our progress, to create the thicket of unreality which stands between us and the facts of life" (Boorstin, 1992, p. 3).

'The struggle lasted for 39 days. The show aired for 14 hours. It changed television forever" (*E! True Hollywood Story* advertisement, 2001).

Survivor, CBS's contribution to the reality television craze, is a novel import hybrid of among other things, ABC's *Who Wants to be a Millionaire?*, MTV's *The Real World*, and Fox's *Cops*; it is a coadunation of the familiar game show, soap opera, and reality television genres. *Survivor's* fusion of conventional elements obscures the fundamental intentions of these genres, to entertain, thrill, amuse, and provide insight into everyday life. Instead, *Survivor* showcases the human tools of trickery, manipulation, deception, and betrayal as justifiable means to a superlative end. In seeking to understand the success of *Survivor*, the works of Daniel Boorstin (1992) are particularly illuminating. Boorstin suggests that members of society use their prosperity to create a "thicket of unreality" which serves as a barricade between unadulterated and contrived reality (p. 3). Boorstin holds that this thicket is composed by Americans' "demand ... [for] illusions which flood our experience" (p. 5). We crave these illusions because "we suffer from extravagant expectations" (p.3). Boorstin holds that, "We expect anything and everything. We expect the contradictory and the impossible" (p.3). Boorstin proposes that Americans are dominated by these extravagant expectations: "Our power to shape the world ... our ability to create events when there are none, to make heroes when they don't exist, [and] to be somewhere else when we haven't left home" (pp. 4–6).

Boorstin suggests, "by harboring, nourishing, and ever enlarging our extravagant expectations we create the demand for the illusions with which we deceive ourselves. And which we pay others to make to deceive us" (p. 5). Boorstin proposes that our extravagant expectations result in our society's shift in attention from authentic events to "pseudo-events," or "synthetic happenings" which are, far more engaging and exhilarating (pp. 2–3). This chapter presents a critical examination of *Survivor* using Boorstin's framework for "pseudo-events" (p. 11). Boorstin avows that a "pseudo-event" possesses the following attributes:

1. The event transpires because it has been designed, orchestrated, or initiated by a person or group.
2. It is chiefly orchestrated with the intention of "being reported or reproduced ... its success is measured by how widely it is reported ... [and] time relations in it are commonly fictitious" (p. 11).
3. The event's relation to the essential reality of the circumstances is imprecise and indefinite. Its appeal arises chiefly from its indefiniteness. The appeal and attraction is in "whether it really happened" (p. 11).
4. By and large it is designed to be a "self-fulfilling prophecy" (p. 12).

Survivor *as a Pseudo-event*

Survivor possesses each of Boorstin's (1992) characteristics for a "pseudo-event." In each iteration, the show's every detail (excluding some castaway interaction) is planned; the location is prudently scouted, a plethora of potential castaways are screened until the "perfect" group is assembled; and the challenges are, for the most part, gamed out before filming begins. Before the scouting and screening, the show itself had to be cultivated until it was ready to be unveiled before a mass audience. Examining the history of *Survivor* provides an inimitable instance in which we can discover how a pseudo-event is engendered.

Boorstin's first and second criteria for the pseudo-event become evident upon examining the evolution of *Survivor*. Foremost, the commencement of a pseudo-event begins with a single cognition. Executive Producer Mark Burnett desired to create a new type of television show. When a friend told him of their idea for *Survivor*, Burnett knew that he had discovered a way to actualize his cognition and bought the rights to the show. CBS's *Survivor* was a result of his unyielding quest to uncover a new way to challenge individuals to participate in what he hoped would become the "ultimate game-show." Burnett began nurturing his ideas for *Survivor* until he had a conglomeration of elements from established genres: drama and fantasy from soap operas, exhilaration and antagonism from game shows, and person-to-person interaction from reality television.

Boorstin's first criterion for a pseudo-event also becomes evident in the examination of the show's design. To begin with, the "shipwreck" that opened the series was a meticulously planned event that would showcase a series of other premeditated events. The ship landed ashore the island of Pulau Tiga, an island that looked like the set of the *Blue Lagoon*, but was actually a dystopia. Pulau Tiga was selected as the location for *Survivor* for its steamy temperatures (the average temperature is 95), jungle-like atmosphere, and less than friendly inhabitants. Among its most alluring characteristics, Pulau Tiga showcased a bubbling mud pit, which served as a reminder that the island had a fiery volcanic past, remnants from the Japanese's brief occupancy of the island during World War II, along with abandoned bungalows and classrooms which stood as jungle swallowed skeletons from a Malaysian university's research closet. The inactive volcano, snakes, jellyfish and stroke-inducing temperatures were the precise ingredients for a seemingly disastrous destination for a pseudo-shipwreck.

An analysis of the show's format reveals a configuration consistent with Boorstin's second characteristic of a pseudo-event. The event was devised to be reported. From its conception, *Survivor* was formulated as a television show. Boorstin suggests, "time relations in [pseudo-events] are commonly fictitious" (p. 11). Although *Survivor* was marketed as "reality TV," it was actually edited to display the most dramatic of events on the island. Lance (2000) reports various instances where shots were shown out of sequence or completely discarded to increase the show's dramatic flair. Consider the example of Rich's nudity on the island. Rich informed Lance that he was "naked a part of almost every day he was on the island; sometimes for hours. Yet the first on-camera mention of his habit of streaking came ... almost halfway into the series in Episode Six" (p. 69). Lance concludes that this instance of selective editing was "used for dramatic effect, to enhance the 'Odd Couple' dynamic between Rich and Rudy" (p. 69). A second example appears when the contestants are invited to an "Ambassador's Summit," a chance for one representative (selected by their tribe) to meet with a representative (also selected by their tribe) from the other tribe the night before the merger was actually incited. Producers looked on this as " a potential night of Bacchanalia in a tented 'fuck hut' on the sand bar" (Lance, p. 81). The "summit" took place with Sean and Jenna as the representatives. When Jenna and Sean (both attractive but unlikely candidates) were chosen as the "ambassadors," Lance asked "Why in God's name ... would the tribe members 'appoint' these two airheads without a nudge from the producers?" (pp. 81–82). Lance's question was answered by Stacy Stillman; the ambassadors were "originally chosen by their tribes, but the producers substituted Jenna and Sean" (p. 82). Lance later discovered that the tribes' choices were Kelly and Greg but "the producers had overruled" (p. 82). The production of *Survivor* also supports the second criterion for a pseudo-event, that "time- relations in it are commonly fictitious," as eighty hours of videotape were commonly reduced to one hour of programming (Boorstin, p. 11). Video was meticulously studied to locate the most dramatic and gripping moments of castaway interaction to create the illusion that the majority of their time was spent struggling for power, respect, and, of course, food. CBS even advertised *Survivor* as if the show were being taped between the weekly broadcasts.

Boorstin further suggests that the prosperity of a pseudo-event can be calculated by how frequently it is reported. Early on, *Survivor* received an immense amount of press-coverage that remained, for the most part, constant features in weekly magazines, daily newspapers, national news, and morning news programs. *The CBS Early Show* featured weekly segments, which included a synopsis of each week's hour of *Survivor* along with an "exclusive interview" with the castaway who had been booted off of their island the night before. Particularly in the first seasons, *Survivor* had an almost ubiquitous presence on television with stories ranging from interviews with Burnett, Moonves (President of CBS), and castaways who "got the boot," to coverage on Richard's nakedness and the *True Hollywood Story*. The tube was not the only saturated medium, the Internet was also congested with the latest *Survivor* scoop. Countless websites, message boards, and chat rooms provided an outlet for *Survivor's* fanatical followers to log on and unite with other fans to rant, gossip, and try to determine the next castaway to be eliminated.

Television and the Internet weren't the only media permeated by *Survivor* anecdotes and advertisements; the popular press was also flooded with *Survivor* lore. In almost every issue, *TV Guide* included a quote from a castaway, a feature story, a behind the scenes look, or advertisement for products endorsed by a former castaway. *USA Today* also featured articles on Burnett, the production, location, and castaways along with reports on the ratings war between CBS and NBC, controversies (the pig slaughter), news (the fire injury) and the culmination/success of the "reality TV" genre. Among others, *Entertainment Weekly, The National Enquirer, Time, People,* and *Playboy* are a few popular press publications that featured stories on *Survivor* and/or its exiled. A succinct investigation of *Survivor's* media presence suggests its fruition as a pseudo-event according to Boorstin's criteria. *Survivor's* pervasive media presence testifies for its prosperity as a pseudo-event, its inclusion in popular outlets is indicative of its prevalence and universality within American culture.

Investigation of the origins/construction of the "Tribal Council" also provides support that the event transpired because it was designed, orchestrated, or initiated by an individual or group with intent to report it, which are again Boorstin's first two criteria for a pseudo-event. The "Tribal Council" itself can be considered a pseudo-event within a pseudo-event. The set for the "Tribal Council" was constructed using columns that framed a fire lava pit, and tiki torches marked a rope bridge used to enter the "Council." The focal point of the set was a sizable treasure chest, which revealed one million dollars of funny money (the winner of the show would actually receive a check). Both the construction and the meeting of the "Tribal Council" took place because they were considered to be necessary elements to ensure *Survivor's* success. Burnett and Dugard (2000) suggest, "without that built in comfort factor the audience would surely cringe as they realize how truly terrifying life on Pulau Tiga will be for the castaways" (p. 12). Burnett and Dugard's inference suggests their awareness that the "reality" of the environment and conditions that they chose for the "castaways" to "survive" in were too brash for their audience to view; therefore, they created a mixture of familiar shipwreck/adventure elements to serve as an anecdote for the harsh nature of the show. The "Tribal Council" wouldn't have been constructed otherwise, nor would the castaways have met every three days to vote one of their fellow castaways off of the island. The "Tribal Council" for *Survivor* was constructed to provide an exclusive and exciting area for the meetings to be held and filmed, for if the "Council" meetings weren't televised they could have been held anywhere on the island.

The assessment of Burnett's screening and selection of potential castaways for *Survivor* is also consistent with Boorstin's first two requirements for a pseudo-event. From the moment Burnett was introduced to the concept of the show, he began to envision the ideal cast. When Burnett began the colossal task of sifting through thousands of applications for the show, he searched for those who would best represent the compilation of castaways in his mind. His aim was to assemble a diverse collection of adventure seekers who would signify a latter-day Gilligan, Skipper, and Mary Ann. The final sixteen men and women embodied a cross-cultural, socioeconomic, representative sample of various ages and occupations.

Burnett's selection of castaways included: a redneck, a homosexual, a retired military man, a God-fearing farmer, a preppie doctor, and among other things, a southern pre-school teacher. They were the "perfect" group for a televised pseudo-shipwreck but a highly unlikely one in *The Real World*. If the shipwreck were in fact real, the group of castaways would more than likely be more homogenous, as a modern day shipwreck would occur in such instances as a pontoon boat full of friends or a cruise ship filled with people who share a similar socio-economic status. Burnett's selection of "castaways" was well calculated; he knew that sending this diverse cast of characters to an uninhabited island for 39 days would make for good television drama in and of itself. (Rudy Boesch, the retired military man, even stated in an interview with the producers that he did not like "queers," and that he would vote someone off of the island solely because they were gay.) Aside from the demographics, the less than hospitable living conditions and the competition against each other would create more intense drama, which would make for "Must See TV."

Boorstin's (1992) third characteristic of a pseudo-event is concerned with the event's relationship to the essential reality of the circumstances. The relationship is imprecise and indefinite, and its appeal arises largely from its indefiniteness, which often leaves audiences wondering if the event really happened. This characteristic becomes evident upon examination of the ways in which *Survivor* was marketed, constructed, and presented to its television audience. *Survivor's* ambiguity began when CBS advertised it as "reality TV," for "reality TV" itself is ambiguous, is it "reality TV" because everything but castaway interaction had been meticulously planned, or "reality TV" because the location, challenges, and castaway interaction were real/unscripted? From its commencement, *Survivor* left audiences wondering if what they were seeing was, in fact real. Lance (2000) suggests that multiple castaways on *Survivor* had fallen victim to Burnett's dastardly production and editing. Lance reports, "Several castaways told me that they'd been unfairly portrayed on the series. They were victims, they alleged, of selective editing" (p. 18). Lance further reports that Stacy Stillman, who believed that she was cast in an unfair light also held that she had been voted off the island at the suggestion of Burnett. Stillman told Lance that shortly after the conclusion of *Survivor*, that she had been informed by Dirk and Sean (two of her former castaways) that Burnett suggested they vote her off the island. When Lance attempted to contact Dirk and Sean, they were less than willing to admit anything. Dirk's response included "I don't have problems with the truth, but I don't know why the truth has to be revealed" and Sean never returned Lance's phone calls (Lance, 2000, p. 251).

From the very moment the castaways arrived on the island the ambiguity was amplified. Had they arrived at a location genuinely untouched by human hands or had it been primed for their arrival by artists and producers? Were their surroundings real or had they been created to look that way? Had the snakes, spiders, and scorpions been imported to the location to maximize the show's appeal, or did they actually reside there in their natural habitat? It was no mistake that *Survivor* locations possessed exotic flair, picturesque landscapes, deadly inhabitants, and extreme living conditions. Burnett chose locations for his "reality TV" show that would feature real human interaction in a pre-determined environment, with an established format, and preset challenges.

Since each segment of *Survivor* was the result of a myriad of hours spent amalgamating the most thrilling moments of castaway interaction into one-hour segments, the ways in which the castaways actually lived on the island were skewed as they were presented to the audience in a nebulous manner. The castaways were rarely shown sleeping, relaxing, bathing, or eating things that didn't crawl—for these activities were far too mundane for a prime time television show. The presence of the castaways was also ambiguous to the viewing audience as they were unaware that each of the castaways had been through a rigorous selection process (psychological evaluations, physical examinations, interviews, etc.) before their appearance on the show. The castaways were selected to comprise a diverse group of Americans for two main reasons: to attract viewers of most ethnic, cultural and socio-economic backgrounds, and to add drama to the show as the producers knew that some castaways had conflicting moral, ethical, and religious beliefs.

The "Tribal Council" meetings and "Immunity Challenges" also increased the ambiguity of the actual circumstances. If the castaways were, in fact, attempting to survive the toils of island-life, they would not have wasted their time worrying over the next "Tribal Council" meeting; rather, they would more than likely have been searching for food, building or maintaining their shelter, or searching for ways to leave and return to civilization. The snakes, spiders, and other predators posed little danger in comparison to that of performing poorly in an "Immunity Challenge." From its conception, the "Immunity Challenge" was incited by Burnett as one of the critical "built in" dramatic elements for *Survivor*.

The "Immunity Challenges" can also be considered as pseudo-events within a pseudo-event, for each challenge transpired as a result of Burnett's planning. The challenges served several purposes, foremost, they were devised to ensure a dramatic element outside of mundane castaway activities (eating, sleeping, bathing), they also guaranteed that the game would unfold in the way in which it was designed. The show was designed in two segments: the first would create unity and allegiance within each tribe, and the second would call for the dismantling of the separate tribes to unify as one. Each "Immunity Challenge" provided an opportunity for both tribes to either unite their individual efforts to prevail in the challenge, allowing them to become stronger as a team, or to lose the challenge rendering hostility and malice within the tribe. "Immunity Challenges" also provided ample conditions for animosity and ill will to be augmented between the opposing tribes, for the reward was so great that the competitions often became fierce. Merging of the two tribes introduced a new type of "Immunity Challenge," for the challenges were no longer team challenges, but individual challenges where each castaway was competing for their own immunity from the "Tribal Council."

Aside from the "Immunity Talisman," the only other bastion from being voted off the island was to rely on each other and form alliances. Alliances were just as necessary a tool for castaway survival as were rice and the first-aid kit. Shortly after arrival, the castaways recognized that their success and survival on the island was just as much in the hands of their fellow castaways as it was their own; therefore, they formed alliances in an effort to preserve their spot. The formation of alliances between castaways allowed them to develop a sense of security, a minute amount, but security all the same. Everyone, despite physical or psychological superiority, had to face the possibility of being voted off the island by his/her peers. If alliances were maintained, castaways would know that they could rely on each other to vote for someone else to be banished from competition, placing them one step closer to winning the game. The formation of alliances also allowed the members opportunities to devise a strategy in which they would determine which of their peers they would vote off and at what time they would do in an attempt to secure their shot at becoming one of the last castaways.

Surviving Survivor

Berger and Luckmann (1966) suggest that reality is a social construct. If reality is indeed socially constructed, the identification and explication of the predominant means used by contemporary society to introduce and maintain the dominant ideology is necessary to achieve a greater understanding of our world. One of the means in which we achieve this understanding of our world is by watching television as it showcases the ways in which individuals live, work, believe, act, and worship. As television is one of the primary socializing agents of contemporary society, it is necessary to determine which programs have the largest viewership and investigate what we are learning from them. An examination of *Survivor* reveals that it is in fact designed to be a "self-fulfilling prophecy," which is Boorstin's final characteristic of a pseudo-event. The show's title and design ensure that "in the end, only one will be the Survivor" (Burnett, 2001, p. 69). By establishing *Survivor* as a pseudo-event, we can identify the elements and ethics employed in this new hybrid of television in an attempt to ascertain what we, as a society, may be learning from it. Boorstin (1992) suggests that once we are enchanted by the magic of pseudo-events, we are enticed to consider them the only momentous events. Our enchantment contaminates "the sources of our experience," yet our enchantment is so splendid that it "spoils our appetite for plain fact" (Boorstin, 1992, p. 44).

Boorstin's conjecture suggests that our society may be in immediate danger; the morals, values, and beliefs of society may begin to digress as a direct result of watching *Survivor*. Lance (2000) reports that in a letter sent to *Time*, the American Psychological Association asked "How are the nation's citizens supposed to maintain functional work relationships if, at the first sign of trouble, they can 'vote someone off their island'" (p. 63). The APA's letter supports the social construction of reality by suggesting that *Survivor's* audience may eventually discard their previous beliefs and assume those, which *Survivor* showcases: trickery, manipulation, deception, and betrayal as *Survivor* is marketed as "reality TV." Classifying *Survivor* as "reality TV" not only leads its audience to believe that it is an exact record of events as they took place, but it also allows the audience to assume that the castaway interaction is a representation of contemporary morals, beliefs, and values. Instead of adopting the values and beliefs of *Survivor's* winners, perhaps we should challenge ourselves to identify real survivors. These survivors, veterans, single parents, orphans, widows, victims of domestic violence, and the impoverished, are often lost in the pseudo-eventian nature of our culture.

References

Berger, P. L., & Luckmann, T. (1966). *The social construction of reality: A treatise in the sociology of knowledge.* New York: Anchor.

Bianco, R. (2001, May 4). Hey, don't have a cow networks. There's always room for improvement. *USA Today,* pp. E1-2.

Boorstin, D. J. (1992). *The image: A guide to pseudo-events in America* (25th anniversary ed.). New York: Vintage.

Burnett, M. (2001). *Survivor II: The field guide.* New York: TV Books.

Burnett, M., & Dugard, M. (2000). *Survivor: The ultimate game.* New York: TV Books.

E! true Hollywood story [advertisement]. *Us Weekly,* 323, 9.

Gabler, N. (1998). *Life the movie: How entertainment conquered reality.* New York: Vintage.

Lance, P. (2000). *The stingray: Lethal tactics of the sole survivor.* Berryville, VA: Cinema 21 Books.

3

Who Owns Your Personality: Reality Television and Publicity Rights

Debora Halbert

Reality programs have multiplied in the past few years, turning everything from highway collisions to wild animal attacks into entertainment. When put into the context of other reality television shows, *Survivor* isn't all that different. *Survivor* continues to blur the line between fact and fiction, as it presents a drama as "reality," and uses "real" people instead of professional actors. It was after I helped a friend download the application for the second installment of the series, *Survivor: The Australian Outback,* that I became interested in the relationship between the contestants and the way in which "reality" was being legally constructed. I read the final portion of the application with great interest. The *Survivor* application contains a "name and likeness release" the potential contestant must sign that gives CBS perpetual rights to all materials related to the television show *Survivor.* There is no possibility of negotiating the terms of the contract; if you want to be considered for the show, this initial contract must be signed. While the public *Survivor* appears to be about competition and winning money, this show is built upon the private contract relationship between the contestants and CBS. This relationship creates some interesting problems because through their contract CBS asserts ownership over the very identities of their new "stars."

All people have publicity rights in their public personas and these rights allow them to control the manner in which others use their image. However, the contract signed by *Survivor* contestants gives CBS control over all rights to publicity for at least three years after the program is aired.

While a television studio may own the publicity rights to a fictional character, the blurring of fact and fiction in reality programming makes the type of ownership CBS has asserted over its *Survivor* cast a bit disconcerting. After all, these people are "playing" themselves on television, not fictional characters.

The contract signed by *Survivor* contestants is just one example of the larger push towards cultural privatization. It goes without saying that Americans live in a cultural world primarily defined by privately-owned cultural symbols. People tend to appropriate from this large cultural morass to create their unique personalities. Assertion of ownership over the public persona of an individual is a logical next step for media interests that already own the underlying cultural content. As public space becomes increasingly subject to surveillance by video camera and webcams, as private information is mined for data to help sell products, and as culture itself is privatized and owned by large corporate interests, the autonomy that each person assumes when establishing both a public and private persona is put at risk.

The identity of a human being, while possibly fractured and always in the process of becoming, is created through both public and private personae. As our cultural identity and personal identities (which are of course inextricably linked to culture) are confronted by the dual forces of property and surveillance, each one of us becomes less able to assert any sort of autonomy over our individual identities. We become divided into a bundle of rights.

By understanding the human body as a collection of alienable property rights, it becomes easier to divide the person from the right. This chapter focuses on the types of property rights in personalities that have been made even more relevant to "average" people by the *Survivor* contract. I would like to examine the implications of corporate owned publicity rights in reality programming. First, I will briefly outline the development of the right to publicity. Second, I will look more closely at the example of *Survivor*. Third, I will discuss the implications of these rights for the individuals involved and the larger implications for how we define ourselves as public persons.

The Right to Publicity

While the right to privacy and the tort of misappropriation of identity are closely linked to the way the law deals with public and private personae (Prosser, 1960; Kahn, 1999; Fleischer, 2000), the right to publicity is most relevant to the *Survivor* show. The right to publicity was first recognized in 1953 by Judge Jerome Frank in *Haelan Laboratories, Inc. v. Topps Chewing Gum, Inc.* (Barnett, 1999; Cordero, 1998; Madow, 1993; Halpern, 1995). Since *Haelan*, the right to publicity has been more thoroughly defined by legal scholars and the Supreme Court. (Madow, 1993; Halpern, 1995) However, only about half the states have a right to publicity, and there is little uniform federal protection (Barnett, 1999; Fleischer, 1999). Some states have statutory protection, some deal with publicity rights through case law, and the right is recognized in the Restatement of Unfair Competition (Stricker, 2000).

As a property right, publicity is "assignable" during life, meaning that an individual can license different uses of their public persona in order to exploit their name and likeness commercially (*Martin Luther King*, 1983). In some states, the right of publicity can be inherited and a public image can remain a property right long after the person has died (Barnett, 1999; Stricker, 2000). Allowing a person to transfer rights to their public persona after death suggests that a person consciously understands their public image as a distinct aspect of their personality and as something they ought to shape, construct, and exploit. Additionally, much like trademarks, one will need to protect one's public image from becoming generic. Once generic, the public image may be less protectable (Halpern, 1995).

Personalities-as-property are justified by arguing that a public image takes work to create. Legal scholars use a Lockean justification to understand the right of publicity as a property right (Fisher, 2000). Sudakshina Sen (1995) clarifies:

> According to this modern application of Locke's labor theory of property, since the celebrity spends time, money, and energy in developing a commercially lucrative persona, that persona is the fruit of the celebrity's labor and entitles her to its rewards. Moreover, in line with the labor theory of property, it is often argued that advertisers who appropriate celebrity personas without permission, much like "pirates" or "free riders," improperly reap what others have sown [p. 739–740].

While it may seem odd to think of one's public persona as a property right based upon the labor invested into the image, the courts have used this analysis in a broad range of cases. In *Uhlaender v. Henricksen* (1970) the court decided that baseball players whose names and statistics have been used by a baseball card company without permission have had their property rights violated. They stated, "It is this court's view that a celebrity has a legitimate proprietary interest in his public personality. A celebrity must be considered to have invested his years of practice and competition in a public personality that eventually may reach marketable status. That identity, embodied in his name, likeness, statistics and other personal characteristics, is the fruit of his labors and is a type of property" (*Uhlaender v. Henricksen*, 1970, p. 1282).

In *Presley v. Russen* (1981), the court utilized the labor analysis to describe the publicity right. Quoting a California Supreme Court case, the *Presley* court stated, "granting protection after death provides an increased incentive for the investment of resources in one's profession, which may augment the value of one's right of publicity. If the right is inheritable, the individual is able to transfer the benefits of his labor to his immediate successors and is assured that control over the exercise of the right can be vested in a suitable beneficiary" (p. 1355). Thus, unlike a privacy right that is inalienable, the right to publicity, based upon the labor one invests in a public persona, is a form of property. Such a position may suggest to some that no such thing as an authentic personality can exist— after all, for legal purposes we are merely investing our labor into a lucrative commercial product, our public persona.

The entertainment industry has long recognized publicity rights for celebrities. As with other forms of intellectual property, publicity rights have seen an extension in their scope over the years (Fisher, 2000; Clay, 1994). A movie star can invoke their "right to publicity" in order to prohibit the use of their likeness to sell products. This right of publicity includes "a person's nickname, signature, physical pose, characterizations, singing style, vocal characteristics, [or] body parts; so long as these are distinctive and the public identifies them with the holder of the right" (Sen, 1995, p. 742). The courts have found a recognized interest in the "commercial value of a person's identity" (p. 741–742). Unauthorized commercial exploitation is limited to appropriation for advertising purposes (Barnett, 1999). For example, publicity rights are balanced with First Amendment rights and the appearance of a celebrity's picture in a magazine or news report does not violate that person's publicity rights.

The right to publicity has been extended in recent years to include a broad array of identifying characteristics, including words associated with a celebrity. Thus, Vanna White has a right to her image, even if the image is a robot dressed in an evening gown turning letters (*White v. Samsung Electronics America, Inc.*, 1992). Bette Midler has a property right in the sound of her voice, and Johnny Carson has a property right in the phrase "Here's Johnny" because the words are associated with his image (Barnett, 1999; *Midler v. Ford Motor Co.*, 1988; *Carson v. Here's Johnny Portable Toilets, Inc.*, 1983).

The picture of publicity rights becomes murkier when one considers the fictional personae that an entertainer might play on television or in the movies. Does an actor have a right to publicity in a famous character they may become associated with? In *Lugosi v. Universal Pictures*, the heirs of Bela Lugosi, most famous for his portrayal of Dracula, argued they should have some degree of control over the Dracula character because Lugosi had played it. The Court argued that the right to publicity did not extend to Lugosi's heirs because Lugosi had not exploited these rights in life and because he was playing a fictional character. In the concurring opinion, Judge Mosk noted that, "merely playing a role ... creates no inheritable property right in an actor, absent a contract so providing" (Sen, 1995, p. 748). The right of publicity extends over a person's identity, not over characters a person may have performed. Lugosi's heirs had no property rights in his portrayal of Dracula because it was a performance Lugosi was hired to do.[1] The court did not take into consideration the blurring between Lugosi's personality and Dracula's based upon the labor Lugosi invested in the character. Thus, the development of personality, if it is a "fictional" character, may be contracted away (Yu, 1998).

While we understand the difference between a fictional character and the actor who plays that character, we may find tensions within the clash of publicity rights that exist when both the "real" and "fictional" people carry rights. A recent example of this problem emerges when both a character and a person have rights as in *Wendt v. Host Intl'l.* (1997). George Wendt and John Ratzenberger, who played Cliff and Norm on the popular television show *Cheers*, sued Host International for using robots that looked like the Cliff and Norm characters in their airport bars. Host International had licensed the use of these characters from Paramount Pictures, the owner of the *Cheers* series. The court found that Wendt and Ratzenberger's publicity rights had been infringed because the value came from the image of Wendt and Ratzenberger used, not the Cliff and Norm characters (*Wendt v. Host Int'l.* 1997; Firsher, 2000). Of course, how does one distinguish between the characters and the real person? Peter Yu (1998) notes:

> Standing in between a human persona and a fictional persona is a hybrid persona, which is commonly found in characters in a television situation comedy. Examples of such persona include "Norm Peterson" from *Cheers* and "Jerry Seinfeld" from *Seinfeld*. Because this hybrid persona contains both the actor's human persona and the character's fictional persona, determining whether works displaying such persona exploit a human persona or a fictional persona is very difficult [p. 377].

There are certainly elements of fictional characters and real persons inherent in any public figure. This hybridization is a challenge to the way the law has constructed fictional and non-fictional identity.

The link between an actor's public image and characters they play is also highlighted in *Hoffman v. Capital City* (1999). In this case, Dustin Hoffman sued the *Los Angeles Magazine,* which is owned by ABC, for creating a computer-generated picture of "Tootsie" modeling a modern evening gown. Hoffman sued for the unauthorized use of his image. His claim regarding his image was independent of the unauthorized use of the character *Tootsie,* an image owned by Columbia Pictures. Thus, there were two overlapping property rights generated by this case. Hoffman can limit the use of his likeness, but Columbia Pictures can limit the use of the character he portrayed in *Tootsie.* In this case, the court found that turning Hoffman into a runway model using computer technology violated his rights to publicity. They stated, "The photographs were manipulated and cannibalized to such an extent that the celebrities were commercially exploited and were robbed of their dignity, professionalism and talent. To be blunt, the celebrities were violated by technology" (*Hoffman,* 1999, p. 873). Thus, the unauthorized use of Hoffman's celebrity image was considered a violation of his dignity.

These cases deal with public figures attempting to protect their public personae from unauthorized commercial exploitation. Publicity rights are assignable and celebrities have negotiated contracts in order to optimize their public value. In all these cases, however, the celebrity retains a right to their own name and likeness. What they contract away is a slice of their persona for commercial use by another party. While they may become associated with a fictional character owned by someone else, their contracts would not preclude them from entering into other agreements dealing with other portions of their persona. The celebrity retains rights over their "core" or "nonfictional" image and merges this image with other images when engaged in new performances.

The development of reality television and the contracts signed by the "stars" provide an interesting challenge to the current state of publicity law and the boundaries between fictional and nonfictional characters. Reality television has created a new group of celebrities who do not own their public image and cannot independently control its use. Thus, contracts associated with the popular television show *Survivor* go beyond protecting CBS's interest in a fictional character to their interest in owning the public persona for the person upon which this character was based (if indeed there is a difference between the person and the character). The emergence of reality television, where "real" people are filmed in a variety of situations brings a new dimension to the ownership of personalities. In order to examine this issue it is necessary to clarify how the contract signed by *Survivor* contestants deals with their publicity rights.

Personalities for Sale

While several seasons of *Survivor* have taken place, I will focus on one particular example: *Survivor: The Australian Outback*. To apply for *Survivor: The Australian Outback*, each applicant was required to answer a series of questions, make a short video, and include a picture. Those chosen from this initial screening traveled at their own expense to a regional interview point for the first in-person interview. After this interview, each possible contestant was flown to LA for the final selection. The final selection included a background check and a physical and psychological examination.

This initial application required the applicant to sign a "name and likeness release." This release signed all rights to publicity in perpetuity over to CBS. The full text of the release reads:

> By submitting this application I hereby consent to the recording, use and reuse by the producers of the Program (defined below) and CBS Broadcasting Inc. and any of their respective licensees, assigns, parents, subsidiaries, divisions, business units, or affiliated entities and each of their respective employees, agents, officers and directors (collectively "Releasees") of my voice, actions, likeness, name, appearance and biographical material (collectively "Likeness") in any and all media now known or hereafter devised, worldwide, in perpetuity, in or in connection with the reality based television series currently entitled SURVIVOR (the "Program"). I agree that Releasees may use all or any part of my Likeness, and may alter or modify it, regardless of whether or not I am recognizable. I further agree that Releasees exclusively own all right, title, and interest in and to the application video that I have provided in connection with the Program (the "Video") and all rights therein and thereto including, without limitation, the right to use the Video and my Likeness in any and all media now known or hereafter devised, worldwide, in perpetuity. I further agree that Releasees may use my Likeness and the Video in connection with any promotion, publicity, marketing or advertisement for the Program in any manner whatsoever. I grant the rights hereunder whether or not I am selected to participate in the Program. I release Releasees from any and all liability arising out of its use of my Likeness and/or the Video. I agree not to make any claim against Releasees as a result of the recording or use of my Likeness and/or the Video (including, without limitation, any claim that such use invades any right of privacy and/or publicity).[2]

In plainer language, this contract grants CBS all rights to the name and likeness of the applicant forever, even if the applicant is not recognizable. It is understandable that CBS would want to have the power to use the application videos to promote the series. However, the scope of the language includes much more than the application video. According to the initial name and likeness agreement, anything related to *Survivor* becomes the property of CBS.

The name and likeness release from the application was only one part of CBS's assertion of publicity rights over *Survivor* contestants. Investigative journalist Peter Lance has written a book detailing his own experiences trying to publish the story of *Survivor* winner Richard Hatch. When CBS demanded control over all *Survivor* related sentences, the book deal between Lance, Hatch, and St. Martin's Press fell through (Lance, 2001). Lance then published a book about his experience trying to publish the book. In *The Stingray*, Lance weaves together information about *Survivor* with stories from Hatch's life and the beginning of an investigative report into the operation of the show. Through a contact he called "Deep Kangaroo," Lance was able to gain copies of the contract signed by *Survivor: The Australian Outback* applicants. These copies are included in the appendix of his e-book.

The contract signed by contestants includes specific language related to their publicity rights. First, in the section entitled "Confidentiality and Life Story Rights" all contestants are barred from using their newfound celebrity status without the permission of CBS for three years from the time the program airs. The contract specifically prohibits contestants from any contact with the media not sanctioned by CBS. Additionally, CBS can sue for damages if the contestant violates this rule. While it is understandable that CBS wishes to keep the show's winner a secret until after the final program has aired, the contract does not limit CBS's control to this topic. Instead, CBS retains all control over appearances made by the former cast and continues to control these appearances long after any potential celebrity status would have lapsed. According to Lance, several *Survivor* cast members have been denied paid celebrity opportunities because of the contract they signed with CBS. If an event can be construed as competitive with any CBS interest, the former cast cannot be involved. For example, former *Survivors* Jenna and Gervase could have made $10,000 each officiating at the opening of a Best Buy store. CBS would not allow them to do the event because it might be construed as competing with Target, a sponsor of *Survivor*.

One of the more revealing sections of the *Survivor* contract deals with the rights to the contestant's life story.

I irrevocably grant and release to Producer, in perpetuity and throughout the universe, the exclusive right, if I am selected as a contestant in the Series, to depict, portray and represent me and my life and all episodes, exploits, events, incidents, situations and experiences contained in or associated or related to my life (including without limitation my experiences in connection with the Series) (my "Life Story") and the Material in theatrical motion pictures, television programs and series, theatrical stage presentations, radio, other audio, visual, audio-visual, and/or print productions, books and other print publications (each, a "Production" and collectively "The Productions"), the production, reproduction, exhibition, broadcast, distribution, advertising, promotion and other exploitation of the Productions in any and all media, whether now known or hereafter devised, and in the exercise of all subsidiary, allied and ancillary rights (e.g., remake, sequel, theatrical, television, radio, publishing, merchandising and other similar rights) in the Productions. Producer may depict, portray me and my Life Story either accurately or with such liberties and modifications as Producer determines necessary as its sole discretion for the purposes of fictionalization, dramatization or any other purposes including without limitation to achieve a humorous or satirical effect, and by means of actors who may or may not resemble me. I hereby grant to Producer the perpetual and worldwide right to use my name, likeness, photograph, caricature, voice, and biographical material in connection with the production, exhibition, advertising, merchandising, and other exploitations of any and all Productions, and the rights therein [Lance, 2001, p. 314–315].

The central theme of this contract is clear. The *Survivor* cast has not only granted CBS the rights to what took place on the television show, but the rights to their entire life story as well. Essentially, CBS controls their ability to appear in public and in what type of venue, their ability to talk about the show, and their life stories. CBS owns their public identities and the rights to disclose their private identities. CBS owns the telling of the experiences that made them who they are. Everything a *Survivor* cast member could communicate to the public might be construed as the property of CBS. Additionally, CBS owns these rights throughout the universe forever.

My initial concern with the *Survivor* contract focused on what I imagined to be an aggressive extension of property rights—the corporate takeover of an individual's ability to control their image. Unlike Bela Lugosi, who was playing a character created by a different person, the *Survivor* applicants "played" themselves. Thus, the distinction between fact and fiction that allows actors and actresses to retain their own public image while contracting with the industry to produce fictional characters is blurred. The public and private personas of these contestants, or

the "fictional" and "nonfictional" aspects of their characters, were indistinguishable—they were living their private lives in public. CBS expected
the cast to tell their thoughts to the other contestants and to the cameras. Stories about their lives and personal history helped provide additional drama for the show. More than one personal revelation was made
(including the fact that Richard Hatch was gay) that added to the dramatic tension. *Survivor* cannibalized the life stories of its contestants to
create a game show/television drama. When viewed in this light, the problems with the contract the contestants signed become evident. While
Dustin Hoffman or George Wendt retained a right to the use of their
public image, and some might argue that they should retain a right in the
fictional characters they have played (Cook, 1999), the *Survivor* cast has
contracted that right away. In exchange for appearing on television and
getting the chance to win one million dollars, the contestants sold their
personal lives and public image to CBS.

One can only speculate about the reasons that a person would sign
such a contract. Perhaps the contestants did not think about the implications of the contract they were signing. Perhaps they did not read the
fine print or seek legal advice.[3] Perhaps they were so excited about the
chance to be on the show that the contract seemed irrelevant. The desire
to be a celebrity may have offset any qualms about the contract. The contestants would not have been as media savvy as professional actors. Perhaps they thought they would be able to trade on their future celebrity
status to re-negotiate a new contract. Additionally, the huge number of
competing applicants kept the pressure on potential contestants to sign
whatever contract they were handed. After all, if they rejected the contract there were plenty of other contestants who would be willing to sign
it. CBS was in a position to take advantage of potential contestants. At
the end of the process, the cast had signed at least four different agreements controlling different aspects of their publicity rights (Lance, 2001).

I wondered how CBS might justify their contract if it became the
subject of a legal debate. Certainly, their first line of defense would be to
argue that these people willingly signed the contract knowing what its
contents were. As rational individuals, they made a choice and now must
abide by their choice. However, CBS might also use a Lockean
justification for their ownership of these publicity rights. The labor theory of property runs throughout publicity rights cases. For example, in
Guy Lombardo v. Doyle, Dane & Bernbach, Inc. (1977), the court agreed that
Guy Lombardo had invested sufficient work into his public persona as
Mr. New Year's Eve to own a publicity right. The majority stated, "Guy
Lombardo had invested 40 years in developing his public personality as

Mr. New Year's Eve, an identity that has some marketable status. The combination of New Year's Eve, balloons, party hats, and 'Auld Lance Syne' in this context might amount to an exploitation of that carefully and painstakingly built public personality" (p. 664).

Thus, the question might be—who invested the labor into the public image that *Survivor* contestants now enjoy? In response to this question, CBS might argue that they are responsible for creating the public persona of the cast member. Without the show, these "average" people with "normal" jobs, would not have a public persona. Whatever persona is known to the world is the result of the CBS's creative editing and public relations. In other words, the individuals on *Survivor* are "raw materials" used by CBS to construct celebrities. CBS invested the labor and thus owns the results.

CBS might go on to argue that the viewing audience only saw what the producers wanted them to see. The producers selected the video footage and "created" the characters as they saw fit. For example, one of the early victims of the first *Survivor*, Stacey Stillman, has since argued that CBS portrayed her in a manner that misrepresented her personality. Stacey was portrayed from the first as a "litigating shrew" (Lance, 2001, p. 40), and it is difficult to know how much this image matches her personality and how much of this image was created by CBS to provide drama and villainy to the show. Lance states, "The fact that she became (as one columnist wrote) the 'most hated woman in America,' may have been the result of nothing more than the fact that Stacey fit some prescripted story line the series producers had drawn from the start" (p. 41). During the post-series reunion when asked about how accurately they had be depicted, *Survivor* Sean Kennif said, "Everyone here including myself is a lot deeper character than anything that you saw on television" (Lance, 2001, p. 182).

Because CBS was responsible for the public images created, they might argue they should retain some control over the public personae, even after the show is completed. Because *Survivor* combines game show competition with reality television drama, it seems that many of contestants felt this may be an opportunity to jumpstart a celebrity career. Instead of returning to their "normal" lives, several of the initial *Survivor* cast moved to California in hopes of making it big. For example, Colleen, who was not a "final four" *Survivor*, appeared in a romantic comedy, in *The Animal*. Thus, the tension between these individuals and the publicity rights owned by CBS becomes heightened by the fact that several of them did not return to their pre-*Survivor* lives. Instead, they have become a new class of "actors" who do not have rights independent of the corporation that has signed them.

To understand publicity rights as CBS has done, one must assume that a *Survivor* cast member has no public personality but the one constructed by CBS. Unlike fictional characters, however, the *Survivor* cast are "real" people. It becomes unclear what the "factual" and "fictional" portions of identity might be in this case. If CBS owns the public persona of an individual, what is left for the individual to own? Is any public display of identity "real"? Is there any private "self" behind these images? Given the contract written by CBS, *Survivor* cast members can no longer claim to be the sole author of their personalities. Thus, the right of publicity, which had been a right created to protect a public figure from misappropriation of their likeness, can now be divided from the "original" author and invested in a new creator. The final section of this chapter seeks to assess some of the implications of this use of publicity rights.

Publicity Rights, Culture, and Communication

In 1905 the Georgia Supreme Court found the appropriation of one's identity for advertising purposes tantamount to slavery (Kahn, 1999). A person's image was sacrosanct, too precious to be crassly commercialized, especially without consent. The court in the Dustin Hoffman case expressed these same feelings of exploitation. Both cases, separated by more than ninety years, assume an identity should not be appropriated without permission. However, once permission is granted, the law is used to contractually divide the person into public and private, performer and performed. I have already detailed how the law interprets and protects a public persona. I would now like to focus on the communicative aspects of reality television. I will do so using the analytical lens developed by Jean Baudrillard (1981/1994). What Baudrillard helps us do is analyze the communicative aspects of *Survivor* as a performance within the larger context of the media. However, this postmodern analysis has deficiencies because it fails to examine what goes uncommunicated. In other words, by only focusing upon the spectacle of reality television, the larger social structure that makes this spectacle possible is ignored. Thus, this final section will begin on the surface and delve into the depths of reality television.

Baudrillard (1981/1994) suggests that our world is one of simulation—that we live in the world of the hyperreal. For all intents and purposes, reality and simulation are the same. The result of the hyperreal is an aetheticized world, one where meaning is lost in the vastly more complex circulation of signs. As Douglas Kellner (1994) writes, "And the narcotized and mesmerized ... media-saturated consciousness is in such a state of fascination with image and spectacle that the concept of meaning itself (which depends on stable boundaries, fixed structures, shared consensus) dissolves" (p. 9). To Baudrillard, "culture is little more than a 'hallucination of the real,' a 'simulational' world characterized by an endless series of copies of previous forms..." (Andersen, 1995, p. 93). If meaning is not communicated by television generally, and reality programming specifically, then what is being communicated?

What is being communicated is the illusion of reality. "As television becomes more of a vast reference to itself, the world of production, corporate practices, and political and social forces becomes more obscure and out of reach. As we negotiate television's terrain, the world outside its boundaries is lost. And as the world is lost, TV grasps for authenticity by relentlessly asserting its 'realness'" (Anderson, 1995, p. 264). Reality television thus co-opts the lives of "normal" people in its effort to cement its claim to portraying reality. What is communicated to the public is the network's myth that they indeed depict reality instead of constructing consumer desires and controlling the ways in which those desires are manifested.[4] Within this context, television producers are far more adept at creating "reality" than everyday people. It takes hundreds or thousands of hours of footage to construct a 30–60 minute program and editorial genius can erase the banality of human life. Any remaining "authentic" personhood is transformed into a simulation of authenticity for the masses—the "reality" of *Survivor* is constructed and these "real" people become TV simulations of themselves. They become the ultimate consumers—willing to do anything for a million dollars and a new car.

Viewers like to believe they can distinguish between what is real and what is fiction. In part, they understand that reality television is anything but real. However, if one were to ask a viewer if they thought a specific character was as stupid or vain as portrayed on the show, the answer almost always seems to be—"well, I know the show is edited, but they did say/do those things." Context is no longer important, and if one says something that becomes immortalized by television, then it must be an accurate assessment of the "real" person, regardless of editorial control. No longer is the individual in charge of communicating their personality, in the world of the hyperreal they are simply another symbol.

Contracting away one's public persona makes it possible to enter the symbolic realm of the hyperreal. The old discourse of power/domination dissolves, as the human personality becomes an object of manipulation. Contestants are objects, not subjects. Their new position as objects in the hyperreal world of television means they too enter the world of signifiers "floating free, so to speak, in communicational space, ... easily attached to particular commodities by the arbitrary whim of advertisers" (Poster, 1994, p. 78). The blurring of fact and fiction along with the willingness to exhibit one's personal life on television illustrates the new system of meanings described by Baudrillard. Perhaps in the new world of reality TV, a life isn't "real" until it has been viewed on television. Thus, it doesn't matter if the identities portrayed are legal property of the network, it doesn't matter if there is a private person behind the public persona, reality is in being viewed and visible. The contestants are unable to control how their personality is communicated to the public. However, they can communicate their validity as individuals by being on television. It matters not at all who owns the image; simply that one has become one. Clay Calvert (2000) suggests in *Voyeur Nation* that, "The youth of today now crave growing up *in* television" (p. 66). This desire seems supported by the thousands of people willing to apply to the very diverse forms of reality programming.

The disturbing element of the hyperreal is the lack of possible resistance and the distinct lack of any analysis of power—in other words, a political perspective. The lack of politics is the inevitable result of a theory of the sign focused exclusively on the surface. At the level of the viewing audience, everything is simulation—there are no external references and thus no politics. This postmodern analysis seems to accurately describe contemporary media culture where meta-narratives have been replaced by aesthetics. However, this postmodern analysis of contemporary culture and communication neglects the realities of production. Andersen (1995) points out:

> The celebration of advertising and symbolic culture as that which constitutes the real is a point of view incapable of looking behind the symbols to an existing material world. Because the magical system of advertising has hidden the social relations of commodity production, they have been theorized and aesthetisized out of the picture. In this sense, consumer society has succeeded in hiding the very economic structure and social relations that account for its existenc. [p. 97].

In order to resist the power of such a mediated reality it is necessary to delve under the image and discover how that image is constructed.

The contractual obligations of *Survivor* contestants highlight the dilemma between postmodern cultural theorists and critical theorists. While it is easy to focus on the surface dimensions of "reality" television, this reality is structured by the contractual obligations of the players. The "reality" of power is invisible to the public who only sees the spectacle. It is important to evaluate what is not communicated as part of reality television—what is taking place at the level of the contract. While the public personas of *Survivor* contestants are easily understood as simulation consumed in a hyperreal world, the real lives of contestants are governed by a very traditional set of power relations. The power relations existing between CBS and contestants are invisible to those living in the simulation, but essential to the very operation of that television reality. Postmodernists deride critical theorists for their interpretation of "culture as manipulation" (Andersen, 1995, p. 115). However, once one reads *Survivor* based on the framework that allows it to exist (i.e., the contract) instead of the product presented for viewing, it becomes clear that the reality of reality television is based upon powerful and manipulative forces. As Andersen (1995) notes, "Postmodern theory, applied uncritically, encourages us to be dazzled by the shining surface of the world of consumer culture. It does not go beneath to decipher the strategies and false promises hidden by that surface" (p. 115). However, to truly assess the implications of reality television it is absolutely necessary to go beyond the surface.

The *Survivor* contract is the unviewed framework that allows "reality" television to work. Without such a contractual release, studios would be unable to use the images of their newly created "stars." All reality television shows must have people sign a release before the show can be aired. This contract signifies the power of the television studio to construct reality on television and control the reality of its products.[5] CBS has the power to narrate the lives of its contestants in any manner it chooses. In fact, the contract makes it impossible for a contestant to offer an alternative narrative of their life or their behavior on the show. All communication by the contestant to the outside world must be mediated through CBS. Any future media related success by a contestant is granted by CBS. Thus, contract controls reality, both the realities portrayed on television and the lived experience of the show's participants.

Because CBS now owns the life stories of all contestants, they have an even larger degree of communicative control. If identity is premised upon the narrative ability to construct our lives through stories, the contract has considerable power. It assumes the existence of an autonomous and rational person capable of signing the contract and then removes the ability of that autonomous person from narrating their own life. The end result is that CBS gains control over a mediated reality. They call the final product, "reality," but it is a reality mediated by the legal matrix of contract law. Any contesting of the reality conveyed by the show is prohibited, both legally and publicly.

This power relationship has been rendered invisible and irrelevant by a reality that is hyperreal. However, it is necessary to understand that the surface and the underlying power structure exist simultaneously. It seems important to make the totalization of hyperreality difficult to achieve. There is a need for both an understanding of Baudrillard's position and that of the critical theorists as Professor Steven Best (1994) argues,

> Just as a feudal mode of production can co-exist with capitalism, so, for example, can disciplinary or "spectacular" forms of power co-exist with the "dead power" of simulation. What we see today is not discipline *or* simulation, the society of the spectacle *or* the world of the panopticon, but a complex interplay of various mechanisms of social control that include discipline, spectacle, simulation, and the classic overt violence of the state [p. 55].

What is equally important to a discussion of publicity rights and culture is not only the specifics of *Survivor*, but also what the publicity rights in general do to our own ability to communicate with each other via cultural symbols and the larger cultural community.

The United States is an extreme example of the merging of commercialism with popular culture. There are few, if any, popular American icons that could be considered public domain. Instead, popular culture is privately owned by Coca-Cola™, Walt Disney™, Hollywood, and Nike™. Images we may consider important to our identity as Americans are the private property of corporations. The implication is that culture is consumed, not created (Madow, 1993). Even public domain material is appropriated when possible and integrated into the corporate intellectual property scheme (Fishman, 2000).

What can *Survivor* teach us about our own culture and how we should view the commodification of culture? If we begin from an understanding of ourselves as socially constructed beings that constantly negotiate the meanings of our identities within the world, it becomes essential to understand culture as something available for personal use when constructing identity. Culture, while understood as a commodity by many producers, is not simply consumed. Rather, culture is appropriated and rendered interesting and unique by each person who interacts with any given symbol (Madow, 1993). This perspective is reinforced by Rosemary Coombe (1994) who concludes, "As the cultural cosmos in which we live becomes increasingly commodified, we will need to define and defend the cultural practices of articulation with which we author the social world and construct the identities we occupy within it" (p. 131). If we are all discursive beings in need of culture to stimulate our own identity building, then the repercussions of monopolizing ownership of individual personalities as well as cultural signs could be damaging to our future creativity.

Ultimately, culture is hurt by the restrictive property limits we impose on cultural creativity. As Coombe (1991) notes, "Everyday life invents itself by poaching in countless ways on the property of others" (p. 1853). Enclosing personality rights even more deeply within the walls of property will only continue the trend towards privatizing culture at the expense of the public domain (Madow, 1993). The extension of the right to publicity allows for those who own rights to further restrict cultural meaning (Sen, 1995). The network of intellectual property rights surrounding *Survivor* can thus inhibit the ability of American culture to "poach" on itself. For example, despite the fact that the *Survivor* idea was appropriated from a Swedish television show, Mark Burnett filed suit against the makers of *Boot Camp* because he argued it was substantially similar to *Survivor*. Thus, the policing of property rights is used as a club to halt cultural innovation, however commercial that innovation might be.

Culture is difficult to define, but most certainly relies heavily upon the ability to exchange meanings in a shared context. As these meanings become further entrenched in property rights, it becomes more difficult for those that are engaged in cultural creation to do so legally or outside the boundaries of the culture industry (Clay, 1994). As Madow (1993) comments, these issues are not just about who should own a particular publicity right, but who has the power and authority to say what a given image means for us culturally: "By centralizing this meaning-making power in the celebrity herself or her assignees, the right of publicity facilitates top-down management of popular culture and constricts the space available for alternative and oppositional cultural practice" (p. 135). Such overprotection stifles creativity (Aoki, 1997). Thus, the current trajectory of publicity rights not only offers serious concerns to the theorist, but also has an impact on the manner in which culture is developed and circulated.

Conclusion

The ways in which our public identities are wrapped around issues of commercialism and property go beyond the publicity rights contract used as an example in this chapter. As Americans become increasingly informationalized via their computers, aspects of their identities become the private property of others. Each time a credit card is used, when a company asserts ownership over phone numbers and other database information, or when our "personality" is invested in electronic forms (like e-mails or web postings) instead of our more tangible bodies, we become the subject of a more complex matrix of property and personality rights. Our personas generally have taken on a digital form as we publicize our personal identities over the web to whomever may want to view us. In this sense, we have all entered the realm of the hypperreal. Thus, the questions of ownership and personal authorship are important not just for potential *Survivor* contestants, but for all people. Keith Aoki (1997) sums up the potential problem best:

> Those who do not have power over the story that dominates their lives, power to retell it, power to rethink it, deconstruct it, joke about it and change it as times change, truly are powerless, because they cannot think new thoughts [p. 546–547].

In a world where ideas and actions are becoming the object of property law, it is important that we avoid the monopolization of culture and the limitations placed upon our ability to create culture. With each step towards greater privatization we come closer to losing what little individual autonomy we may have left.

Endnotes

1. Since the *Lugosi* case the California legislature has passed a law providing the heirs of a celebrity with protected rights. See: Stricker, 2000.
2. Copy of Contract/Application for *Survivor: The Australian Outback* on file with author.
3. At least one of the initial survivors (Dirk Been) consulted a lawyer before signing the contract and was advised against signing (Lance, 2001, p. 248). He signed the contract anyway and now is willing to live with the consequences (p. 250).
4. For an excellent critic of consumer culture see: Thomas Frank and Matt Weiland's (1997) *Commodify Your Dissent*.
5. One might wonder why many people sign these contracts, especially on the talk show versions of reality television or a show like *Cops*. However, as Calvert (2000) reports, people will do a lot to be on television and most contracts provide monetary rewards for signing (p. 98).

References

Andersen, R. (1995). *Consumer culture and TV programming*. Boulder, CO: Westview Press.

Aoki, K. (1997). Using law and identity to script cultural production: How the world dreams itself to be American: Reflections on the relationship between the expanding scope of trademark protection and free speech norms. *Loyola of Los Angeles Entertainment Law Journal, 17,* 523–547.

Barnett, S. R. (1999). "The right to one's own image": Publicity and privacy rights in the United States and Spain. *American Journal of Comparative Law, 47,* 555–581.

Baudrillard, J. (1994). *Simulacra and simulation.* (S. F. Glaser, Trans.). Ann Arbor: University of Michigan Press. (Original work published in 1981)

Best, S. (1994). The commodification of reality and the reality of commodification: Baudrillard, Debord, and postmodern theory. In D. Kellner (Ed.), *Baudrillard: A critical reader* (pp. 41–67). Cambridge, MA: Blackwell.

Calvert, C. (2000). *Voyeur nation: Media, privacy, and peering in modern culture.* Boulder, CO: Westview Press.

Carson v. Here's Johnny Portable Toilets, Inc., 698 F.2d 831 (6th Cir. 1983).

Clay, S. C. (1994). Starstruck: The overextension of celebrity publicity rights in state and federal courts. *Minnesota Law Review, 79,* 485–517.

Cook, A. D. (1999). Should right of publicity protection be extended to actors in the characters which they portray. *Journal of Art & Entertainment Law, 9,* 309–351.

Coombe, R. (1994). Author/izing the celebrity: Publicity rights, postmodern politics, and unauthorized genders. In M. Woodmansee & P. Jaszi (Eds.), *The construction of authorship: Textual appropriation in law and literature.* Durham, NC: Duke University Press.

Coombe, R. (1991). Objects of property and subjects of politics: Intellectual property laws and democratic dialogue. *Texas Law Review, 69,* 1853–1880.

Cordero, S. M. (1998). Cocaine-cola, the velvet Elvis, and anti-Barbie: Defending the trademark and publicity rights to cultural icons. *Fordham Intellectual Property, Media and Entertainment Law Journal, 8,* 599.

Deyhimy, L. (1998). Why seeing is no longer believing: Misappropriations of image and speech. *Loyola of Los Angeles Entertainment Law Journal, 19,* 51–73.

Fisher, K. M. (2000). Which path to follow: A comparative perspective on the right of publicity. *Connecticut Journal of International Law, 16,* 95–116.

Fishman, S. (2000). *The public domain: How to find copyright-free writings, music, art and more.* Berkeley, CA: Nolo.

Fleischer, S. M. (2000). The right of publicity: Preventing an identity crisis. *Northern Kentucky University Law Review, 95,* 985–1020.

Frank, T., & Weiland, M. (1997). *Commodify your dissent.* New York: W.W. Norton.

Kahn, J. (1999). Bringing dignity back to light: Publicity rights and the eclipse of the Tort of Appropriation of Identity. *Cardozo Arts & Entertainment Law Journal, 17,* 213–272.

Kellner, D. (1994) Introduction: Jean Baudrillard in the Fin-De-Millennium. In D. Kellner. (Ed.), *Baudrillard: A critical reader* (pp. 1–23). Cambridge, MA: Blackwell.

King, J. (2000, Spring). The protection of personality rights for athletes and entertainers under English intellectual property law: Practical difficulties in relying on an action of passing off . *Sports Law Journal, 7,* 351–373.

Guy Lombardo v. Doyle, Dane & Bernbach, Inc., 396 N.Y.S.2d 661 (1977).

Haelan Laboratories, Inc. v. Topps Chewing Gum, Inc., 202 F.2d 866 (2nd Cir. 1953).

Haemmerli, A. (1999). Whose who? The case for a Kantian right of publicity. *Duke Law Journal, 49*, 383–492.

Halpern, S. (1995). The right of publicity: Maturation of an independent right protecting the associative value of personality. *Hastings Law Journal, 46*, 853–873.

Henley v. Dillard Dep't Stores, 46 F. Supp. 2d 587 (N.D. Tex. 1999).

Hoffman v. Capital Cities/ABC Inc., 33 F. Supp. 2d 867 (Dist. Court. Central Dist. of CA 1999).

Hyde, A. (1997). *Bodies of law*. Princeton, MA: Princeton University Press.

Lance, P. (2001). *The stingray: Lethal tactics of the sole survivor: The inside story of how the castaways were controlled on the island and beyond* (E-book edition). Cinema 21.

Madow, M. (1993). Private ownership of public image: Popular culture and publicity rights. *California Law Review, 81*, 125–240.

Martin Luther King, Jr. Center for Social Change Inc. v. American Heritage Products, 250 Ga. 135 (S.C. Georgia 1982).

Martin Luther King, Jr., Ctr. For Social Change, Inc. v. American Heritage Products, 694 F2d 674 (11th Cir. 1983).

Midler v. Ford Motor Co., 840 F.2d 460 (9th Cir. 1988).

Perry, M. M. (1999). Fragmented bodies, legal privilege, and commodification in science and medicine. *Maine Law Review, 51*, 169–210.

Poster, M. (1994). Critical theory and technoculture: Habermas and Baudrillard. In D. Kellner (Ed.), *Baudrillard: A critical reader* (pp. 68–88). Cambridge, MA: Blackwell.

Presley v. Russen, 513 F. Supp. 1339 (U.S. Dist. Ct. New Jersey 1981).

Prima v. Darden Restaurants, 78 F. Supp. 2d 337 (U.S. Dist. Ct. New Jersey 2000).

Prosser, D. (1960). Privacy. *California Law Review, 48*, 383.

Sen, S. (1995). Fluency of the flesh: Perils of an expanding right of publicity. *Albany Law Review, 59*, 739–763.

Stricker, B. (2000). In memory of lost heroes: Protecting the persona rights of deceased celebrities. *McGeorge Law Review, 31*, 611–622 .

Uhlaender v. Henricksen, 316 F. Supp. 1277 (U.S. Dist Court, Minnesota 1970).

Wendt v. Host Int'l, Inc., 125 F.3d 806 (9th Cir. 1997).

White v. Samsung Electronics America, Inc., 971 F.2d 1395 (9th Cir. 1992).

Yu, P. K. (1998). Fictional persona test: Copyright preemption in human audiovisual characters. *Cardozo Law Review, 20*, 355–414.

4

From *Dragnet* to *Survivor*: Historical and Cultural Perspectives on Reality Television

Sean Baker

In recent years, television programming in the United States has changed significantly. For instance, the congressional deregulation of telecommunications in 1996 instigated numerous mergers, restructurings, and deal makings that accounted for billions of dollars in yearly revenues. Digital television signals have begun to demonstrate the potential to broadcast multiple programs on one channel. Production costs have increased dramatically, while household penetration rates have begun to fall. Consequently, networks must compete aggressively for each audience member they can get.

The continuing shift in network programming to reality-based television represents another aspect of this metamorphosis (Littleton, 1997; Tobenkin, 1995). One can glance at a television schedule and see titles such as *Survivor*, *America's Most Wanted*, *Cops*, *Real Videos*, *Early Edition*, and *Prime Time Live*. In fact, Lin (1995) argues that the amount of broadcast prime-time reality programming doubled in the late 1980s. However, reality television may not be such a recent phenomenon as many researchers and practitioners assert. Shows from previous decades such as *Candid Camera* and *Real People* are often cited as the instigators of this genre (NTVS, 1997). Even earlier series such as *Dragnet* and *The Big Story* exhibited notable characteristics of reality-based television. One purpose of this examination is to describe the historical precedents of reality television.

A second intention is to identify the relevant factors that have contributed to the appearance of reality television in prime-time network schedules. First, reality television must be defined.

Reality Based Programming Defined

One definition of reality television is, "nonfictional programming in which the portrayal is presumed to present current or historical events or circumstances. The production presents itself as being a realistic account" (NTVS, 1997, p.272). This interpretation is broad, including news and public affairs programming, talk shows, entertainment programs, sports coverage, news magazines, documentaries, docu-dramas, movies "inspired by real events," and cinéma vérité formats. Kilborn (1994) presents a more specific definition:

> Reality programs involve (a) the recording, "on the wing," and frequently with the help of lightweight video equipment, of events in the lives in individuals or groups, (b) the attempt to simulate such real-life events through various forms of dramatized reconstructions and (c) the incorporation of this material, in suitable edited form, into an attractive packaged television program which can be promoted on the strength of its "reality" [p. 423].

This analysis will employ Kilborn's definition of reality television. However, a distinction between the most recent verité formats is necessary. Programs like *Survivor*, *The Mole* and *Boot Camp* differ from traditional verité formats such as *Cops* and *Rescue 911*. The primary difference lies in the involvement of the participants. The latest forms tend to show everyday people in constructed situations as a basis for the programming. Participation is voluntary and their actions are structured around the program itself. For example, the participants on *Survivor* and MTV's *Real World* are on television because they chose to be there. Thus, production values and techniques guide their activities. This represents a marked difference from previous verité formats whose participation tends to be involuntary, or at least participants are unaware of their potential appearances on television until they meet the production team by chance. Similarly, most current reality programming tends to focus on tasks or games. As part of the story, the performers are required to participate in activities, which in turn are constructed into a narrative. In contrast, older programs focus on actions and events as a common narrative structure. Accordingly, they attempt to represent more of a "slice of life" story rather than focusing on everyday people.

Here a new distinction is proposed based on participants' involvement on the program and the setting of the program. The first type may be termed *Artificial Person in Ordinary Settings (Artificial/Ordinary)* that primarily consists of docu-dramas based on real events and reenactments of events. Programs in this category tend to focus on criminal justice activities by highlighting the normal activities of solving crimes. *Dragnet* is the most notable example. The second distinct type is the *Artificial Person in Extraordinary Settings (Artificial/Extraordinary)*. It is similar to the first, where the content is organized around real-life events with reenactments and narratives based on real-life stories. Both employ professional actors and actresses. However the activities in this group are outside of normal daily events and often involve intense and dangerous situations. For example, *Combat* highlights the extreme conditions that soldiers faced during WW II. The third type, *Real People in Ordinary Settings (Real/Ordinary)*, emphasize everyday actions of people, but the participants are not professionals. Much of the content employs hand held cameras and submitted home video. The participants voluntarily accept their role on the program and are involved in common everyday activities. For example, people on *A Dating Story* are aware of the cameras prior to the filming and are doing an average activity—going out on a date. Finally *Real People in Extraordinary Settings (Real/Extraordinary)* revolve around non-professionals and tends to employ cinéma vérité formats. The distinction lies in the extreme activities and conditions that the participants are exposed to during shooting. Generally, participants choose to be on the program and they are involved in events that are purely constructed by the creators of the program. On *Survivor*, participants volunteer to participate in activities that are outside of what is considered to be "normal" —being stranded in a remote and dangerous location, eating bugs. Also, there is generally a single narrative (often the pursuit of a goal) that is presented throughout multiple episodes. Each category is discussed in detail below.

Typing Reality Television from 1950 to 2001

Table 1 lists prime-time reality programs that were ranked in the top 25 from the 1950 through 2001.[1] Across nearly all seasons, at least one reality program achieved a high standing, according to Nielsen rankings. For each season, all listed series are cross-referenced with detailed program descriptions.[2] Using this data, we can further illustrate reality television shows-types—as defined by this essay's typology.

TABLE 1.
Reality Television Programs by Year and Nielsen Ratings

Program	Year	Rank	Rating
The Big Story	1950–51	25	33.7
Gangbusters	1951–52	14	38.7
Dragnet	1951–52	20	36.3
Dragnet	1952–53	4	46.8
Gangbusters	1952–53	8	42.4
Dragnet	1953–54	2	53.2
Treasury Men in Action	1953–54	15	33.9
Dragnet	1954–55	2	42.4
Dragnet	1955–56	8	35.0
The Lineup	1955–56	17	30.8
Dragnet	1956–57	11	32.1
The Lineup	1956–57	15	31.4
The Life and Legend of Wyatt Earp	1957–58	6	32.6
The Lineup	1957–58	18	28.4
The Life and Legend of Wyatt Earp	1958–59	10	29.1
The Life and Legend of Wyatt Earp	1959–60	20	25.0
Candid Camera	1960–61	7	27.3
The Untouchables	1960–61	8	27.0
Candid Camera	1961–62	10	25.5
Candid Camera	1962–63	2	31.1
The Defenders	1962–63	18	23.9
Candid Camera	1963–64	7	27.7
Combat	1964–65	10	26.1
Dragnet	1966–67	21	21.2
The F.B.I.	1967–68	22	21.2
The F.B.I.	1968–69	18	21.7
Dragnet	1968–69	20	21.4
The F.B.I.	1969–70	24	20.6
The F.B.I.	1970–71	10	23.0
The Partridge Family	1970–71	25	19.8
The Partridge Family	1971–72	16	22.6
The F.B.I.	1971–72	17	22.4
The Partridge Family	1972–73	19	20.6
Project U.F.O.	1977–78	19	21.4
That's Incredible	1979–80	3	25.8
Real People	1979–80	14	22.1
Real People	1980–81	12	21.5
That's Incredible	1980–81	22	20.5
Real People	1981–82	21	19.7
That's Incredible	1982–83	22	18.3
TV's Bloopers and Practical Jokes	1983–84	14	20.3
TV's Bloopers and Practical Jokes	1984–85	22	17.1
Unsolved Mysteries	1988–89	17	17.4
America's Funniest Home Videos	1989–90	5	20.9
America's Funniest Home Videos	1990–91	7	16.7
America's Funniest People	1990–91	13	16.3
Unsolved Mysteries	1990–91	16	15.7
Unsolved Mysteries	1991–92	13	16.5
America's Funniest Home Videos	1991–92	20	14.5
America's Funniest People	1991–92	25	13.8

Program	Year	Rank	Rating
Rescue: 911	1992–93	12	15.1
Unsolved Mysteries	1992–93	21	14.2
Survivor[3]	1999–2000	2	22.5
Survivor: The Australian Outback	2001	1	20.1
Survivor: Africa	2001–2002	8	14.7
Survivor: Marqesas	2002	8	13.4

Source: *The Complete Directory to Prime Time Network and Cable TV shows, 1945-Present*, By Brooks and Marsh (2000) and Nielsen Media Research.

ARTIFICIAL PEOPLE IN ORDINARY SETTINGS

Reality programs in this category tend to draw attention to the commonplace activities of specialized occupations, often by focusing on solving crimes. Using dramatic reenactments and story lines based on real-life events, this group has the longest history in prime-time television. For example, *The Big Story* (1950–51) presented actual case histories about journalists who solved crimes or performed momentous public service activities. The sponsor, American Tobacco Company, awarded a five hundred dollar cash prize to the reporter whose story they featured. At the end of each program the journalist received "Pall Mall Award." One may assume that no journalists whose story highlighted health risks associated with the use of tobacco was earned this "honor." Given its minimal writing requirements and casting costs, the program's format inspired other series to try reality-based approaches.

The next season (1951–52) marked the appearance of Jack Webb's *Dragnet* on television. During the first two seasons *Dragnet* altered its weekly time slot with *Gangbusters*, another highly rated police anthology docu-drama. *Gangbusters* explicitly stated in the opening dialogue that the cases were "taken from actual police and F.B.I. files." Perhaps the most unique aspect of the show was in that at the end of each episode pictures of society's most wanted criminals were televised and viewers were asked to phone the authorities if one knew of his or her location. Hence, *Gangbusters* was the thirty-year predecessor to *America's Most Wanted*. Unfortunately, *Gangbusters* altered its weekly time slot with *Dragnet*, broadcasting's first formula packaged crime program. This ultimately led to *Gangbusters'* cancellation in 1953 (Marc, 1996). *Dragnet* emerged as enormous hit for NBC. More than that, it became a cultural icon (Marc, 1996; Marc & Thompson, 1992). In addition to being a formula format prototype, *Dragnet* was important for other reasons. It was the first to use law enforcement language, adding to the "realistic" nature. Also, it was the first to win an Emmy. In fact, it won "Best Mystery, Action, or Adventure Program" for three consecutive years . Indeed, *Dragnet* ensured the creation of a new television genre, the police show.

Jack Webb's programs were known for their dramatization of true events—and their use of "journalistic chronology" (Marc, 1996, p.75). *Dragnet* opened each episode with the voice of the rigid crime fighter, Sgt. Joe Friday, stating that this episode was based on real police files and "the names were changed to protect the innocent." From the start of each episode, viewers are presented with real cases where the victims are protected and criminals punished. In nearly all episodes, the criminals were caught and the sentence was pronounced as the stiff arm of justice prevailed over society. Of course, one could always discern Webb's conservative philosophy in these shows: good triumphed and evil paid the price (Marc & Thompson, 1992). *Dragnet* was highly successful, six years in the top 25 with a peak in 1954–55 when it climbed to number two on the Nielsen chart. Webb created numerous other series in his unique style, as well, but only *The Defenders* and *Project U.F.O.* reached *Dragnet's* popularity. Other shows inspired by *Dragnet* included *The F.B.I.* which, like its predecessor, revealed pictures of outlaws and requested citizens' help in locating the wanted criminals.

The window to reality presented in Artificial/Ordinary programs exemplifies a cultural fascination with realism. These programs emulate real-life by presenting content that attempts to illustrate what it is like to be a police officer, crime fighter or investigator. The use of actors and actresses represents a significant difference from many current reality based programs. This tendency sterilized the content when compared to newer programs. Technological limitations that forced the use of fixed camera shots and angles assisted in this process by creating an overly-produced look and feel to the programs. However, actual reality was emphasized by indicating that these programs were based on real case files and by frequently displaying images of suspects. Overall, these programs are the simplest and most banal of this genre.

ARTIFICIAL PEOPLE IN EXTRAORDINARY SETTINGS

This category is similar to the first except that it consists of programs that are based on pre-existing famous people or events, or has content where the actors and actresses are involved in extreme situations. The tendency to use well-known stories as structuring mechanisms marks an important departure from other series discussed in this essay. For example, from 1957 to 1960 *The Life and Legend of Wyatt Earp* earned a place among the top-25 Nielsen rated programs. This series in included because

Wyatt Earp was, indeed, a real personage from American history. My assumption is that viewers perceived this program as rendition of historical facts. Interestingly, even though the program was a Western, Wyatt Earp was a man of the law and the program's content documents his experiences as a lawman. Similarly, the 1960–61 season rendered a series based on Oscar Fraley's biography of Eliot Ness, *The Untouchables*. Again, episodes were presumed to be historically accurate descriptions of the vicious conflicts between Ness and organized crime. The program's most notable consequence was that it inspired a congressional investigation into the effects of media violence (Marc, 1996). Military dramas such as *Combat* managed to do fairly well, nonetheless. *Combat* illustrated a United States Army platoon fighting in Europe after D-Day. The inclusion of authentic World War II battle footage indicates the emphasis on realism. It was a mud-splattered series that emphasized realism by providing a microcosmic look at the lives of front-line infantryman and exposed viewers to the horrors of war. The cast was even trained at an actual army boot camp for a week prior to the onset of production (Brooks & Marsh, 2000).

The significance of these programs lies in the dramatization of real-life events and people. The entertainment value of these programs is emphasized by its realistic nature. At the same time, by using scripts, multiple takes, and professional actors and actresses, these programs are heavily produced, creating a genuine yet fashioned experience for viewers. This allows audience members a visceral thrill where they are able to experience actual events while still being entertained. The experience of historical events within the context of dramatization and professional programming standards establishes a new televised reality that acts as a social safety valve where viewers are able to experience these events within a sterilized setting that is shaped by the program producers and the content itself.

REAL PEOPLE IN ORDINARY SETTINGS

In 1960–61 a new style of reality programming rose to seventh in the Nielsen Ratings. Allen Funt's *Candid Camera* gained intense popularity and departed from previous models. The series promised a glance into comical reactions of ordinary people in ordinary settings—dealing with humorous situations. Given its use of real people, *Candid Camera* required a minimal cast and was, therefore, less expensive to produce. Similarly, *Real People* and *That's Incredible* showcased "slice of life" events of interesting people. Using footage of unconventional professions, hobbies and interests, *Real People* presented appealing commentary on offbeat persons, places, and things. Programs like these innovated reality television by bringing audiences into the lives of real people, often leaving the "set" altogether. In this way, these sorts of shows inspired a high degree of audience interaction. Shows like *America's Funniest Home Videos* and *America's Funniest People* took audience participation to an extreme. In each of these programs, viewers submitted video clips to win cash awards.

A consistent theme in Real/Ordinary programs is the presentation of actual people who are involved in commonplace settings. These "slice of life" windows have influence reality television today. For example, litigants on *Judge Judy*, *Divorce Court* and *Animal Court* want to settle their disputes on a televised courtroom reality program. The Learning Channel's *Life Unscripted* block programming also exemplifies this category by depicting makeovers, blind dates, wedding days, and baby births—everyday people confronting real life events. The key lies in the selection of ordinary people, not professional actors and actresses.

Real People in Extraordinary Settings

The final category also includes "typical" people—at least as "typical" a people who might be selected by network casting experts. Yet their activities are anything but typical. In fact, many of the activities would never occur outside of the content of the program itself. For example, Fox's *Temptation Island* consisted of unmarried couples who chose to vacation in exotic locales and date sexy singles to test the strength of their relationships. None of the authors in this volume can recall a similar situation in their lives—but this might simply reflect bias in the sample.

Rescue 911 is the only true cinéma vérité reality program that has achieved a top 25 rating. It documented heroic efforts of police, firefighters, paramedics, etc., often with footage from the actual efforts. *Rescue 911* and other Real/Extraordinary programs were inspired by *Cops*, another verité style program. With action-packed narratives, these police verité programs present an excessive view of reality that many viewers do not regularly face. Viewers confront minute details of program participants where it is common to hear the intense breathing of a police officer chasing a criminal or encounter the sights and sounds of a paramedic conducting an emergency procedure. Rarely does someone experience first hand tragic accidents or the violent subduing of a fleeing criminal suspect. The result is an enrichment of the potential vicarious experiences of these extreme situations similar to the window to the world presented in *Combat*.

In 2000, *Survivor's* extreme situations and competitions exaggerated this kind programming. Numerous clones of this format now exist, including imprisonment in a house (*Big Brother*), a race around the world (*Amazing Race*), or finding one's way back to the U.S. from an unidentified and remote location (*Lost*) to name a few. The blending of fact and fiction is elaborated in these programs yet the circumstances are slightly different. Here, authentic people (not professional actors) are subjected to artificial and constructed situations. Participants are not actually stranded on a desert island. Rather they voluntarily participate in the program with the chance of the reward. Also, if an accident occurs there are emergency paramedics and transportation opportunities if necessary. This did occur on *Survivor: The Australian Outback* where one participant was suffered serious burns and was removed from the island by a helicopter. Thus, *Survivor* is extreme, but not *that* extreme.

Each program in the last two categories pushes everyday people into the media spotlight—offering a chance for fame and recognition. For instance, "freed" members of *Survivor* and *Big Brother* are often guests on *Today, Early Edition, Late Night with David Letterman*, among other talk and entertainment programs. Other opportunities arise for contestants. Many are now topics of both television and print advertisements, feature films, and magazine articles from *People* to *Playboy*. This secondary coverage pushes the common person into the limelight and creates a new breed of professional actors and actress with minimal (if any) training. This potential resonates into society where teenagers attempt to reach stardom by trying out for a limited chance to appear on these programs (Tan, 2001).

The Economy and Attraction of Reality Television

Television is a resource intensive medium. Recent stories of actors demanding salaries of one million dollars an episode are convincing examples of skyrocketing expenses. Other aspects of the production process are rising at astronomical rates. For example, licensing fees increased 45% from 1985 to 1991 (Coe, 1991). To address this problem, networks can either raise advertising costs or cut production expenses. The latter technique is utilized with complimentary outcomes (Foisie, Brown, & Flint, 1991). In fact, "losses in audience-related advertising revenue are more than offset by savings in production costs" (Atkin & Litman, 1986, p.42).

Employment of the reality television format offers a successful strategy to accomplish this goal. Obviously, programs like *Cops* and *Rescue 911* have minimal, if any, casting expenses. Also, these programs can follow police officers, paramedics, and firefighters for a short period of time and record enough footage that can be edited into multiple episodes. Further, the content of *America's Funniest Videos* and *Real TV* primarily consists of viewer submitted videotape. Technological improvements in recording devices have advanced the rise and endurance of reality television. In recent years, the reduced cost of lightweight, sophisticated cameras have provided amateur video makers the ability to produce broadcast quality sound and video. Accordingly, this situation has assisted in the introduction and maintaining of reality based television, particularly the Real/Ordinary and Real/Extraordinary categories as programming strategies.

The occupational culture of television programmers also plays an important role in the popularity of reality television. Programmers confront ambiguity and uncertainty when deciding which television series will be successful in forthcoming seasons. They have no trustworthy guidelines for predicting whether audiences, advertisers, and critics will embrace the series. Also, they encounter multiple and often contradictory assessment criteria (Bielby & Bielby, 1994). To legitimate their decisions, programmers often justify their scheduling decisions by choosing new programs that are created from established writers or producers (Bielby & Bielby, 1994). Another strategy is to mimic other hit series. This is obvious from the similarity of numerous shows listed in Figure 2 and the numerous *Survivor* clones that have come to dominate network schedules. Economic considerations play an important role in the evolution of reality programming as a genre.

Macroeconomics facilitated the introduction of reality television as a modern genre. In an increasingly competitive market, networks are often forced to create new and exciting formats in an attempt to increase market share (Litman, 1993). For example, in the late 1970s ABC matured, widening its market share and legitimizing itself as a competitive network. Consequently, ABC producers increased program expenditures and developed new formats (Litman, 1979). Attempting to regain audiences, NBC and CBS also enhanced program quality and diversity. *That's Incredible* (ABC), *Real People* (NBC) and other Real/Ordinary series resulted from their efforts. The success of these series prompted numerous cloned reality programs. Thus, the financial environment of television adds to the explanation of the proliferation of contemporary reality programming. However, economics alone does not justify the existence of this genre. Indeed, without viewers, a series will fail.

Part of the attraction reality television stems from the "real" portrayals. People tend to perceive these formats as more realistic representations of life than pure fictional programs (Geiser-Getz, 1995). The news-like format that many reality programs utilize exaggerates this relationship. The voyeuristic quality of reality television allows viewers to "participate" in law enforcement and other activities. The audience experiences intrusions into homes, vivid images of tragic events, and detailed descriptions of crime scenes. In short, viewers are exposed to social artifacts that, previously, had been viewed as private (Andersen, 1995). Contemporary Real/Extraordinary programs such as *Survivor* exaggerate this characteristic.

The interactivity of many reality television programs also contributes to their popularity. Shows like *America's Funniest Home Videos* construct viewers "in relationship to the ritual of audience participation" (Caldwell, 1995, p.277). Viewers watch these sorts of program to formulate ideas for potential clips from their lives that may win cash prizes. In this way, the audience is drawn to watch and participate in the television experience. Indeed, reality television reduces the social distance between viewers and program events (Manning, 1996). As a result, exposure becomes an interactive affair. For instance, *America's Most Wanted* nurtures active participation by empowering viewers to search for criminals and report suspects to the program center in Washington, D.C. Thus, viewers identify with crime control, and are encouraged to watch next week and see if surveillance induces the arrest of fugitives (Cavender, 1993). Networks encourage this process to enhance internalization of meaning and boost ratings (Caldwell, 1995). On *Big Brother* audiences had the opportunity to participate in creating the content itself by voting on who should be removed from the program. *Big Brother 2* also uses this technique where there is a weekly choice to determine an amenity that is added to the house.

These simulated worlds of television culture where narratives are constructed around highly produced and choreographed events embody a new reality that is neither fact nor fiction. As these messages increase, the implications are that what we call to be truth is questionable in U.S. society. Now that reality based television stars are celebrities the traditional distinction between professional celebrities (e.g., film stars) and accidental celebrities (e.g., topics of news like Monica Lewinsky) is becoming blurred. Today, new media icons are people who participate in extreme events as opposed to traditionally ones who must have significant talent that assists in their becoming stars. Socially, meaning and importance is ascribed to these new media figures. As they become icons in a society fascinated with the new and improved, the difference between television reality and actual reality is reduced.

Television presents a mediation of culture. Culture, ideology, and normative social and individual functions are presented and interpreted by television, creating memories that are based on mediated nostalgia not reality (Ventura, 1995). Postmodern aspects of television demonstrate that culturally we are attracted to reality based television programming, yet the images are artificial constructs. "The simulacrum denies not reality, but the difference between the image and the real," resulting in a homogeneous ideology that is experienced solely through mediation (Fiske, 1996, p.57). Thus, viewers' experience with "reality does not exist in the objectivity of empiricism, but is a product of discourse" (Fiske, 1996, p.56). Essentially, the artificial worlds of reality television become real for viewers and the ideas and values embedded within them become truth while the mediation and manipulation of culture are masked behind the "reality" itself.

It is evident that reality-based programming has been and continues to be a notable and popular programming type. Reality television originated in the 1950s with programs like *Dragnet* and *The Big Story* and has continued throughout the history of U.S. television into contemporary versions like *Survivor*. This chapter has tracked the endurance and popularity of reality television while commenting on its cultural significance. Also a new distinction of current reality television based on participation levels of the "stars" and program setting was offered. This new distinction allows for a better understanding of social and cultural implications of reality television by illustrating novel differences between current programs. As argued in this chapter, the voyeuristic and realistic portrayals of social life that are presented in reality programming obscure the traditional distinctions between fictional and non-fictional television. The problem lies in the seemingly realistic depictions that are often heavily produced and choreographed. The potential ramifications for viewers are significant where it is becoming increasingly difficult to ascertain the difference between fact and fiction. The point of view discussed here is a valuable foundation for scholars and industry personnel to think about reality television within different contexts, allowing for a much richer and comprehensive understanding of this ever-mutating genre.

Endnotes

1. The inclusion of only the top 25 programs may introduce bias into this analysis. Some reality television programs may not have obtained a Nielsen rating this high, which would exclude them from this analysis. However, I am presenting a description of popular series, and the top 25 is a reasonable cut off point. Also, I am arguing that reality television has existed throughout television history, thus,

the potential bias is in favor of excluding programs and invalidating this assumption.

2. The program descriptions were compiled by Brooks and Marsh (2000). Therefore, I am trusting that their descriptions are fair and accurate. Any fault in their analysis would resonate into this essay. Their accounts are similar to those presented by Marc and Thompson (1992). Also, I have been exposed to some of these programs and feel that Brooks and Marsh's descriptions are correct. I coded television shows as reality based if they (a) were dramatizations based on true events or facts; (b) were based on actual historical persons or figures; (c) employed a cinéma vérité technique; (d) filmed people in authentic situations in which the program was not a news magazine or documentary; or (e) represented or simulated real-life events, people, or situations.

3. Since each *Survivor* series follows a non-traditional scheduling format, comparisons to other programs are problematic. The rankings for each *Survivor* program are based on their overall ratings from each premiere to the finale.

References

Andersen, R. (1994). "Reality" TV and criminal justice. *The Humanist, 54,* 8–13.

Andersen, R. (1995). *Consumer culture and TV programming.* Boulder, CO: Westview.

Atkin, D., & Litman, B. (1986). Network TV programming: Economics, audiences, and the ratings game, 1971–1986. *Journal of Communication, 36,* 32–50.

Bielby, W., & Bielby, D. (1994). "All hits are flukes": Institutionalized decision making and the rhetoric of network prime-time program development. *American Journal of Sociology, 99,* 1287–1313.

Brooks, T., & Marsh, E. (2000). *The complete directory to prime time network and cable TV shows, 1946-present.* New York: Ballantine Books.

Caldwell, J. (1995). *Televisuality: Style, crisis and authority in American television.* New Brunswick, NJ: Rutgers University Press.

Cavender, G. (1993). Fear and loathing on reality television: An Analysis of *America's Most Wanted* and *Unsolved Mysteries. Sociological Inquiry, 63,* 305–317.

Cavender, G. (1998). In the "Shadows of Shadows": Television reality crime programming." In M. Fishman & G. Cavender (Eds.), *Entertaining crime: Television reality programs.* New York: Aldine De Gruyter.

Coe, S. (1991). The rise and rise of program prices. *Broadcasting, 121* (13), 44–45.

Fiske, J. (1996). Postmodernism and television. In J. Curran & M. Gurevitch (Eds.), *Mass media and society.* London: Edward Arnold.

Foisie, G., Brown, R., & Flint, J. (1991). One of TV's best-kept secrets: How ABC, CBS, and NBC have taken the bite out of program costs." *Broadcasting, 121* (24), 3–4.

Geiser-Getz, G. (1995). *Cops* and the comic frame: Humor and meaning-making in reality-based television. *Electronic Journal of Communication, 5,* 1–22.

Kilborn, R. (1994). "How real can you get?": Recent developments in "reality" television. *European Journal of Communication, 9,* 421–239.

Lin, C. (1995). Diversity of network prime-time program formats during the 1980s. *The Journal of Media Economics, 8,* 17–28.

Litman, B. (1979). The television networks, competition, and program diversity. *Journal of Broadcasting, 23*, 393–410.

Litman, B. (1993). The changing role of television networks. In A. Alexander, J. Owers, & R. Carveth (Eds.), *Media economics: Theory and practice*. Hillsdale, NJ: Lawrence Erlbaum.

Littleton, C. (1997). Long arm of reality. *Broadcasting and Cable, 127* (2), 35–36.

Manning, P. (1991). Dramaturgy, politics, and the axial media event. *The Sociological Quarterly, 37*, 261–278.

Marc, D. (1996). *Demographic vistas: Television in American culture*. Philadelphia: University of Pennsylvania Press.

Marc, D., & Thompson, R. (1992). *Prime time, prime movers*. Boston: Little, Brown and Co.

Mulvey, L. (1984). Visual pleasure and narrative cinema. In B. Wallis (Ed.), *Art after modernism: Rethinking representation*. New York: D.R. Godine.

NTVS. (1997). Television violence in "reality" programming: University of Texas, Austin study. In *National television violence study: Volume 1*. Newbury Park, CA: Sage.

Tan, C. (2001, August 21). Almost famous: MTV generation thinks star statue is just an audition away. *The Baltimore Sun*, E1.

Tobenkin, D. (1995). Real stories of a crowded genre. *Broadcasting and Cable, 125* (4), 16–20.

Ventura, M. (1995). Report from El Dorado. In D. George & J. Tribus (Eds.), *Reading culture: Contexts for critical reading and writing*. New York: Harper Collins.

II

LESSONS ABOUT PLAYING SOCIAL GAMES

5

Reel Life: The Social Geometry of Reality Shows

Ellis Godard

"But most importantly, the show was real. You could watch how people handled situations and relationships that weren't concocted. ...This was a mentally demanding social experiment" [Hatch, 2000, p. 122].

Reality shows are the edited footage of unscripted interactions, broadcast as a television series about participants' naturally occurring social life.[1] Both scripted and unscripted television programming concerns cast behavior in a sequence of structured events on a uniquely designed set, drawn from more footage than could be affordably broadcast. But the content and casts of reality shows are distinct. They may involve seven strangers living in a plush urban loft courtesy of a television network, sixteen strangers reducing their number until one becomes a millionaire, six singles chained together until two find love, or pairs of strangers racing each other around the world. What makes them *reality* shows is the resulting naturalness of social interaction, including familiar patterns of confrontation. Their casts, who participate with almost no scripted dialogue, interact in patterns that can be described with the same theoretical statements that describe social life in any setting. While the settings are atypical, the social life is theoretically normal.

Interactions on reality shows, while natural, are nonetheless highly structured. They have no scripts, but they *are* productions and many of their details are by design (see Roth, chapter 2): Sets are constructed through art and "prop" (property) departments, participants are cast from among thousands of applicants, producers shape and sequence the events, and editors finalize the broadcast segments. But beyond conventional production processes, reality shows are also structured through sociological processes. For example, participants' ability to interact with each other, the crew, and others affects their proximity to adversaries and their access to supporters (Black, 1993). Production decisions about parameters such as these affect participant behavior by limiting, prohibiting, or even conducing behavioral patterns. In particular, they affect what patterns of conflict are available to be filmed, and thus help determine the content of these shows. Although producers are not aware of it, available theory explains the results of sociological decisions they already make.

In this chapter, I contrast the social structures of eleven reality shows and the moral patterns these structures induce. Anecdotal[2] comparisons illustrate the extent to which this content mirrors everyday social patterns, as well as manners in which production decisions structure that content. In the next two sections, I introduce the strategy of explanation that I employ and then introduce a series of observations about the mobility and isolation provided by sets, the diversity of cast members selected, and the stratification, organization, and intimacy of their participation. I conclude by summarizing theoretical lessons for producers.

Theoretical Approach

My sociological account of reality shows employs an explanatory strategy and theoretical model developed by Donald Black, initially to account for variation in police behavior (1971 and 1973; see also 1980), then expanded to account for all forms of conflict management (1976)[3] and, later, a range of social behavior including medicine, ideas, and art (1993), religion (1995), and science (2000a). Black's work employs a revolutionary conception of sociology (1995), constitutes an entirely new kind of sociology (1997; 2000b), and represents a significant scientific breakthrough in sociological explanation (1995; 2000a). His strategy, model, and theory have been employed in a growing body of literature that explicitly applies his ideas to a variety of social settings (e.g., Baumgartner, 1988; Horwitz, 1984; Morrill, 1995; Senechal de la Roche, 1996; Tucker, 1999). Here, I employ these ideas to relate aspects of participation on each reality show to variation in conflicts observed on them. First, I introduce Black's explanatory strategy of pure sociology, descriptive model of social geometry, and theory of conflict management.

STRATEGY OF PURE SOCIOLOGY

The theoretical strategy of pure sociology (Black, 1997; 2000a) "purifies" the discipline (Black, 2000b) of the facts and accounts of other disciplines, including anything remotely psychological, such as the intentions or motivations of participants (Black, 1976). Instead, it addresses observable variation in social interactions, such as the extensiveness or exclusivity of interactions. The approach permits explanations not of the behavior of individuals as such, but of the social life that occurs between and among them. Violence and crime, for example, are not what one person does to another, but things that occur between them, under specifiable *sociological* conditions.[4]

The content of reality shows can similarly be accounted without any regard for the intentionality of participants. Their patterns of confrontation are often attributed to characteristics of participants as individuals, such as motivations, independent of the social context on each show. Johnson (2001b), for example, wrote that, "Whether chaos actually erupts [on *Big Brother*] is up to the fools who volunteer to be on camera 24 hours a day. [In the show's first season], a group of mostly nice people opted to bond with each other, leaving the chaos to the production staff." However, whatever erupts can be attributed in part to the production itself— not merely to the fact that the interactions are filmed, but aspects of them settled before filming begins. Shows may need "the right mix of people to produce sparks—belligerent, romantic, or otherwise" (Johnson, 2001a). But contexts produce sparks, as well—and belligerence is not uniformly displayed in all contexts. Even "mean" contestants will be eruptive only under certain sociological conditions. Neither interest in cash prizes nor personal ethics need to be imputed in order to explain variation in moral life on reality shows. Participant interactions, and the structures provided for them, suffice.

MODEL OF SOCIAL GEOMETRY

Black also developed the idea of explaining social life with its "social geometry," envisioning moral life as occurring within a multidimensional social space (Black, 1976; 1995) His model includes five dimensions of social space: Interactions vary vertically, horizontally, culturally, organizationally, and normatively. The *vertical* dimension is the unequal distribution of wealth: Participants (and tribes) can be more or less impoverished, and any two adversaries can have more or less equal resources. The *horizontal* dimension addresses the distribution of relations among individuals, both within society and directly: Participants can be more or less involved with others, so have more or less equal integration—and they may have more or less direct relations, so be relationally closer to or more distant from each other. The *cultural* dimension addresses both the quantity of expressiveness—such as variation in symbols and artifacts—and cultural distance, such as ethnic differences. Reality shows can have more or less cultural content, their participants can be more or less culturally conventional, and their casts are more or less culturally diverse. The *corporate* dimension addresses the capacity for collective action: Participants can be more organized or more atomized. Finally, the *normative* dimension concerns variation as a result of conflict management itself: Those who have been previously labeled deviant (or otherwise wrong) have lower normative status (and, the theory below predicts, are more likely than others to be subjected to further conflict management). Participants in any case, such as an instance of violence, can be located according to their relative status on any of these dimensions.

The distance between participants varies and can be assessed, such as their relative wealth (their vertical distance) or their relative degree of integration (their radial distance). The relative locations of participants in a setting, and the distances between them according to these dimensions, thus define the social geometry (Black, 2000a) of that setting.[5] For example, reality shows vary in whether they have greater relational distance or heightened intimacy, and stratification of resources or marked equality. Groups and settings can similarly be compared in terms of the variation in the distance among their participants—i.e., their social diversity (see Black, 1976)—and this varies among reality show casts, as well. Social geometries describe instances of social behavior, by specifying the relative locations of participants within social space, and by the direction of that behavior (such as in an upward direction, from lower to higher corporate status). That is, any case of social life has a social geometry. The model thus describes cases and settings as a step in specifying the sociological conditions conducive to certain quantities and forms of behavior. It can similarly be used to specify the reality show designs likely to produce or exclude desired patterns of filmable content.

Theory of Conflict Management

A growing body of theory utilizes the model to explain patterns of interactions. Black's theory of conflict management uses it to explain moral behavior. For example, violence may occur in a more or less stratified setting, and from a lower status person towards someone of higher status or vice versa. Moreover, the behavior of moral life—the geometric patterns in which individuals express grievances and thereby manage their conflicts—is now known to have stable patterns. Black's theory of conflict management (esp. 1976; 1993; 1995) identifies the conditions under which participants act alone (1983; 1984b; 1990) and whether they act decisively, directly, or not at all (1993). It explains variation in the quantity, structure, and form of conflict management with the relative social characteristics of participants (Black, 1976), that is, with their social geometries. The *quantity* of conflict management (Black, 1984a; 1993) varies according to the social location of participants. For example, it is observed more often among acquaintances than among strangers and more often among those who are integrated than among those who are nomadic or otherwise marginal (Black, 1976). The quantity of conflict management also varies with its direction in social space. For example, it is most likely to be observed when integrated persons manage outsiders and when higher status persons manage inferiors (Black, 1976). In other words, conflict management has a radial direction and a vertical direction: It is more likely outward than inward, and downward rather than upward. Each dimension of social space conveys a kind of status—vertical *wealth*, relational *intimacy*, cultural *conventionality*, corporate *organization*, or normative *respectability*—that serves as a structural defense against confrontation. The quantity of conflict management thereby increases as distances between participants increase, and is highest where there are relational differences, vertical segmentation, and normative events that identify wrongs (Black, 1976).

Conflict management also varies in its *structure*. It may involve only principal adversaries, who act unilaterally through self-help (Black, 1998) or bilaterally. It may also involve third parties, either as partisans (Black, 1993) or as settlement agents (Black & Baumgartner, 1983). An example of settlement agents would be a producer intervening to resolve a conflict, as *Real World* producers have done by removing cast members who hit other cast members. But settlement is unusual in all shows observed. More common are partisans, available onlookers who take sides with one side or adversary in a dispute. Partisanship occurs with variation in intimacy, arising as "a joint function of social closeness to one side and social remoteness from the other" (Black, 1993, p. 126–128). It occurs in reality shows not only in the context of conflicts, but also in the negotiation of voting alliances. The alliances themselves trigger conflict and further partisanship, by adding variety to the intimacy among participants, bringing some closer together while isolating others.

The *form* of conflict management also varies according to specifiable conditions (Black, 1990). For example, upward conflict management (from lower to higher status) is rebellion, while discipline is downward (Black, 1993). But vertical segmentation alone is not sufficient for either rebellion or discipline: Each also requires social distance, inequality, functional unity, and immobility (Black, 1993). These are the precisely conditions between staff and crew that generated a threat of mutiny on the first *Big Brother*. But rebellion rarely occurs in other reality shows, since they do not have the same degree on social distance and immobility. Vengeance is even more rare. While it flows laterally between immobile equals such as are found on many reality shows, it also requires functional independence and organization (Black, 1993). Participants on reality shows are often interdependent yet disorganized. Where they are both organized and independent, such as with the tribes of *Survivor* or even more so during *Real World / Road Rules* challenges, vengeance is common. Reality shows do have the conditions for settlement—"the handling of a grievance by a nonpartisan third party" (Black, 1993, p. 85)—including organizational asymmetry and relational distance. However, settlement occurs only between cast and crew, as casts themselves are too relationally close and equal (see Black, 1993). Avoidance is found where there is an absence of hierarchy and individuation (Black, 1993), both of which many reality shows encourage. However, avoidance also requires social fluidity, fragmentation, and independence (Black, 1993), absent from most shows. Cast members thus avoid each other except when there is hierarchy, organization (e.g., alliances), and interdependence (typically forced if present on some shows, while endemic to the nature of other shows). In each reality show, as in any setting, social conditions may restrict some forms of conflict management and allow others to predominate. But social differentiation diversifies moral life (Black, 1976), and some shows are sufficiently diverse to produce even unusual forms such as violence and settlement (Black, 1993).

The theory of conflict management is remarkably powerful. It allows the moral life of reality shows to be explained with structural aspects of each show, rather than with storylines or the motivations of participants. Variable aspects of show design structure the situations in which participants interact, establishing parameters on their interactions and thus dictating, in part, the quantities, structures, and forms of moral life present. The structured social geometry of each reality show—the exclusivity of its sets, the diversity of its casts, and the relations of its participants— explains the variation in which its participants identify and manage each other, as well as the crew and others.

Set Exclusivity

The sets of reality shows vary widely. Most of each *Real World* is filmed in a house or apartment, *Road Rules* casts travel in an RV, and *Lost* participants travel by any means available. *Survivor* has been on an island, the Australian outback, and an African game preserve. *Love Cruise* takes place on a boat, as did one season of *Road Rules*. Some of these sets are more exclusive than others. *Real World* casts come and go from the set as they please, *Big Brother* participants have no view beyond the yard of their five-room set, and *Chains of Love* participants leave the set only under prescribed conditions (prearranged "dates"). Exclusivity in the physical structure of sets effects variation in social structures, including whether participants must interact with each other and whether they can interact with others. Some sets allow temporary escape (whether to be alone or to interact with family or friends) whereas others restrict cast mobility (from each other and towards third parties) and thus structurally limit available forms of conflict management. Sets also vary in participant exposure to crew. Some sets are exclusive in both of these regards, while others allow some combination of cast mobility and/or crew exposure.

Cast Mobility

Reality shows vary in the degree to which they allow participants to roam and leave a central set, and thus interact less with other cast members and more with non-cast persons. Whereas the casts of many reality shows interact almost solely with each other, *Real World* participants are able to leave the set overnight, and indeed spend much of their time elsewhere. They meet and express grievances to (and about) friends, love interests, strangers, families, producers, coworkers, clients, professors, and more. Their mobility widens their social geometries to include third parties, providing forms and structures (even adversaries) not permitted in most reality shows. *Survivor's* cast is much less mobile than *Real World's*, limiting conflict management patterns to within the cast, but more mobile than *Big Brother's*, allowing alliances and other aspects of conflict management to remain covert, hidden sometimes even from the crew. *Survivor* contestants wander from camp to gossip or avoid—not as extensively as on *Real World*, but more easily (and more often) than on *Big Brother*, where one cast resorted to whispering its grievances. Contrarily, *Chains of Love* participants are literally bound together, so their conflict management is necessarily local and public. The cabins of *Love Cruise* provide some opportunity for relational distance (and variation), but apparently not enough to prevent overt confrontation even in the first few days.

Whereas individual mobility adds structural alternatives (as through third parties), group mobility removes them. *Lost* and *Amazing Race* teams travel freely worldwide, but most of their interaction remains within those two-person teams, with little flexibility for the management of conflicts. *Lost* teams are quickly dispersed and then never near one another. *Amazing Race* teams often meet up when, for example, they wait for a common flight. Since only the slowest team is removed from each leg in the competition, those in front sometimes cooperate to protect their lead. But their alliances are as fluid as their intimacy, evidenced when two teams were abandoned in Paris by another team with whom they had been cooperating. As on *Eco-Challenge*, most conflicts remain within teams, and other teams are as likely to provide partisans as adversaries. More diverse moralism requires *individual* mobility. The *Road Rules* cast is similarly nomadic, with frequently changing third parties all remaining distant. But while the group is mobile, individual mobility from the group is restricted. The participants, physically confined on the road to an RV, are thereby *structurally* confined. As a result, moralism is turned inward, and participants frequently blame each other. The restrained closeness, combined with a lack of consistent third parties, generates intense moralism that comes in bursts and fits, including frequent screaming not seen on other shows. Confined intimacy thus *can* produce intense moralism.

Mobility can either be restricted or increased. Introducing mobility alters cast geometries and so can also produce moralism. Several *Real World* casts took trips abroad, bringing the members closer together but further from whatever non-cast third parties they had near the main set. These trips provide new physical sets, such as small cabins in an African train where gossip generated a mean prank that affected the relational and normative status of several participants upon their return to the main set. But restricting mobility does not generate exclusivity if the cast has partisans who are themselves mobile. The exclusivity of *Big Brother* is broken through periodic interviews by crew, but also because non-cast partisans hire planes to fly banners over the set while cast members use the 24-hour webcast, allowing limited bi-directional communication with the outside world—something not possible on *Survivor*, taped remotely in undisclosed foreign locations and aired after completion. Through banners, particular cast members receive messages of encouragement or derision. But even those derided gain status by having a banner: When a banner from Nicole's husband alleged intimacy with another participant, the cast defended and consoled her. External partisans appear to raise the status of participants.

CREW EXPOSURE

Staff exposure on most reality shows is kept to a minimum, at least in what is broadcast. *Survivor* producer Mark Burnett acknowledges (2000) that crew interactions can affect the course of participant events. Thus, when a *Survivor* cast member burns his face and hands, or when a flood or tide washes away supplies, cameramen know they would be fired for interfering. But their very presence matters, both theoretically and empirically. There is variation among shows in how accessible crewmembers are, with consequently variable effects on social structure and moral life. Despite Burnett's protestations, his crew is more sociologically involved than others. The extent to which participants interact with the show's production staff varies, as does the extent to which such interaction is shown in the final edits. *Big Brother* participants are filmed by 28 stationary (including infrared) cameras, with actual cameraman concealed behind one-way mirrors. While there are hidden cameras on *Survivor, Real World,* and *Road Rules*, their contestants are also followed, often on foot, by camera crews they come to recognize, if not interact with. Even on *Survivor*, billed as having a marooned cast, participants are never really alone. Interaction with crew allows moralism to be revealed via gossip, which becomes particularly frequent and complex at the off-set crew compound (Burnett, 2000). These interactions, and the constituent gossip, are evidenced by answers to specific questions not only during solo interviews but also directly by host Jeff Probst at the periodic tribal councils, where voting takes places and thus moralism is at its highest. Probst precedes each tribal council with a lengthy interrogation of members in front of each other, including explicit and repeated questions such as, "Is there an alliance?" Unlike *Big Brother* contestants, who have less interaction with staff and almost no group feedback based on those individual interactions, *Survivor* members face greater revelation of their social life because that show's crew is involved, not in the face of physical threats but in the geometry of sociological threats.

Although crews (including Probst, and producer interviews on many shows) do engage the social geometries of participants, they rarely settle disputes—professionally because their premise is to capture natural behavior, but also structurally because their status is so much higher. Producers intervene most often on *Real World,* where crews are more accessible than those of most reality shows. They are sufficiently close to generate two cast/crew relationships and at least three instances of settlement (discussed below). Though not broadcast, higher amounts of gossip and other forms probably also arise from the crews' greater proximity. On *Making the Band*, by contrast, producer Lou Pearlman criticizes participants directly. He disciplines them, and his structural position—a status superior who is more organized than any of the participants but in frequent contact with them—allows and explains his behavior. It also explains the behavior of the participants, who (like *Survivor's* cast towards Probst) defer and do not rebel—at least on the show.

Cast Diversity

Giving explanatory weight to storylines, the *Big Brother* competition—involving confined spaces, virtually no outside interactions, and elimination towards a sole $500,000 winner—ought to generate more moralism than *Real World*, where members cooperate incrementally with no risk of loss and plenty of outlets moralism. *Big Brother* participants have fewer moral alternatives, and more to lose from being stigmatized. But structural variation on *Real World* generated more conflict than the monetary competition of *Big Brother*, at least in its initial configuration of structural homogeneity. Reality shows vary in the amount of social diversity the casts include, and social diversity generates moral diversity (Black, 1976). Some social variation emerges from the casting process. Other variation emerges within the events of each show, subject to the structural design of that show.

SOCIAL DIVERSITY

"The cast of *Survivor* is diverse in age, experience, and background—and, yes, in race, religion and sexuality—which yields plenty of interesting conflict" (Denhart, 2000). While diversity may widen a show's potential audience appeal, some shows are broadcast to narrow audiences so employ less cast diversity. The casts of *Real World*, selected to fit the youthful demographic of MTV's audience, are of a narrower age range (18–24) than most reality shows, and appear more culturally and vertically similar, as well. But while *Real World* casts members arrive more similar than do those on *Big Brother* or *Survivor*, they become more differentiated structurally by assigned roles such as weekly producer of a radio show or business manager of a clothing startup. They also have access to resources (including money, and places to spend it) and more interaction with non-cast members (who add radial, relational, organizational, cultural, and normative variation). And not all are strangers: On one *Real World* season, two cast members were prior friends, making the cast more relationally diverse than "seven strangers." Structural diversity generated moral variety, adding avoidance, violence, and even settlement (with examples of each discussed later in this chapter).

Some variation emerges through resource differentiation. *Survivor* cast members are under the strain of scarce food and shelter, but relieving that strain can awaken moralism. Food, tools, and other supplies are unevenly distributed by reward challenges. The higher status tribe typically experiences the most internal confrontation. The other tribe lacks food and strength, thus weaker in immunity challenges and more vulnerable to having to vote off one of their own. Their lower vertical status and more tenuous position generate lower levels of conflict, sometimes to the point of sullenness. But the richer tribe experiences rich eruptions, such as between Alicia and Kimmi screaming at each other (2/22/01), first over whether to eat a chicken won during a reward challenge and then over the confrontational style of Alicia, who exclaimed, "I will always point my finger in your face!" Diversity also emerges through conflict management itself, which both labels someone as having committed a wrong and subjects the labeled participant to further criticism (Black, 1976). Conflict is itself sometimes deviant, so that claiming to have been wronged can itself be wrong. The social life of each show thus changes as the show progresses. Relational histories are established, and participants are no longer strangers. As their social space becomes differentiated by competition, contribution, and confrontation, new patterns of conflict management emerge. The participants are cast, but their social life continues to evolve.

SELECTIVE STRATIFICATION

Each setting allows diversity to emerge among participant interactions, if only through scant differences in relations and growing patterns of normative labeling. But diversity can also be part of the design of a reality show, and producers alter designs in order to increase diversity. *Real World* moved from exclusively residential in the first four seasons to cooperative ventures among cast members, increasing both role variation and relational histories. Changes in *Road Rules* have been even more significant. Competitions became for individual rewards rather than for the team, differentiating cast members by their relative wealth rather than merely their contribution to a group effort. Then, for each two missions not completed, cast members had to vote off one of their own, to be replaced by the producers. This innovation allowed an outlet for moralism, but also introduced relational variation when a replacement was added. It also allowed patterns of partisanship and deception not apparent in earlier seasons.

Significant changes have also been made to *Big Brother*. Whereas *Real World* casts typically live in a flat, the original *Big Brother* was *structurally* flat. Despite the lack of mobility and third parties, cast members' interactions were not sufficiently diverse to generate conflict. Few production choices allowed individual differentiation or social distance. Almost all of the other reality shows discussed include various opportunities for individual reward and advancement. But *Big Brother* competitions were almost all group efforts, such as everyone having to eat a pie, dress up as one another, ride a bike, jump rope, or complete a domino rally. The only structural distinction among the cast came through nominations for banishment, and those were doled out weakly: Each cast nominated two others for eviction (rather than one, as on *Survivor*), and the two with the most nominees were put to a phone-in vote by the viewing audience. What little social distance there was (largely normative) was eliminated through nominations. After the few members who were conflictual were nominated and banished, and without sufficient distance to identify clear deviants, few cast members assembled many nominations. Ties were frequent, so that the audience often had to choose between more than two contestants. By midway through the season (8/24/00), the nominations were a six-way tie, as indecisive as the cast could get. While there is not evidence that they had *planned* such indecisiveness, several called it "cool." Anything more decisive may not have fit their social geometry. Indeed, the cast worked throughout the season to eliminate conflict amongst themselves, directing their grievances outward in critiques of the voting process and the show generally. After completing a required "roast" of each other, they threatened to walk off the set and forego the cash prize rather than continue to be eliminated by an external, unobservable and unknown audience, and ruled over by a distant crew. They thus employed rebellion (see Black, 1993), one of the few instances of it on reality shows. They did not have the social diversity necessary for the generation of divisive alliances. Their only distance was from the show's production team, and their only alliance was against it.

Big Brother producers attempted to generate social differentiation within the cast by providing information about nominations, audience elimination votes, and even extraneous rankings such as the public's "favorite" contestant. They added interactions with non-cast members, including reward challenges that brought letters and calls from home. Each of these interfered with the pace and premise of the show—that contestants are isolated from the outside world—without enhancing moral life. Despite these efforts at distancing participants from each other, little about the first season was decisive. Even nominations, contestants' one opportunity to invoke morality explicitly, were not absolute: The audience, not the cast, selected between the two nominees. The show was treated with "critical ridicule" (Kenevey, 2001), with some blame placed on the casting. The problem, however, was not a "shockingly dull cast" (Johnson, 2001a) but a structurally dull design. Even CBS president Leslie Moonves conceded, "the design of the game could have been better" (Kenevey, 2001). So, the producers changed it.

Big Brother II was structurally new, generating more moral content for broadcast. Competitions were no longer joint efforts for the good of the entire household, but individual-oriented events that stratified participants. Some were team events for food luxuries, and others individual competitions for items such as a car. But the core competitions were for the weekly "head of household," who makes sole use of the only lockable room, as well as food and other luxuries. Moreover, nominations no longer came from the cast at large, but from the head of household. Elimination was then decided not by a distant audience but by participants (those neither nominated nor head of household). And victory among the final two was decided by evicted members (drawing on the moral order of *Survivor*), which allows alliances to have social force even after their members are gone. The second season's cast was thus stratified on dimensions that were uniform in the first season. The second was more relationally differentiated, vertically segmented, and morally empowered—and more morally active. Whereas the first cast first nominated those who introduced conflict, the second cast first removed those who were being frivolous and then those who struck up an alliance. Vengeance then arose with a "civil war" among cigarette smokers (8/7/01). While moral conflict was still less frequent and less intense than on some other shows (such as the actual violence of *Real World*), the second *Big Brother* was more competitive, and developed explicit alliances.

Some producers use the voting process creatively to exaggerate moral life. On *Love Cruise* (10/16/01), the final vote was preceded by a day of interaction between the final contestants and those already banished—a day filled with intense moralism, including name calling, shouting, and sporadic attempts at alliances. Adding to the social distance, two of the final four had powerful "switch cards," and one of those two had been banished and then brought back into the game. Her uniquely intermediate position attracted rebuke from many of the banished, and she responded disciplinarily, accusing Toni, one of the banished, of bribery. Another of the banished, Anthony, rebelled in several ways, first by stirring up the

Toni-Jeanette conflict during the pre-voting day of interaction, and then during the final "hot seat" by asking Melissa about a boyfriend prior to the show. Then producers allowed one of the banished couples to qualify for the final selection, which could have allowed *any* couple to win. The entire series became a tool to stigmatize players, a social geometry for its own sake, with the prize potentially accidental.

ORGANIZATION AND ALLIANCES

Even though *Survivor* is ultimately won as an individual, having participants vote each other off offers the opportunity for strategic voting alliances. Alliances among the first *Survivor* cast were active and decisive: "if you haven't figured out by now that building alliances is an essential survival secret, then you didn't see the show" (Hatch, 2000, p. 23). Such alliances would be similarly strategic in other shows with elimination competitions—but they do not similarly appear. Their appearance is predictable in part by structural patterns and affinities among the participants, rather than by each show's storyline. If for *Survivor*'s first winner, "Happiness is being challenged" (Hatch, 2000, p. 11), he would be happier on some reality shows than on others. While his pre-planned strategy of voting alliances worked on *Survivor*, other shows present structural impediments. Among reality shows, *Survivor* was not the strongest challenge to Hatch's plan.

Even where alliances are more plausible, partisanship attracts derision. Social control is more likely in a direction towards less organization than towards more (Black, 1976)—and, indeed, the very purpose and behavior of these organized alliances is to systematically extract exile on other contestants. Participants on the first *Survivor* denied an alliance, suspecting that as an organization they would be subject to more conflict management. Participants on other shows were not as sociologically astute. "Chilltown," an alliance on *Big Brother II*, was flaunted and subject to collective liability (see Black, 1993), as others removed them one by one. Some producers manipulate parameters in order to discourage alliances. On *Survivor*'s third installment (and fourth), alliances were split and geometries disrupted. One tribe was split by age into two alliances, and the youth quickly outnumbered the elders four to three. The youth tried to get the remaining elders to distribute their votes so as not to disadvantage the youth. (Past votes have been used to settle tribal council ties.) But the elders instead all voting for youth leader Silas, an act of rebellion (not, as he said, of revenge) against him individually and against the youth alliance. Then, in a series twist (11/8/01), each team of six was told to send off three of their own, who were swapped and sent back to opposite tribes. This geometric disruption was followed by a reward challenge that required teamwork, particularly difficult given that disruption. Moreover, the earlier ageist alliance, which had been became a liability: Silas was stranded from his three compadres, and recognized in his new tribe as a post-merger threat precisely *because* of his alliance. Silas' distance made his banishment certain but reduced open confrontation, as apparent at the next tribal council, where Probst noted "not near as much talking."

Sometimes the activities of the show construct alliances that would otherwise be unnatural—that is, some shows manufacture real but unusual social patterns. Participants on *Love Cruise* vote in gender blocks, each voting off one member of the other. But contestants are also repeatedly paired off as male-female couples, to spend 48 hours at a time sharing cabins and competing as a team—i.e., building intimacy and dependence. The forced interaction establishes cross-gender ties, which complicate other patterns of social life and generate more complex forms of alliance and deception, including participants hiding their own affections and flirting with other competitors. The resulting mix of structural strategies with the tender emotions of new love interests generates a great deal of moral heat.

Where the decision to remove participants is external, there is no strategic (or structural) incentive to form alliances. On the first *Big Brother*, the audience supplied both nominations and votes. In the face of an external threat—an empowered "big brother"—conflict itself was considered deviant. And on *Making the Band*, in which a large group of hopefuls is whittled down to a pop quintet, one character said, "We are a chain, and if there's one weak link...." and shrugged. Another said, "Anybody that is not of that mindset will probably get kicked out or forced out or drop out." Alliances do not fit the social geometry of an external threat, so generally nonconfrontational interaction ensues. On *Amazing Race* and *Lost*, there are no provided means for conflict management, no constructed events such as banishments, evictions, or nominations. Competitions are not incremental events, for a portion of the overall money available to win such as on some *Road Rules,* an amount of food such as on *Survivor,* or a period of a chosen "luxury" such as on *Big Brother II.* Each mission is critical to continuance. Teams survive or fall on their own, and what other teams do only matters if they do it faster. Participants do not initially engage in moral life—or interaction whatsoever—except with their own teammates. But moral life within teams becomes intense under the pressure of entirely nontrivial circumstances, such as literally racing vehicles through South African streets. Without structural alternatives—such as interaction with other teams—that pressure stays within teams until it erupts. The first episode of *Amazing Race* was almost constant yelling among the members. But by the second episode, as noted, the teams at the front united—and collective action diversified moral life again.

Cast Intimacy

When relational distance varies, so does moralism, on reality shows as everywhere (Black, 1976). Relational variation is structured in part by variation in sets, such as whether participants are filmed in close quarters or wherever they wander. Relational distance is thus most uniform on *Chains of Love*, approximately uniform on *Big Brother*, and most diverse on *Real World*. Relational distance is also generated by the filming and voting schedules for each show—that is, variation in the length of filming and the length of participant tenure. Participants are filmed in situations that range from one day to many months. Whether they remain the entire time also varies, among shows and within casts: On some shows, participants typically remain the entire length, whereas on others eliminations begin within days or even hours. Those who are together for longer do not behave in the same way as those who have only been together for a few days. Those who will be together at least a day and perhaps three do not behave the same as those who will be together at least a week and maybe eight. Participants know at least the range of their tenure, and act accordingly. They play the role dictated by their scripted tenure range, not dramaturgically but sociologically.

Relational Distance and Histories

In elimination competitions, those voted off first are usually relationally distant, such as Kel, the loner on *Survivor: The Australian Outback* who is gossiped about while gone and then kicked off in the second episode, or the one contestant on *Chains of Love* who takes less part in conversations. The first ones kicked off *Love Cruise* were an openly confrontational woman (addressing another's breast implants) and the man who then comforted her in her cabin—that is, the one too normative for the comfort of strangers and the one who spent the least time with them, and in both cases the ones most marginalized by their own behavior. As one participant, noted, "It's easier to vote off the person that you don't see" (9/25/01). Relational distance varies not only within a cast but also among reality shows. *Love Cruise*, for example, offers intermediate variation in relational distance: Participants are all on the same ship, but cabins and decks allow some escape and variation in intimacy. Some shows offer greater relational distance, while others offer less. On *Real World* and *Amazing Race*, there are great differences between some participants who are quite intimate, others who rarely see each other, and some in between. But on *Survivor* and *Big Brother*, participants are seen more or less equally, and there is less relational differentiation. Initial votes are not for those relationally distant, because no one is. Initial conflicts focus instead on physical strength or normative behavior, as when Debb, who had been outspoken and abrasive, was the first voted out of *Survivor: The Australian Outback*. Her confrontational style did not fit the society of strangers. But there are few explicit criticisms for being absent from the group, as if the geometry of the group *needs* relational distance.

Real World casts live together for much longer—as many as four months, compared to as little as six weeks on *Road Rules*—and these longer "relational histories" (Black, 1976, p. 41) generate greater moralism, with frequent conflicts in almost every season. Moreover, the conflicts of *Real World* reach greater heights than any other show. Not only is there sufficient intimacy for love and marriage to develop, but also sufficient relational histories to generate a condition for violence (Black, 1993) as well as settlement. David was removed from the second season for a physical act against another cast member (pulling bed sheets off Tami, then attempting to reveal her body). Thenceforth, removing any participant who physical confronts another became a "rule" of the show—but one to be broken, as other instances of violence (including one on *Road Rules*) occurred without dismissals.[6] On no other reality show has there been purported a physical attack.[7] *Real World* has more intimacy than other shows, and longer relational histories than even *Road Rules*. As a result, it has more, and more diverse, moral life.

But while *Real World* generates intimacy through lengthy relational histories within the context of the show, the race versions of reality shows typically include participants who have such histories from long before filming. *Eco-Challenge* teams train together for a year or more prior to each expedition, and *Amazing Race* teams included a mother-daughter, two fraternity brothers, and several married couples. The participants are not strangers from the start, as is true on most residential and elimination reality shows, and their moral life on camera is different. Under the right conditions, their greater intimacy can generate ongoing intensity, such as the frequent bickering between Frank and Margarita on *Amazing Race*. But when intimates are put in the presence of many others, the overtness of their moralism withers. Frank and Margarita only bickered when away from the other teams. Similarly, on *Eco-Challenge*, conflicts often surface at the stopping points after each leg, as teams re-organize and navigate the next leg. But these are the same points at which many others are in close proximity, including other teams as well production crew, "race managers," and medical personnel. Open criticism in these contexts is rare, and grimaces are clarified during editing by splicing in interviews taken at later times.

RELATIONAL DISTANCING AND STRANGERS

Relational movement also explains behavioral patterns. For example, participants in *Chains of Love* begin as strangers, four members of one gender literally chained with one member of the opposite gender—such as one man with two women on either side, or a woman with four men—and separated only for short bathroom breaks. The participants are together for less than 72 hours, and so do not develop lengthy relational histories. Their interactions are also restricted to the household, with little opportunity for outside interaction or events. The proximity of strangers generates conflicts more quickly than on *Love Cruise*, for example. Without the option of avoidance, the presence of third parties, or the diversifying effects of relational histories, the strangers are eruptive, challenging each other's morals explicitly. But the variety of their moralism is greatly restricted: There is no violence, little opportunity for gossip, and few of the conditions for vengeance (see Black, 1993). Eruptions almost always come from the central figure (outward rather than inward) at the time that he or she votes off a potential date—i.e., at the moment of exile, when the accused is pushed away with finality.

Each *Chains of Love* episode features three dramatic moments at which a tall and darkly dressed man in sunglasses (the Key Man) requires the central participant to eliminate one of his or her remaining choices. The central player must award each exiled player, upon their release from the chains (and the show), a portion of the money available to be split among the five participants. Moralism is expressed both in the amount of money chosen and in what is said. Exit comments are sometimes softened with compliments about first impressions, but are generally harsh and abrupt, and include criticisms not apparent prior to the banishment. Conflict earlier in the show is across what social distance exists, as in the first conflict of the first episode with the woman farthest from the man in the middle (and who emphasized that she was culturally different from the rest). After two of the potential matches are eliminated, each of the other two take the central player on a "date," during which the third person remains attached but now with a slightly longer chain. Dates typically include gossip and snide comments about the third person, even though they are perhaps only a few dozen feet away, as the burbling moralism finally finds an outlet in even the slightest amount of relational variation. The gossip comes from each of the competing two—who have for the entire sequence been focused on the central player—about the other. But it comes unwelcomed by the central player, who shifts attention between the two dates without gossiping about either and then, in making a choice between the final two, occasionally notes gossip and snideness as a reason for that final banishment. Relational distance generates moral life, but moral life also generates relational distance.

On *Temptation Island*, rather than binding strangers together, intimates are separated. Three[8] (heterosexual, so far) couples participate, with the three males put in an encampment of 13 single women, and the three females in an encampment of 13 single men. Dates are arranged to allow members of each participating couple to explore other relationships, thereby challenging themselves socially and morally. Whereas on other shows the mixing of strangers results in conflict content, here the ties within the dates are weak relative to the pre-existing ties within the couples. Periodic communication within couples—such as the viewing of one-minute confessions, or of short segments of partners' dates—serves simultaneously to reinforce those pre-existing ties and to identify the deviance of having been intimate with others. Conflicts (particularly gossip, given the distribution of participants) ensue within each gendered trio about their respective partners as those partners are pushed apart, increasing their distance and attracting further grievance expressions that foment as gossip. The show achieved strong ratings despite (or perhaps in part due to) almost universal critical derision about the ethical questions raised. But regardless of ethical content, ratings suggest that viewers want to see *moral* content, as when intimates are pushed apart.

Lessons for Producers

Asked about reality shows, NBC president Jeff Drucker said, "The best programs will always survive." (MSNBC interview, 9/4/01). If success is identified by ratings market share, and to the extent that ratings are affected by the actual content of each show, series and network executives could benefit by applications of Black's work. Producers currently make decisions according to the dictates of a show's storyline, with expectations about participant behavior that are uniformed by available theory. They could instead employ *sociological technology* (Black, 2001), making practical application of sociological theory. In addition to designing tasks and casts—and explicit tools for moralism, such as banishment procedures—they could design moral patterns, through planned socio-structural conditions. Structuring unscripted content by geometrically maximizing the likelihood of desired social patterns could make better programs. They could understand the social geometry they film, how it differs from the geometries of other reality shows, and how those differences affect content. They could even understand when social structural conditions supercede other preparations they may have made.

Conventional production design is insufficient, and may even impede geometric effects, as a final anecdote illustrates. Four *Survivor* cast members were brought into the *Big Brother II* household overnight for two distinct competitions. The first challenged each cast (distinguished by black or white costumes) to assemble its show's name from a scattered set of blocks as ominous background music played. But the competition was not moralistically black and white. Participants danced about gleefully. Will, in black, said, "I'm a ballerina ninja." His teammates rejected his suggestion to play dirty by throwing a "V" into the pool, perhaps because they knew the *Survivors* only as celebrities, deferring from cheating against status superiors. But the *Survivors* were much closer to each other (having known each other for nearly a year, on and off their set), and had interacted more (though unidirectionally) with the *Big Brother II* cast (having seen them on the show gaining similar celebrity status). Being structurally wrong, they acted wrong—and threw a "B" in the pool. But before the second competition, the *Big Brother* members were shown fan websites created for each of them, signifying to them their *own* celebrity status. This allowed the structural conditions necessary for the mixed-pair competition that followed, mollifying differences within each pair and thereby reducing structural friction.

The lessons for producers are clear: To encourage vengeance, add intermediate relational distance but remove vertical distance; to discourage vengeance, force intimacy and/or introduce status variation. More generally, the lesson is to rely on revolutionary theory about social geometries rather than costumes, colors, and music. Producers who only employ production tools conventional to scripted settings do so at the risk of producing something boring, or at least less appealing than competing shows. But those who precisely manipulate the natural geometry of interaction can determine moral outcomes. Reality shows are in part "a game of people against people" (Probst, 10/4/01 preview to third season). But they also pit people against geometries, and producers are engaged in that struggle.

The struggle can be greatly reduced. We know how the design of show parameters such as the selection of participants and the flexibility of interaction can impact patterns of confrontation among participants. It is theoretically possible for *Chains of Love* to have the fits and hits of *Real World*, and for *Road Rules* to achieve the shifting alliances of *Amazing Race*—but only if their social geometries are redesigned. Reality show producers can take advantage of the theory of conflict management to generate social life they believe will achieve ratings or artistic success. They can literally produce more or less conflict, or conflict of particular forms or styles. They can also make reality shows appear more or less real, by manufacturing unnatural quantities of grievances—or they can make reality shows peaceable (even boring) by eliminating the structural conditions necessary for any grievance expressions. They may even wish to tailor induced conflict patterns to particular audiences, generating toleration for a children's network but quick aggression for adult networks. Given desired moral patterns,[9] they could produce a sociological blueprint for each show, a scripted social geometry, including appropriate amounts of mobility, isolation, diversity, stratification, organization, relational distance, and relational histories.

Such engineering would entail a peculiar danger: Situations such as trying to be the longest person still standing on a pole in the South China sea are already atypical, which makes them entertaining. But engineering patterns of conflict management that are also atypical may make the shows confusing. While the patterns may be geometrically (or otherwise theoretically) consistent with what occurs elsewhere, that elsewhere may be limited or even unknown. If the crafted social geometries are unfamiliar, the theoretically subsequent patterns may be as well. Audiences might appreciate a show's storyboard but not its participant behavior, its task sequence but not its social life. While exotic locales and events may entice audiences, exotic quantities or forms of conflict management might repel them. How the typicality and familiarity of social geometries affect a reality show's ratings is among the questions producers should pose. The producers of *Big Brother II* illustrated how to help generate cutthroat alliances—but did those generate higher ratings than would separatist individualism? Moreover, while variation in moral content does not account for all ratings differences, what additional role do participant interactions (including distances and diversity) play independent of moral content? More generally, if the best reality shows will survive, what is their social geometry?

Endnotes

1. To distinguish them from what is sometimes called "reality TV," "reality shows" concern interactions within a group (rather than of a police officer's or department's interactions with those pursued, such as on *Cops*) and over a period of days to months (rather than hours, such as on *Fear Factor*).

2. Though complete data on all of the interactions of participants on all reality shows was not possible for this project, I have seen at least three episodes of each show discussed, including each of the first nine seasons of *Real World* and *Road Rules*, as well as all episodes of several shows, including each season of *Survivor*. My data is more substantially limited by the editing of days or weeks of events into less than an hour of broadcast observations. It is not possible to examine all participant interactions, since some were not taped and only a small fraction is aired. However, the utilized data is sufficient to illustrate patterns observed, and to indicate that alternative patterns are unlikely to have occurred but been concealed.

3. The literature employing this theory regards "conflict management" as interchangeable with "social control." Both refer to the observable identification of and response to deviance (Black, 1976).

4. As a form of handling grievances, each is distributed precisely according to sociological parameters (Black, 1993; and 1983 & 1984b, respectively) without regard for individuals as such. See also "the elimination of people" (Black, 2000a, pp. 347–348) and "the ghost of the person" (Black, 2000a, pp. 362–363).

5. Black also pursues social geometry at a multidimensional level. Aggregate measures combine to generate a useful typology of settings (Black, 1990)

6. Social geometry explains what rules, norms, and laws cannot. Moreover, it explains the behavior not only of participants, but producers as well. Regardless of stated principles, "geometry is destiny" (Black, 2000a).

7. One cast member of *Big Brother II* was removed for being threatening while holding a knife, although no contact was made. That member did have a history of violence and a legal record (which, his "victim" accuses in a lawsuit, the producers knew and should have excluded him on). But another member of the same cast was isolated by producers and warned for having threatened another player, then *not* removed—and nearly won. Contrarily, while *Survivor* is known for its conflicts, its most eruptive moment came in the final tribal council words of banished Susan to finalist Kelly—that is, from someone already labeled deviant after she separated from group, as great a distant as *Survivor* contestants experience.

8. During filming of the first season, a fourth couple was discovered—through gossip among the potential dates—to have had a child, violating a condition that participants be childless. They were removed from the show—an instance of settlement—but not sent home. Instead, they were relocated and provided therapists, then revisited for additional content.

9. The theory of conflict management only tells us how to structure shows geometrically to produce desired moral content. It does not tell us what moral content is desired. Producers can employ sociological technology to structure the outcomes of filming without conventional scripts, but they must at least script the desired outcomes.

References

Baumgartner, M.P. (1988). *The moral order of the suburb*. New York: Oxford University Press.

Black, D. (1976). *The behavior of law*. New York: Academic Press.

Black, D. (1971). The social organization of arrest. *Stanford Law Review, 20*, 1087–1111.

Black, D. (1973). The mobilization of law. *Journal of Legal Studies, 2*, 125–149.

Black, D. (1980). *The manners and customs of the police*. New York: Academic Press.

Black, D. (1983). Crime as social control. *American Sociological Review, 48*, 34–45.

Black, D. (1984a). Social control as a dependent variable. In D. Black (Ed.), *Toward a general theory of social control: Volume I: Fundamentals* (pp. 1–36). Orlando, FL: Academic Press.

Black, D. (1984b). Crime as social control. In D. Black (Ed.), *Toward a general theory of social control: Volume 2: Selected problems* (pp. 1–27). Orlando, FL: Academic Press.

Black, D. (1987). Compensation and the social structure of misfortune. *Law and Society Review, 21*, 563–584.

Black, D. (1990). The elementary forms of conflict management. In *New directions in the study of justice, law, and social control* (pp. 43–69). New York: Plenum Press.

Black, D. (1993). *The social structure of right and wrong*. San Diego: Academic Press.

Black, D. (1995). The epistemology of pure sociology. *Law and Social Inquiry, 20*, 829–870.

Black, D. (1997). A strategy of pure sociology. In D. Black (Ed.), *Theoretical perspectives in sociology* (pp. 149–168). New York: St. Martin's Press.

Black, D. (2000a). Dreams of pure sociology. *Sociological Theory, 18*, 345–367.

Black, D. (2000b). The purification of sociology. *Contemporary Sociology, 29*, 704–709.

Black, D. (2001). The geometry of law: An interview with Donald Black. Interviewed by M. G. Justo, H. Singer, & A. B. Buoro. Forthcoming in *Brazilian Review of Criminal Sciences* (English version, from the author).

Black, D., & Baumgartner, M.P. (1983). Toward a theory of the third party. In K.O. Boyum and L. Mather (Eds.), *Empirical theories about courts* (pp. 84–114). New York: Longman.

Burnett, M. (2001). *Survivor II: The field guide*. New York: TV Books.

Burnett, M., & Dugard, M. (2000). *Survivor: The ultimate game*. New York: TV Books.

Denhart, A. (2000, July 12). *Big Brother*, meet *Survivor*; *Survivor*, meet *The Real World*—What reality TV shows should learn from one another. *Salon*. Retrieved from the World Wide Web: http://www.salon.com.

Denhart, A. (2001, July 3). *The Real World* refuses to grow up—The show that spawned reality television comes back for its 10th season, forgets lessons it taught everyone else. *Salon*. Retrieved from the World Wide Web: http://www.salon.com.

Hatch, R. (2000). 101 *Survival secrets: How to make $1,000,000, lose 100 pounds, and just plain live happily*. New York: The Lyons Press.

Horwitz, A. V. (1984). Therapy and social solidarity. . In D. Black (Ed.), *Toward a general theory of social control: Volume I: Fundamentals* (pp. 211–250). Orlando, FL: Academic Press.

Hughes, C. (2000, September 19). Italy's *Big Brother*. Associated Press Newswire.

Johnson, M. D. (2001a, June 30). Getting a grip on reality TV—The highs and lows of television's megatrend. *The Partial Observer*. Retrieved from the World Wide Web: http://www.partialobserver.com.

Johnson, M. D. (2001b, July 8). *Big Brother 2*: Righting some wrongs—CBS tries to make a winner out of a loser. Retrieved from the World Wide Web: http://www.partialobserver.com.

Kenevey, B. (2001, January 10). *Survivor* factor shifts CBS lineup. *USA Today*, p. 4D.

Kronke, D. (2000, September 11). BBC America show features the real survivors. *Santa Cruz Sentinel*, p. A-10.

Lance, P. (2000). *The stingray: Lethal tactics of the sole survivor*. Portland, OR: Cinema 21 Group.

Mendoza, M. (2001, July 9). *Big Brother* reworked—2nd Installment has better editing. *San Jose Mercury News*, p. 8C.

Millman, J. (2000, April 3). Men II Boyz: The new reality series *Making the Band* exposes the emasculating truth about boy bands. *Salon*. Retrieved from the World Wide Web: http://www.salon.com.

Morrill, C. (1995). *The executive way: Conflict management in corporations*. Chicago: The University of Chicago Press.

Nock, S. (1993). *The costs of privacy: Surveillance and reputation in America*. New York: Aldine de Gruyter.

Senechal de la Roche, R. (1996). Collective violence as social control. *Sociological Forum, 11*, 97–128.

Tucker, J. (1999). *The therapeutic corporation*. New York: Oxford University Press.

Wolk, D. (2001, May 14). Signs of intelligent life: "A.I.'s" mysterious and masterful promotional campaign. Slate. Retrieved from the World Wide Web: http://www.slate.com.

For comments on earlier drafts, the author thanks Dave Ballard, Donald Black, Kristen Godard, Allan Horwitz, Roberta Senechal, Matthew Smith, and Andrew Wood.

6

The Nonverbal Communication of Trustworthiness: A Necessary *Survivor* Skill

R. Thomas Boone

There is considerably more to the TV show *Survivor* than slick advertising and good casting: The heart of *Survivor*'s appeal is the social psychological situation it creates and viewers' ability to think of real-life situations that are flavored with the same agonizing decisions about whom to trust and with whom to form alliances. To appreciate how this tension is created, *Survivor* must be recognized as a variant of a social dilemma, any situation in which individuals' short-term gains are pitted against the long-term interests of the collective (Komorita & Parks, 1996). Several factors clearly make *Survivor* a social dilemma. First, no person is an island unto him- or herself; votes at tribal council are what decide who stays and who wins. Alienating other people by refusing to cooperate or by being too competitive will get a person voted off in a hurry. Alliances are also crucial in deciding who stays or goes; having a group of people who will not vote you off affords you some protection. However, entering into an alliance requires being willing to abide by collective decisions rather than individual preferences. Throughout the game, each contestant must carefully walk the line between self-interest and collective partnerships.

Winning in *Survivor* also means carefully balancing competence at the various immunity and reward challenges and managing the social milieu. Despite how important it is to win the challenges, the social

97

impression that each contestant creates is what really decides who stays, who goes, and who wins. Likeability, particularly in the early stages of the game, helps determine who will make it to the next round. However, if someone is not doing so well in the popularity contest, or even if an individual is doing well, alliances clearly dictate who will stay in the game. Ultimately, the final choice between the last two contestants is made by a jury of the seven most recently ousted members, and the three final choices we have seen so far seemed to have been more socially determined rather than decided by some measure of competence at the various challenges.

Given the social dilemma structure and the critical importance of being liked and accepted into an alliance, the ability to appear trustworthy and the ability to assess trustworthiness are a critical part of success in the game of *Survivor*. The ability to read or decode trustworthiness provides an advantage by allowing an individual to select more loyal alliance partners or determine whether a partner is considering a change in allegiances. The ability able to convey or encode trustworthiness would make an individual more attractive as an alliance partner or allow him or her to have multiple alliances. Viewing trustworthiness this way casts it as a quality capable of being communicated with varying degrees of success and accuracy. Of course, the challenge is that everyone who is playing *Survivor* should be trying to appear as trustworthy as possible.

Oddly enough, despite the importance of trustworthiness in real life and in *Survivor*, social scientists have not really considered trustworthiness per se as a construct to be communicated. Instead, the focus of research on interpersonal perception has been on the question of deception and its detection (DePaulo, Stone, & Lassiter, 1985; Zuckerman, DePaulo, & Rosenthal, 1981) or on general overall impressions of honesty and credibility (Zebrowitz, Voinescu, & Collins, 1996). Both research areas are certainly related to trustworthiness, but do not fully capture the construct since trustworthiness also implies at least conditional cooperation in a social exchange. Researchers interested in exchange theory discuss situations that lead to greater or lesser degrees of trust (Messick & Kramer, 2001; Yamagishi, Cook, & Watabe, 1998), but the focus of the research tends to exclude interpersonal variables. Researchers investigating individual differences in the willingness to trust have found that people who are high-trusters tend to be better at decoding nonverbal information (Sabatelli, Buck, & Dreyer, 1983). However, this research has not been extended to include what aspects of others behaviors might be used to assess trustworthiness or whether high-trusters are more accurate in assessing other people's trustworthiness.

A Model for the Communication of Trustworthiness

Deciding whether a target individual is trustworthy is an attributional judgment. Attribution, the process by which we make inferences about stable traits or characteristics, can be modeled using the Lens Model (Petrinovich, 1979), shown in Figure 1, which can readily be adapted to most forms of communication. In the Lens Model, there is an actor (or construct) with a set of stable internal characteristics that can be encoded into a set of observable cues. There is also an observer who decodes these cues to arrive at a judgment about the internal state of the actor. The process by which these cues are encoded is called *cue validity,* and the greater these cues accurately reflect the true internal state of the actor, the more successful the attribution process or communication is likely to be. The process by which these cues are decoded is called *cue utilization,* and the better schema that the observer has for matching the cues to their underlying behavioral state, the more successful the attribution process or communication is likely to be. Given such a model, the cues themselves are critically important in that they serve as the sole interface between the actor and the observer and any failure in the communication process must be a function of either the encoding or decoding of these cues. Much of the research in nonverbal communication involves the identification of observable cues associated with a given psychological construct.

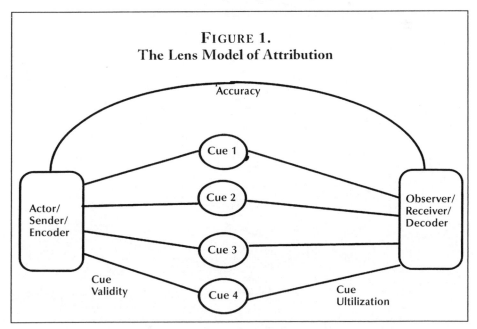

FIGURE 1.
The Lens Model of Attribution

Accuracy

Cue 1

Cue 2

Actor/
Sender/
Encoder

Observer/
Receiver/
Decoder

Cue 3

Cue
Validity

Cue 4

Cue
Ultilization

At first glance, this model seems straightforward and, well, simple. In the case of a communication or attribution in which the actor wants to be easily read, the model is pretty basic. However, when the attribution process is derailed, intentionally or unintentionally, the model demonstrates its greater value. Consider the case of deception, depicted in Figure 2: The actor, who is intentionally trying to mislead the observer, will emit a series of cues that do not accurately reflect his or her true internal state. If the actor is successful in emitting false cues, the observer will not be able to make an accurate inference. In fact, if the observer is to have any chance in detecting the actor's true state, the actor must emit some veridical cues that do reflect his or her true state. In the case of detecting deception, the observer's task is now considerably harder; the observer must use the veridical cues and ignore the false cues. Any observer who utilizes a cue or series of cues that are not veridical to the actor's true state will be misled.

Trustworthiness is similar to deception in that an actor who is

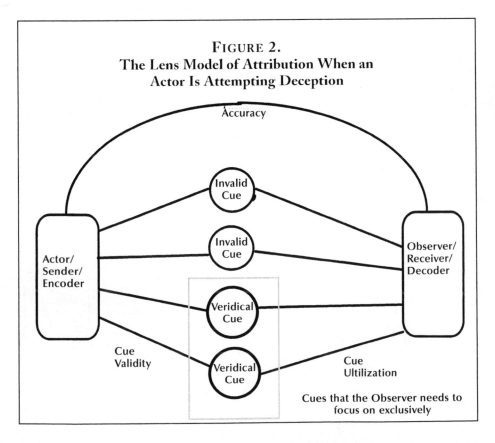

FIGURE 2.
The Lens Model of Attribution When an
Actor Is Attempting Deception

Accuracy

Invalid
Cue

Invalid
Cue

Actor/
Sender/
Encoder

Observer/
Receiver/
Decoder

Veridical
Cue

Cue
Validity

Veridical
Cue

Cue
Ultilization

Cues that the Observer needs to
focus on exclusively

untrustworthy will want to hide his or her true nature and, subsequently, should attempt to emit a series of false cues. However, there are differences between the constructs, mainly due to the difference between the act of deception and the stable quality of trustworthiness. Specifically, a liar merely seeks to deflect the observer from identifying the true state of affairs, while the untrustworthy person is specifically trying to appear trustworthy, arguably a more stable and global characteristic. Given the strong social pressure to be judged as trustworthy, both trustworthy and untrustworthy individuals will be actively engaged in emitting what should be the same set of cues that indicate trustworthiness. Consequently, a discerning observer should be more interested in searching for cues that suggest that a person is untrustworthy rather than potentially misleading cues about trustworthiness. Due to the lack of research that specifically addresses the quality of trustworthiness, no specific set of cues has been generated for this construct. However, two areas of research are clearly related to the concept of trustworthiness, specifically, research on deception and research on having an honest demeanor.

Detection of Deception

Some researchers have portrayed the relationship between the ability to deceive and the ability to detect deception as an evolutionary footrace (Bond & Robinson, 1988). To be successful in detecting deception, the perceiver must recognize the cues that the deceiver is emitting when lying. If there were a set of "marker" cues that were always present when an individual lied, this task would be straightforward. The perceiver would simply need to attend to those marker cues and ignore the rest. Unfortunately, no such cues exist. Instead, there is a cluster of cues (shown in Table 1) that are likely, but not guaranteed to be emitted by the deceiver (DePaulo, 1994; DePaulo et al., 1985; Zuckerman et al., 1981). Such cues, when emitted, are the cues that perceivers should attend to when judging whether someone is lying.

However, perceivers have another set of cues that they believe indicates when someone is lying, also shown in Table 1 (DePaulo, 1994; DePaulo et al., 1985). Some of these cues are associated with lying; other cues are distractor cues and will act to decrease the accuracy of deception detection. For instance, liars are no less likely to look you in the eye than truth tellers. A good liar will capitalize on the belief that liars are less likely to look someone in the eye and make an effort to look people in the eye. The observer may notice the increased pitch in the liar's voice, a true

TABLE 1.
Perceived and Real Cues That Reveal Deception[†]

Cues that are associated with deception	Cues that people believe are associated with deception
Greater speech hesitations	**Greater speech hesitations**
Speaking in a higher pitch	**Speaking in a higher pitch**
Greater number of speech errors	**Greater number of speech errors**
Having somewhat shorter responses	Taking longer to respond to questions
Making more negative statements	Avoiding gaze
Making more irrelevant statements	Are more likely to shift posture or fidget
Overgeneralizing	Are less likely to smile
Using less immediate references (distancing self from the situation)	Speak faster
Increased pupil dilation	
Increased use of adaptors (rubbing, scratching, etc.)	
Increased blinking	
Appearing more rehearsed	
Having greater interchannel discrepancies (nonverbal messages from the voice do not match nonverbal messages from one of the other nonverbal channels such as the face)	
Having more discrepant microexpressions (fleeting facial expression that flash across the encoder's face)	

[†]*This table was generated using information primarily from DePaulo et al., 1985, but also Zuckerman, DePaulo, & Rosenthal, 1981; Ekman, O'Sullivan, Friesen, & Scherer. 1991; and Riggio, Tucker, & Widaman, 1987.*

cue, but ignore or downplay this cue because the liar is looking him or her in the eye. Indeed, research examining overall accuracy rates shows that most people seldom do better than guessing when attempting to detect deception (DePaulo, 1994; DePaulo et al., 1985; Zuckerman et al., 1981). Despite the fact that people are identifying some of the correct cues, their use of the false cues interferes with arriving at a correct decision. If there is a footrace, the liars are ahead.

Given the consistent finding of chance level accuracy for the detection of deception, research has changed its focus to consider whether some people are better than others in detecting deception and whether there are some situations in which people are better at detecting deception. Training and being alerted to the fact that there may be some on-going deception in a given situation often aid people in their ability to detect deception (Zuckerman, Koestner, & Alton, 1984). Some occupations provide hands-on exposure to such experiences and individuals in such jobs (i.e., Secret Service agents) often perform better than the general populace at the detection of deception (Ekman & O'Sullivan, 1991; Vrij & Semin, 1996). Certain situations also trip up would-be liars. In particular, liars tend to perform less well when they are strongly motivated, often revealing their deception through a greater number of the nonverbal cues which indicate arousal (DePaulo, Kirkendol, Tang, & O'Brien, 1988).

It is hard to imagine that there is not a considerable amount of deception going on in *Survivor*. Certainly, no one walks into *Survivor* thinking that everyone is going to be truthful. However, given that most people do not take lie detection courses and rarely hold jobs that afford the opportunity for feedback about accuracy, lie detection skills are likely to be rudimentary at best. However, the social context should help in letting people know when deception is more likely to occur. Some deception is likely to be related to mundane issues, such as honesty about hygiene. Other deceptions are likely to be more serious, involving allegiances and loyalty to an alliance.

Clearly one component on *Survivor* that involves deception is the voting process. Though contestants discuss voting options openly, the voting is done individually and no one is assured that any other contestant will honor an agreement to vote a specific way. Being able to judge both other contestants' loyalty while they are voting and their surprise when the votes are read would be a valuable skill. Such a skill most likely would involve assessing the feeling state of other individuals and should allow a contestant to detect alliances and assess loyalty. In *Survivor: Africa*, Teresa voted for Lex in the first tribal council after the merge, but much to his consternation, Lex was unable to determine at the tribal council or in subsequent questioning over the following two days who had actually voted against him. In the end, he focused on the wrong individual and Kelly was ousted, blamed for a defection she did not commit.[1]

The second kind of serious lying that probably occurs in *Survivor* involves direct confrontations and promises of allegiance. In some ways these lies may be the most interesting since, due to the presence of the "side-bars" to the camera, viewers are allowed a rare opportunity to evaluate various contestants' negotiations with *a priori* knowledge of the truthfulness of these negotiations. In the first season of *Survivor*, Jeff Probst directly asked Rich, Susan, and Kelly in turn about the presence of an alliance. The audience, having watched numerous asides in which several of these individuals openly discussed the alliance, knew that each of these people was lying. Rich, not surprisingly, was the most convincing. He laughed it off and then, making an irrelevant comment, said he was "all about catching fish." Susan, certainly not as skilled Rich, took longer than usual to respond, made a grimace which turned into a smile, and then said no, also attempting to laugh it off. Kelly, interestingly, said yes, then laughed and said, too quickly, just joking, and then shortly and simply no. In all three cases, there was evidence that these people were lying, yet, at least as far as what the audience was shown, none of the other contestants appeared to doubt the lies of these alliance members. In fact, this interrogation took place at a critical juncture; if all the remaining contestants had banded together or had been able to enlist Kelly to their side, the alliance would have remained vulnerable and the outcome would have likely been different.

More obvious forms of lying played a critical role in *Survivor: The Australian Outback* as well. Colby specifically lied to Jerri and Amber about his allegiance to them. It was harder to evaluate what cues Colby may have emitted since this conversation was videotaped via infrared camera; however, he did not face either of them directly and he kept his voice low and controlled. Clearly it was a convincing presentation since both Jerri and Amber believed him. The other pivotal event that involved the question of deception was the confrontation between Jerri and Kel, in which Jerri accused Kel of hoarding food. No evidence was provided that there ever was any food or how Kel may have evaded the security procedures designed to protect against such a violation of the rules, making it more likely that Kel was telling the truth. However, the contestants clearly sided with Jerri and ousted Kel, at a considerable loss since Kel would have been helpful in the following immunity challenges. What was really striking about this outcome was that the audience seemed more willing to believe Kel, or at least less willing to believe Jerri. Apparently, Jerri appeared much more trustworthy in person.

Appearing Trustworthy—An Honest Demeanor

Appearing trustworthy means more than the ability to avoid getting caught as a liar. Trustworthiness also implies a willingness to cooperate, if only conditionally, in a social exchange. We trust a wide range of people in a variety of roles to be reliable in their promises to uphold their end of a social contract. Since no one wants to be exploited by an uncooperative partner in social exchange, most of us are invested in assessing who might be trustworthy as quickly as possible. In fact, game theorists have shown that the long-term advantage in a series of social exchanges goes to those individuals who lock into a cooperative relationship early (Orbell & Dawes, 1993). Other research has shown that people demonstrate a much wider range of cooperation levels when given the chance to leave their partner, some people becoming much more cooperative and others much less cooperative, compared to when they are forced to remain with the same partner (Boone & Macy, 1999). The implication of these findings is that people probably have a heuristic for assessing trustworthiness that is readily available and strongly activated during first impressions.

Physical appearances definitely play a role in appearing trustworthy. Baby-faced people, individuals who have faces similar to those of babies by having a round-shaped face, large eyes, high forehead, small nose, and a less pronounced jawline, are more likely to be perceived as dependent, likeable, and honest (Berry & McArthur, 1985). In contrast, more mature-faced people, people who are less baby-faced, are perceived to be more independent, intelligent, and less honest. Attractiveness is also related to babyfaceness in that people who are more babyfaced are generally rated more attractive, probably leading to an overall impression of honesty. However, appearances can be deceiving: While babyfaceness and attractiveness affect the appearance of honesty, there is only modest evidence that either construct predicts actual honesty.

People on *Survivor* and people watching *Survivor* clearly have definitive opinions about who is trustworthy and who is not. Such impressions are obvious right from the outset. Based upon appearance alone, who *appeared* more trustworthy: Gretchen or Susan? Kelly or Jenna? BB or Rudy? Michael or Keith? Jerri or Alicia? In each of the pairing, each of which is roughly matched for age, Gretchen, Jenna, Rudy, Michael, and Alicia are more baby-faced than their partners. If we had just met each of these pairs, research suggests we should think that the more baby-faced individuals are the more trustworthy. Having watched these people in action, we probably have some opinions, which may support the idea that the more baby-faced people are more trustworthy. However, it should be noted that Richard has a baby-face and most people did not find him to be trustworthy, though he did keep his word to the members of his alliance.

Attractiveness also plays a role in appearing honest. As previously mentioned, attractiveness and babyfacedness are correlated. However, attractiveness has a halo effect that goes beyond just babyfaceness. We just like people who are attractive more and we are more willing to assign them positive traits. Jerri was not as baby-faced as some of the other contestants, but most viewers reported her as attractive. Does anyone think that she would have gotten away with so much if she had not been attractive? The only good news is that eventually the attractiveness wore thin and the halo was tarnished. It is also interesting to note that in all three initial *Survivor* seasons, the first person ousted was one of the older, less attractive females.[2]

In addition to these appearance-based judgments, demographic variables predict who is likely to be perceived as more trustworthy. Gender is certainly an important factor. In general, women are perceived as more honest than men by both men and women (DePaulo, Epstein, & Wyer, 1993). Despite these clear gender stereotypes, belief does not always match reality. When asked directly, women often rate themselves as more honest and cooperative than men (DePaulo et al., 1993). However, when asked through daily journal rather than self-report, women reported lying about substantive issues at the same level as men (DePaulo et al., 1993). Thus, while women are rated more favorably on honesty, there appears to be no significant difference in actual honesty as a function of gender. This bias may also extend to trustworthiness.

There have been several confrontations throughout the *Survivor* series that involve a male squaring off against a female over an issue of trust. Most notably, the aforementioned confrontation between Jerri and Kel comes to mind. Jerri was more attractive than Kel, but her gender also may have given her an advantage. Additionally, there was a confrontation over trust between Diane and Clarence in the first episode of *Survivor: Africa* over the consumption of critical rations. While it was clear that Diane and Clarence both ate the food, the issue involving trust was about Clarence's motives and the decision process used to determine whether it was acceptable to eat the beans. Diane claimed that it was Clarence's idea, while Clarence claimed that it was more Diane's idea. The group sided with Diane in terms of how they felt about Clarence, possibly because of gender, though certainly race and other factors could have played a role.[3]

Finally, the final decision in the first *Survivor* series appeared to revolve, in part, around questions of trust and gender. In Richard vs. Kelly, Richard's penultimate partner Rudy continued steadfast in his support of Rich at the final tribal council, though Rich had arguably put him in make-it-or-break-it position by leaving him alone on the pole with Kelly in the final immunity challenge. In contrast, Kelly's friend and partner Susan had a considerably different reaction when Kelly decided to have Susan kicked off. In Susan's now famous speech, she clearly indicated that her single biggest problem with Kelly was one of trust. No one quibbled about trust with Rich; Rich himself made no claims about trustworthiness. One interpretation of Rich's victory is that he won because he did not violate gendered expectations about issues of trust, whereas Kelly did. Because we expect women to be more trustworthy and honest, it comes as a bigger shock when they betray this belief.

In addition to looking trustworthy, there are other behaviors that can be used to indicate trustworthiness. One such behavior is smiling, which when emitted spontaneously is a universally recognized expression of happiness (Ekman, 1994; Izard, 1991). Smiling is also used as a more symbolic form of communication; people smile to indicate approachability and assurance that they are trustworthy. Unlike a spontaneous display of happiness, a smile for indicating approachability and trustworthiness is a posed expression (Buck, 1988). Researchers have argued that it is possible to distinguish between posed and spontaneous expressions. To distinguish between the two types of smiles the critical feature is the orbicularis oculi muscle which is contracted in a spontaneous smile, causing wrinkles or crow's feet to form at the corners of the eyes (Ekman, Davidson, & Friesen, 1990). Spontaneous smiles are perceived as more genuine but there is no research examining whether people who smile more often or smile with more genuine appearing smiles are more trustworthy.

People smile a good deal on *Survivor* and not every smile is meant to reflect happiness. When losers congratulate winners at the various challenges, they often smile and even hug, though no one expects the losers to be happy. Certainly, such occasions provide opportunities for insight into how genuine people might be. In addition to situational differences, there are also individual differences in expressivity. When Elisabeth or Colby smiled, they appeared more genuine than Silas or Jerri. Kelly did not smile well, but Colleen certainly did, and the audience liked and appeared to trust Colleen considerably more.[4] Perhaps the most clear cut example of a difference in smiling occurred in *Survivor: The Australian Outback* when Jerri and Colby returned from the Great Barrier Reef. Colby, having formed some attachments among the group appeared happy to see people and enjoyed bringing back trinkets for the remaining contestants. Jerri stood by smiling, but not quite so convincingly. In her latter aside to the camera, Jerri congratulated Colby on his "move," and she smiled, but underneath her smile it looked as if she had just swallowed a wasp.

Advice for Future Survivor Contestants

The focus of this chapter has been on the perception of trustworthiness, a valuable skill in general and certainly to contestants on *Survivor*. Would-be contestants should be advised to attempt to hone their skills in detecting deception and assessing who is likely to be honest and cooperative. In many ways that is the underlying competition: Find cooperators and lock into a secure alliance with such people.

To increase the likelihood of detecting deception, contestants should pay careful attention to the arousal level of their peers. If someone seems to be more agitated than usual, then something may be afoot. Microexpressions, momentary emotional expressions, could be particularly telling. Careful examination of people's faces, particularly when they are beginning and ending conversations or when they are turning around, could reveal relevant information. It is also possible to create situations in which you may have the opportunity to observe a peer when he or she is lying. If so, note his or her behavior, particularly whether the person appears to blink more or be more fidgety. Of course, learning to manage your own presentation is also of critical importance. Avoid lying whenever possible. If forced to do so, be as relaxed as possible. Other people may be watching you to see if you reveal the same set of cues.

More research needs to be done to determine if there are any reliable cues that reveal who is trustworthy based upon demeanor. However, there is probably some limited ability to make yourself look more trustworthy. Certainly presenting yourself as attractive, particularly in the beginning, is a good start. Realistically, given the conditions under which the contestants live, most differences in attractiveness are moot within a quick span of time. It certainly is possible to be more open and friendly; smile and smile often, when appropriate. Being upbeat, particularly when it appears to be genuine, will increase the likelihood that people will like and trust you. Finally, being negative, even when appropriate, is problematic. As much as people may want to commiserate, they will also associate you with that negativity and may remember your negative facial expressions.

Conclusion

Most of us probably do not live in an artificial world so full of intrigue and backbiting that it is necessary to be chronically suspicious and obsessed with nonverbal nuances. In their daily jobs, only a few specialized groups of people appear to be exposed to enough feedback to demonstrate increased accuracy in lie detection. However, while *Survivor* is a game, games often have us practice valuable skills that we may not encounter in abundance in everyday life. Part of enjoying the show is assessing whether your detection of trustworthiness is any better than the ability of people who are playing the game. Of course, the other aspect of the show, perhaps a darker theme, is the ineluctability of what happens. Most people willing to go on *Survivor* are probably low-trust individuals. As such, they probably have poor emotion decoding skills. If as you watch the show you wonder why these people cannot figure out whom to trust, there is your answer. *Survivor* has taken people with low social perception skills, put them in a situation that requires high social perception skills, and then documents their efforts as they attempt to work it out. There is a chance that there are lessons for us all in these performances.

Endnotes

1. Ironically, Lex claimed that he had a gut feeling for whom he could trust and whom he could not: He may have sensed Kelly's dislike for him but she was, in fact, trustworthy. Instead, Lex trusted Brandon, who played it straight with Lex, but was less than trustworthy with his own long-term partners.

2. For seasons two and three, I have had students make ratings of the contestants starting with the first episode. In both cases, Debb and Diane, both received the lowest relative attractiveness ratings—looks appear to determine who is the first to go.

3. While the members of the Samburu tribe clearly handed the indictment to Clarence, they voted Diane off at the next tribal council. Having seen what happened in *Survivor: The Australian Outback*, these members were not going to risk weakening their collective strength by losing Clarence while the tribes were competing.

4. Colleen was actually one of the most expressive people to appear on *Survivor* and it is not surprising that she was the first one to get a significant movie role.

References

Berry, D.S. & McArthur, L.Z. (1985). Some components and consequences of a babyface. *Journal of Personality and Social Psychology, 48,* 312–323.

Bond, C. F., & Robinson, M. (1988). The evolution of deception. *Journal of Nonverbal Behavior, 12,* 189–204.

Boone, R. T., & Macy, M. W. (1999). Unlocking the doors to the prisoner's dilemma: Dependence, selectivity, and cooperation. *Social Psychology Quarterly, 62,* 32–52.

Buck, R. (1988). *Human motivation and emotion.* New York, NY: John Wiley and Sons.

DePaulo, B. M. (1994). Spotting lies: Can humans learn to do better? *Current Directions in Psychological Science, 3,* 83–86.

DePaulo, B. M., Epstein, J. A., & Wyer, M. M. (1993). Sex differences in lying: How men and women deal with the dilemma of deceit. In M. Lewis & C. Saarni (Eds.), *Lying and deception in everyday life* (pp. 126–147). New York: Guilford Press.

DePaulo, B. M., Kirkendol, S. E., Tang, J., & O'Brien, T. P. (1988). The motivational impairment effect in the communication of deception: Replications and extensions. *Journal of Nonverbal Behavior, 12,* 177–202.

DePaulo, B. M., Stone, J. I., & Lassiter, G. D. (1985). Deceiving and detecting deceit. In B. R. Schlenker (Ed.), *The self and social life* (pp. 323–370). New York: McGraw-Hill.

Ekman, P. (1994). Strong evidence for universals in facial expressions: A reply to Russell's mistaken critique. *Psychological Bulletin, 115*(2), 268–287.

Ekman, P., Davidson, R. J., & Friesen, W. V. (1990). The Duchenne smile: Emotional expression and brain physiology II. *Journal of Personality and Social Psychology, 58,* 342–353.

Ekman, P., & O'Sullivan, M. (1991). Who can catch a liar? *American Psychologist, 46,* 913–920.

Ekman, P., O'Sullivan, M., Friesen, W. V., & Scherer, K. R. (1991). Invited article: Face, voice, and body in detecting deceit. *Journal of Nonverbal Behavior, 15,* 125–135.

Izard, C. E. (1991). *The psychology of emotions.* New York, NY: Plenum.

Komorita, S. S, & Parks, G. D. (1996). *Social dilemmas.* Boulder, CO: Westview Press.

Messick, D., & Kramer, R. M. (2001). Trust as a shallow form of morality. In K. Cook (Ed.), *Trust in society* (pp 89–117). New York: Russell Sage Foundation.

Petrinovich, L. (1979). Probabilistic functionalism: A conception of research method. *American Psychologist, 34,* 373–390.

Orbell, J., & Dawes, R. (1993). Social welfare, cooperators' advantage, and the option of not playing the game. *American Sociological Review, 58,* 787–800.

Riggio, R. E., Tucker, J., & Widaman, K. F. (1987). Verbal and nonverbal cues as mediators of deception ability. *Journal of Nonverbal Behavior, 11,* 126–145.

Sabatelli, R. M., Buck, R., & Dreyer, A. (1983). Locus of control, interpersonal trust, and nonverbal communication accuracy. *Journal of Personality and Social Psychology, 44,* 399–409.

Vrij, A., & Semin, G. R. (1996). Lie experts' beliefs about nonverbal indicators of deception. *Journal of Nonverbal Behavior, 20,* 65–80.

Yamagishi, T., Cook, K. S., & Watabe, M. (1998). Uncertainty, trust, and commitment formation in the United States and Japan. *American Journal of Sociology, 104,* 165–194.

Zebrowitz, L. A., Voinescu, L., & Collins, M. A. (1996). "Wide-eyed" and "crooked-faced": Determinants of perceived and real honesty across the life span. *Personality and Social Psychology Bulletin, 22,* 1258–1269.

Zuckerman, M., DePaulo, B. M., & Rosenthal, R. (1981). Verbal and nonverbal communication of deception. In L. Berkowitz (Ed.), *Advances in experimental social psychology* (Vol. 14, pp. 1–59). Orlando, FL: Academic Press.

Zuckerman, M., Koestner, R., & Alton, A. O. (1984). Learning to detect deception. *Journal of Personality and Social Psychology, 46,* 519–528.

I would like to dedicate this chapter to my brother, Christopher Robert Boone, who urged me to watch Survivor *during the summer of 2000. I would also like to thank Nellie Harari and Molly Hitzges for their comments on earlier drafts.*

Correspondence concerning this article should be addressed to R. Thomas Boone, Department of Psychology, St. John's University, 8000 Utopia Parkway, Jamaica, NY 11439. Electronic mail may be sent via Internet to booner@stjohns.edu.

7

Metaphors of Survival: A Textual Analysis of the Decision-Making Strategies of the *Survivor* Contestants

Kathleen M. Propp

"By their metaphors ye shall know them" (Cowell, 1972, p. 114).

Mills (1967) argued that small-group researchers needed to trace "latent group processes such as feelings, wishes and unconscious assumptions" as well as to examine the "transformations of long-term groups from their origin to their dissolution" (p. 8). While few group researchers have heeded this call, the television airing of the "real-life" game show *Survivor* provides an excellent opportunity to meet Mill's challenge. By examining the interaction of the group members as they attempted to achieve the goal of individual survival, one can explore the group dynamics and decision-making dialectics inherent in this "mixed-motive" game.

The show provides a unique case study of two groups' development and dissolution. Moreover, by analyzing the metaphors revealed in the contestants' narratives, one can determine the conscious and unconscious motivations that drove their behavior and decision-making processes. The purpose of this study is to describe the system of metaphors used by the tribe members to frame their reality and guide their decisions. And as Koch and Deetz (1981) argued in their analysis of organizational metaphors, "Because the description is presented in the members' own language, it retains the implications of their world independent of the subjective inferences of the researcher" (p. 13).

Mixed-Motive Decision Making

The rules of the *Survivor* game created a rather unique series of decision-making processes and tasks that were interpreted, weighted, and striven for in different ways by the two assigned tribes and the individual contestants. First, they made decisions that would ensure their physical comfort and survival. These decisions revolved around using the available resources of the island, as well as winning reward challenges that offered items to ease the physical hardships of island life. Second, they made decisions about their social survival—decisions to ensure that they built relationships with one another so that they would not be expelled from the game. Third, they made decisions to ensure their tribe's survival given initially immunity was granted at the tribal level. Consequently, if the tribe lost a competition, they had to decide who were the members least or most essential and who should be voted off the island. Finally, the contestants made decisions to ensure their individual survival. These decisions incorporated the need to survive the votes, gain individual immunity, and have the jury select them as the winner.

The interdependence and juxtaposition of these primary decisions created a mixed-motive game for the contestants; the ability to integrate them effectively was the ultimate determinant of the winner of the game. The inherent paradox in all group settings is that although members are dependent on the group for identity, members also feel a need to express their individual independence (Smith & Berg, 1987). *Survivor* took this paradox and multiplied it exponentially by requiring the players to expel a fellow competitor each episode. Ultimately, the players had to rely on each other for physical, social, and tribal survival, but could not fully trust one another because of the demand for individual survival. Negotiating this metaphorical minefield was the ultimate challenge of the game.

Centrality of Metaphors

A metaphor can be most simply defined as "saying that one object is another" (Kendall & Kendall, 1993, p. 150). In other words, a metaphor is based on an analogy that identifies certain attributes of one symbol with another (Cowell, 1972). Metaphors allow us to take feelings, thoughts, or concepts that are difficult to understand or communicate to others and express them through more familiar experiences or concepts. Metaphors represent a compact, yet rich, tool of expression that pervades our language use. Analyzing a person's metaphors provides a window into the thought processes of the speaker, and allows a fuller exploration of a person's behavior and decisions than more direct methods. This is because while the meaning is often in the metaphor, we may not be linguistically conscious of this (Embler, 1966). Consequently, metaphors reflected in subtle linguistic choices cannot be manipulated easily.

Kendall and Kendall (1993) argue that metaphors are "intimately interconnected with the way we think" (p. 149). Further, they argue that metaphors lead us to conceptualize or see the world in certain ways. Researchers and theorists have identified many related functions of metaphors in everyday usage. First, metaphors articulate what we find important or unimportant (Hill & Levenhagen, 1995). Second, they create the range of potential actions and determine how we will act (Lissack, 1997). Third, they structure our current reality, but also have the power to create new realities (Lakoff & Johnson, 1980). Finally, they can reduce uncertainty by providing models for how to act (Choi, 1993). Put simply, metaphors are fundamental in shaping our reality and the behavior that ensues from those perceptions. Subsequently, metaphors are not merely ornamental; rather they are "direct expressions of evaluation" (Hayakawa, 1978, p. 109). Thus, analyzing metaphorical expressions provides a lens through which to view the perceived social reality that guides the decision-making processes of group members.

Method

Koch and Deetz (1981) laid out the methodological procedure used for the identification of the metaphors in this study. In the first step, all of the contestants' talk was examined, and from this data the metaphors were isolated. Specifically, metaphors used when referencing decision-making strategies or justifications for behavior were identified. Some of the metaphors isolated were explicit uses of figurative language, such as "It's a chess game." Others that were isolated were "nested" metaphors with implicit objects of comparison. For example, "I don't want to *play* with him" would imply a game metaphor. In the last stage of isolation, the metaphorical phrases were reduced to the base metaphors they displayed (see Table 1).

In the second step of the analysis, the metaphors were sorted into coherent clusters (Koch & Deetz, 1981). After repeatedly sorting the base

TABLE 1.
Base, Root, and Secondary Metaphors of *Survivor* Contestants

Base Metaphors	Root Metaphors	Secondary Metaphors
Economic Game Sports Contribution Weakness	Equation	
Murder Hunt Cannibalism Bomb Spying Military Fight	War	
Family Team/Group Friendship Tribe	Tribe	
Alliance Dirty Gang	Politics	
Spirituality		Spirituality
Journey		Journey
Drama		Drama

metaphors, patterns began to emerge, clustering around "main" metaphors that had similar underlying attributes. By creating clusters of similar metaphorical expressions, root metaphors guiding decision-making were identified in this step, as well as secondary metaphors that were used to justify behavioral choices. Finally, to gain insight into the worldview of the contestants, the interpretation and entailment of each metaphor was accomplished through the systematic extension and elaboration of the metaphors (Martin, 1990). Further, patterns of usage within and between the clusters were examined (Ivie, 1987).

In addition to the determination of the root and secondary metaphors, Owen's (1984) criteria for identifying themes in discourse were employed. Owen argues that three criteria should be present to identify a theme: (1) recurrence—two or more metaphors had the same thread of meaning, even though different wording was used,(2) repetition—explicit use of the same wording, and (3) forcefulness—nonverbal behavior serving to stress the metaphors.

Identification of Metaphors

Almost 200 individual metaphorical expressions regarding decision-making strategies and justifications emerged from the series. Seven clusters of metaphors emerged that guided the decision-making strategies and justifications for behavior of the group members (see Table 1). After seven metaphors had been identified, distinctions were then made based on the primacy and commonness of the metaphors. Four primary, root metaphors emerged that met Owen's three criteria of recurrence, repetition, and forcefulness, and served as the underlying foundations for making decisions and/or for determining what actions should be taken to achieve the goals of group members. The root metaphors that emerged included survival is (1) an equation, (2) war, (3) tribe, and (4) politics. The three remaining metaphors were secondary to the worldviews encapsulated by the root metaphors. These metaphors were used far less frequently and usually were more evaluative, focusing on the justification of behavior. The three secondary metaphors that emerged included behavior is (1) a journey, (2) a drama, and (3) spirituality.

IDENTIFICATION AND EXTENSION OF ROOT METAPHORS

Survival is tribe.

The first root metaphor used to guide the decision making of contestants equated survival to the tribe. This metaphor centered on the relational dimension of the group. Put simply, decisions based on this perspective suggested that one's value was based on how much you were liked or if you were able to work with others in your tribe. Thus, contestants were evaluated on their contributions to the relational dimension of the group and were held accountable to one another and the norms of the group. This metaphor implies caring, sharing, and friendship, and suggests that one should protect other members of one's tribe and could potentially have to sacrifice oneself to help the tribe. As one member stated, "It's not about I, it's about *us.*" Contestants using this metaphor often made metaphorical references to the cohesion of their tribe, using terms such as "*stick* together," "bonded," and "tight." From this perspective, members were judged on whether they made a perceived connection with their tribe. As one contestant said, she was not worried about receiving votes because, "I feel safe—I *get along* with people."

It is important to note that while the producers of the show created "tribes" at the beginning of the show, this did not create an inherent feeling of "groupness" for all of the contestants. Rather, the individual members of each tribe had to define for themselves what it meant to be a part of the tribe, if they accepted the metaphor as meaningful at all. Some perceived the tribe as an artificial creation of the show, and rejected its imagery by acting independently or forming their own sub-groups. Contestants who rejected the tribal imagery rarely used metaphors reflecting that they perceived themselves as a "team" or "family." Subsequently, contestants with this perspective viewed the tribe as a collection of individuals assigned to the same living space, and acted accordingly. Others contestants embraced the concept of being a "tribe," and imported social norms for behavior associated with being a member of a cohesive group.

Recurring themes clustered under this root metaphor and used by contestants who accepted it included references to family, team, or friendships. For example, when one contestant knew that he would perform poorly in an upcoming competition he argued, "They have to compensate for me—that's what a *team* does." Another contestant expressed the difficulty of voting for tribe mates saying, "I can't imagine, fathom voting someone off this *team* tonight." Perhaps the clearest expression of the group as a family came from a contestant when forced to vote for a fellow tribe member, "It's like taking a piece of our *family* away." Words repeated in this metaphor included "friend," "team, " and "group."

Survival is an equation.

The second root metaphor clustered around expressions that equated survival in the game to an equation. This metaphor represented a very logical and calculated basis for making decisions—a rational weighing of the potential costs and rewards for given decisions. Contestants using this metaphor focused on what contributions were made by other members in regard to the multiple tasks of the group (e.g., food, shelter, competitions, etc.). Use of this metaphor implied that the choices made were not personal or emotional; decisions were made on the "merits" of each contestant.

Two recurring themes created the root metaphor of survival as an equation. The first recurring theme was that decisions should be made based on a model of economic exchange. Contestants were voted off the island because they had "cost" the team, were not "contributing" enough, or were viewed as a "liability." On the other hand, contestants attempted to increase their chances of staying in the game by providing a service that was valuable to their fellow contestants. For example, one contestant talked about how he had to "up his *value*" and "squeeze every ounce of *credit*" out of providing fish as a food source. Words representing this theme that were repeated included "pull his or her weight," "lazy," "getting the fish," and "contribution."

A second recurring theme that made up the root metaphor of survival as an equation expressed the equation in terms of a game or sport with decisions being made based on the calculation of payoffs or losses associated with potential choices. From this metaphorical perspective, behavior is based on strategy and viewed as a series of moves and countermoves. As one player put it, "It's a *game* and I have had a strategy from day one." Another stated, "This is just a chess *game*." While similar to an economic exchange, contestants were evaluated based on who "*played* the *game* better," or who was "the reason we *lost*." Words that were repeated that represented this theme were "game," "weakest," and "competition."

Survival is war.

The third root metaphor clustered around images of survival as war. Contestants often made references to the game being a "battle," "fight," or "free for all." A war metaphor implies strategy and calculations much like the equation metaphor, but the choices made are not as logical or impersonal. This metaphor entails doing whatever is necessary to achieve one's goal, including spying and deception. One might need to "sleep by an *enemy*" and "turncoat" to achieve one's end. This metaphor also was depicted by many images of death and violence, such as "slitting throats" and "digging a knife" into one's back.

Many recurring themes constituted the root metaphor of survival as war. The most common theme was that of murder. For example, one contestant referred to the members of the other tribe as "sitting around with a red dot pointed to their head" and also admitted that her team was "leading lambs to the *slaughter*." Other recurring expressions representing death included "*wipe* them *out*," "*kill* them all," and "face the *firing squad*." Words or phrases that often were repeated included "bloodbath," "burning," "back stabber," and "*pick off* one by one."

Another recurring theme in the root metaphor of survival as war was that of the hunt. Some contestants expressed this when they envisioned themselves as hunters of their fellow contestants. For example, one contestant said, "I am a *hunter*. And I've got both *guns loaded* all the way and I'm gonna *fire them* full blast." Another contestant said, "There are analogies between my going out there and hunting fish and my *picking off* the tribe members one by one. I have been *stalking* them since before I got on the island." Those who felt they were being hunted also expressed this theme. For example, some group members referred to themselves as a "bull's-eye," or a "sitting duck." Within this theme the one word that was repeated was "hunt."

A third recurring theme that fell under the rubric of survival as war was that of cannibalism. One contestant explained the choices of contestants in the game by saying it was "what happens when you put a big chunk of cheese in a maze and let all the mice go at it—see *who eats who*." The same contestant predicted the actions of the other team; "They're going to pick people off until it gets down to three and then *start eating* each other." The words "eat" and "eating" were repeated often within this theme.

Two final recurring themes that were clustered within the metaphor of survival as war included references to bombs and spying. For example, one contestant compared the expulsion of a teammate to "dropping an atomic *bomb*," and another said "I bit off more than I could chew and then it all *exploded*." Expressions that reference spying included "*played both sides* of the fence" and the repeated phrases of "double agent" and "under the radar."

Survival is politics.

The final primary root metaphor equated survival to politics. The emphasis of this metaphor was the need to form subgroups and alliances in order to achieve a base of power over fellow contestants. A primary entailment of this metaphor includes voting along party lines (or sub-party lines). This metaphor recognizes the need to have others follow you or at least vote in your interest, as power ultimately comes from the willingness of others to support you. However, political alliances were not relationships based on friendship as they were in the tribal metaphor. Rather, connections were made based on mutual needs, promises, and ensuing obligations. From this perspective, one did not have to fully trust or even like the people in one's alliance. One member of an alliance expressed this lack of trust when he threatened retaliation if the other members of his alliance didn't follow support him, "Their *word* better be good. If they *betray* me, I'll get even with them."

The primary recurring theme of survival as politics incorporated explicit and implicit expressions of sub-group alliances. Contestants talked about "*ganging* up" and "getting together." One contestant referred to her alliance as "three against the world." Another contestant argued, "*Alliances*, little teams within bigger teams, don't detract from the larger group." The word that was repeated within this metaphor was "alliance."

IDENTIFICATION AND EXTENSION OF SECONDARY METAPHORS

Three additional base metaphors were identified that did not cluster in the root metaphors identified in the last section. Metaphorical expressions revealing the secondary metaphors were far less common and were focused on actions taken rather than on decisions. The secondary metaphors are best interpreted as extensions of the primary or root metaphors, and can be conceptualized as new ways of indicating the experiential structure of the contestants (Koch & Deetz, 1981). The secondary metaphors typically were used by contestants to evaluate their own and others' behaviors in terms of what was deemed fair, ethical, moral, or responsible.

Behavior as a journey.

The secondary metaphor of survival as a journey reflected the view that there was a path one had to take if one were to achieve one's goals. This metaphor was primarily used as an extension of the root metaphors of war and politics. It was used as a justification for employing behaviors that others might deem unethical. As one contestant said to the others, "I would hope that you appreciate what I've done to *get here.*" Another contestant said that they had to do "whatever it took to *get to the end.*" In the end, this metaphor was an attempt to exonerate a contestant from the negative evaluations of others.

Behavior as drama.

Another secondary metaphor that was an extension of the root metaphors of politics and war was the equation of behavior to a drama. Equating one's behavior to a drama alleviates one from taking responsibility for his or her actions. Expressions constituting this metaphor made references to being on a "stage" and playing a "role." For example, one contestant said, "I'm playing the *role* of a redneck and hopefully the redneck will burn the city slicker." Equating one's behavior with a role in a drama allows a person to enact behavior that might be viewed as unethical by others, but then rationalizes the behavior as play acting rather than taking responsibility. One contestant summed up this perspective the best when she said, "We're not evil, we just *play* bad people on TV."

Behavior as spirituality.

In contrast to the secondary metaphors of behavior as a journey or role, others expressed their behavior as spirituality. Using spiritual references entailed Judeo-Christian references that implied ethical guidelines for judgment. Examples of spirituality metaphorical expressions included, "seeing the light," "prophecy," "forgiveness," and "redemption." The spirituality metaphor was primarily an extension of the root metaphor of survival as a tribe. This metaphor implies that people can change (like a spiritual conversion), and therefore, they should be judged on their most recent behavior. For example, one tribe member argued she should not be voted off the island because she had "*redeemed* herself" by changing her behavior.

In addition, the spirituality metaphorical perspective focuses on the need to do what is ethical. As one contestant said about another's behavior, "He stepped on some toes and people ain't gonna *forgive* him." Contestants seeing through the lenses of war or political metaphors saw this perspective as naïve. For example, one contestant clearly rejected this metaphor and its implied ethical judgments when he said; "Sean says '*do unto others.*' Time for you to go, bud."

Implications for "Survival"

Having identified the root and secondary metaphors used by the contestants of *Survivor*, the final stage of this analysis was to examine how these metaphors guided the behavior and decisions of the contestants and to explore the group dynamics created by the varying metaphors. At this point in the analysis, metaphoric usage was contextualized in two ways—by tribal affiliation and stage of the game. First, primary metaphors used by the original members of the Pagong and Tagi tribes were separated. Second, metaphors were distinguished by whether they came before or after the merger of the two tribes. Separating the metaphoric usage in these two ways allowed interpretations to be drawn about differences between the two tribes, as well as differences based on the developmental stage of the game.

METAPHORS BY TRIBE BEFORE THE MERGER

In the first stage of the game, the Pagong and Tagi tribes competed against one another as two distinct groups. Therefore, at this stage in the game, decisions had to account for not only what was good for one's own survival, but also what was good for the tribe. Assuming some level of group orientation was needed at this stage of development the root metaphors can be distinguished best by the reasoning style employed. At one end of a continuum, decisions about what was best for the group and oneself could be based on purely rational reasoning. On the opposite end, decisions could be based on a more instinctual level.

Two root metaphors represent the rational end of the continuum: survival as an equation and survival as politics. What these two metaphors have in common is that they both are relatively impersonal in nature. Respectively, the metaphors call for decisions to be made on the basis of value to the group or value to the sub-group. Whether one was "likeable" or a friend had little to do with what decisions were made if one was using the lens of survival as an equation or politics. At this stage, the only strong difference between the two metaphors on the rational end of the continuum at this stage was whether one was judged based on contributions to the group as a whole or contributions to a smaller sub-set of the group.

The other two root metaphors represent the instinctual end of the reasoning style dimension: survival as tribe and survival as war. Both metaphors are based on the instinctual need for self-preservation, but present different solutions. A focus on the tribe is based on the instinctual need of humans as social creatures to make connections with others and build relationships, as there is safety in numbers. A focus on war also is based on an instinctual need, but it is to maintain (or perhaps even increase) one's territory. These two metaphors are really reflections of one another with one focusing on the preservation of the in-group (tribe) and the other focusing on the destruction of the out-group (war).

The Tagi tribe before the merger.

The metaphors displayed by the Tagi tribe before the merger revealed a strong reliance on the two root metaphors at the rational end of the continuum: equation and politics (see Table 2). The most common metaphoric themes encapsulated the use of the survival as equation metaphor. Numerous references were made to economic exchange and game themes, revealing that decisions were based primarily on the value of an individual at this point in the game. Tribe members were judged to be "contributors" or "lazy," and if one was perceived as "weak" or a "liability" he or she was voted off at the tribal councils. While not as prevalent, the survival as politics metaphor also emerged in the Tagi's rhetoric prior to the merger. This metaphor was compatible with viewing survival as an equation, but incorporated a strategy for forming and voting as an alliance to ensure one's own safety.

There was much less evidence of the metaphors that fell on the instinctual end of the continuum. Very few references were made to the need to be a "tribe" or to make friends. Rather, most of the Tagi tribe members appeared to be focused solely on winning the game, and did not feel it necessary to make social connections with one another. There were even clear rejections of this metaphor by the Tagi tribe members. For example, one Tagi member said, "I'm not out here to make *friends*."

Table 2.
Tagi Tribe's Metaphoric Usage Before Merger of Tribes
(abbreviated quotations)*

Root Metaphors

War	Equation	Politics	Tribe
Military, one in charge	*Getting the fish* (3)	Get women together	Tight group
Band together,			
cut throats	Don't get along	Gang up	Think of the *team*
Kicking and screaming	Tough call	Stick with it, keep self *safe*	*Team* morale
Brute force	*Game* and I had strategy	Develop *alliance*	I get along, feel *safe*
Keep under wraps	*Game*	Not here to make friends	
Free for all	Doesn't move her ass	Finally went along w/ *alliance*	
Thin ice	Cost them	Three against the world	
Thing blows up	Reason we lost	Little teams in bigger teams	
	Liability		
	Weakest link		
	Weakest member		
	People who work versus *lazy*		
	Not successful, think I'm *lazy*		
	Gave it my best		
	Tired of feeding people		
	who don't do anything		
	I'm entertaining, make		
	people laugh		
	Contributing the most		
	Athletic *competition* that		
	we have to win		
	Contributed		
	Failed at everything		
	Can't stand the complaining		

Secondary Metaphors

Spirituality	Journey	Drama
Do unto others	Get there from here	

Repetition noted in italics

The Pagong tribe before the merger.

Much like the Tagi, the Pagong tribe members prominently displayed the rational metaphor of survival as an equation (see Table 3). Tribe members made repeated references to the need for members to "pull their weight" and "contribute," as well as references to the need to "stay competitive." One Pagong member even expressed her concern recognizing that her tribe mates were guided by this perspective when she stated, "My leg [of a race] *lost* and it makes me feel *vulnerable* in the vote tonight."

Unlike the Tagi tribe, the Pagong tribe also displayed evidence of

TABLE 3.
Pagong Tribe's Metaphoric Usage before Merger of Tribes (abbreviated quotations)*

ROOT METAPHORS

War	Equation	Tribe
Dropping atomic bomb	Stay *competitive*	Great to have friend
Dug his own grave	Want to *compete*?	What a *team* does
	Have to win *competitions*	Keep *team* strong
	Board game Sorry	Fun to play with
	Get out of jail free card	Bonded
	Free ride	Struggling w/group life
	We're hurting	Take a piece of family
	Gets things done	Everyone clicked
	Pull her weight	It's about us
	Pull his own weight	Stick together
	Least want to play with	Lose someone
	Needs to win less	All about charm
	Work ethic	Condescending, "Moo"
	Contributes least	Ice breaker—laughing
	Contribute	We all like each other
	Not a champion	
	Voted for me	
	My leg lost, vulnerable	
	Haven't done anything bad	
	Can't have lazy people	
	Too little too late	

SECONDARY METAPHORS

Spirituality	Journey	Drama
Self-fulfilling prophecy		
Judgment day on earth		
Redeemed herself		

*Repetition noted in italics

heavily relying on the instinctual metaphor of survival as tribe. Numerous references were made to being a "team," "group," and "family," and decisions about expulsion were based on this as well as what individuals contributed to the tasks of the group. One Pagong member appeared to disdain this way of thinking and said, "I'm not trying to win a personality contest …I'll do what I want to do." The power of the tribal metaphor was made clear when he was the first person voted off by the Pagong tribe, despite the fact that he had contributed greatly to the tasks of the group (equation). Other Pagong members also were voted off because they violated the social norms of the tribe.

It should be noted that the secondary metaphor of behavior as spirituality was also evident and supported the tribal metaphor. Pagong members used phrases like "*judgment* day on earth" and "self-fulfilling *prophecy*" to explain their judgments of fellow tribe mates who were seen as violating the expectations of what it meant to be a member of the tribe.

Metaphorical expressions of survival as war or politics were almost non-existent for the Pagong tribe in this stage of the game. A virtually equal weighting of survival as an equation and survival as tribe created a difficult dialectic for the tribe members to overcome when making decisions about whom to expel. On the one hand, they were trying to make logical and rationale choices based on the task value of tribe members, but on the other hand they were evaluating people instinctually based on their contributions to the social life of the group. The focus of the tribe on the social dimension created much more angst in the tribal council when the Pagong tribe was forced to vote one of their own off the island. While the Tagi appeared to view the vote as a way to strengthen their chances of winning the game, the Pagong lamented the fact that they had to "*lose* someone" or that "a piece of their *family*" was being taken away by the vote.

The Merger: Creation of the New Tribe Rattana

In the second stage of the game, the two original tribes were merged to form one large tribe called Rattana. This change in the rules of the game added a new dimension along which the root metaphors rested. The contestants now had to decide whether an orientation of loyalty to a group was still necessary or if a more individualistic or independent orientation would be more effective. The orientation dimension at one end encompassed "affiliation" where one recognized the interdependence of the contestants. Autonomy was at the opposite end and reflected a desire to act independently. Utilizing the previous reasoning style dimension and adding the new dimension of orientation, the four root metaphors can now be seen to fall into four distinct quadrants (see Figure 1).

First, survival as politics is a metaphor of rationality and logic in that it does not rely on personal friendships and is relatively impersonal—one does what one has to do to win. Yet despite the lack of stress on relationships and friendships, the political metaphor acknowledges that one needs to build alliances to gain power. It is, therefore, affiliative, but in an impersonal, calculating way. Second, survival as tribe is also affiliative, but the connections one makes are based on friendship and normative values. It is instinctual in this need for social relationships. Third, the survival as equation metaphor is very rational as one logically determines

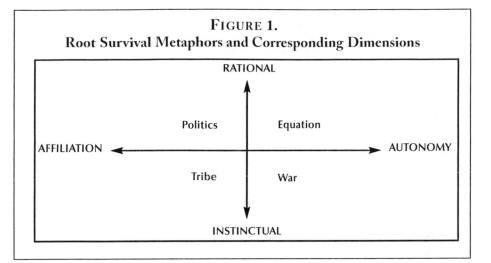

FIGURE 1.
Root Survival Metaphors and Corresponding Dimensions

RATIONAL

Politics   Equation

AFFILIATION ←—————————————→ AUTONOMY

Tribe   War

INSTINCTUAL

the highest relative rewards for a given behavior. At this point in the game, however, it was possible to adapt its use to take an autonomous orientation. In other words, rather than determining what was best for the group, it was now possible to retain this metaphorical orientation and focus on what was best for the individual alone. One Pagong member explained these changes in orientation as the groups were merged. She argued that one had to go from an orientation of "who's strongest in your tribe to keep, to who's strongest in this one tribe to get rid of." Finally, as stated before, the survival as war metaphor fell on the instinctual side of the reasoning dimension, but also was adaptable to an autonomous orientation in that one can "hunt" or "kill" to retain one's own territory rather than the tribe's territory.

The Tagi tribe after the merger.

The Tagi tribe displayed three primary root metaphors in the second stage of the game (see Table 4). Members of the tribe still used some metaphorical expressions reflecting the survival as equation metaphor. However, use of this metaphor reflected a more individualistic orientation at this point. One Tagi member illustrated this change in logic by voting for someone because she was "tired of getting beat at the competitions." While still retaining some equation metaphors, overwhelmingly the two metaphors used in the second stage of the game by Tagi members were metaphors of war and politics. Having to make "dirty" choices became a repeated theme in association with the "alliance" theme. Metaphors of war became the most common and they were much more vivid than they

Table 4.
Tagi Tribe's Metaphoric Usage after Merger of Tribes
(abbreviated quotations)*

Root Metaphors

War	Equation	Politics
Joined forces	Up my value	Still have a team (alliance)
Backstabber (2)	Squeeze every oz. credit	She had to go
Bloodbath	*Competition*	Got burned
Bloodbath has begun	No more *competition*	Time to get dirty
Not a *blood bath*	Beat at *competitions*	Regret *alliance*
Burn the city slicker	Slackers on other team	Went along with *alliance*
Burning, taking down	Chess *game*	Not a politician
Sleeping by enemy	Playing a *game*	Next leader
Tortures me	Approach to *game*	Fulfilling obligation
Turncoat	Just playing a game	Never was a tribe
Uphill battle	Played the *game* better	Not here to make bosom buddies
Slit my throat	Strong work ethic	Deal with the devil
Self-preservation	Least objectionable	Time to get *dirty*
Digging knife in backside		Have to get a little *dirty*
Number was up		Conniving and *dirty*
Hunting fish and picking off	Not gonna f... her, burn her	
Stalking them		Betray, I'll get even
Leading lambs to slaughter		
Had them lined up		
Hunter, both guns loaded		
Firing squad		
Red dot pointed to their head		
All exploded		

Secondary Metaphors

Spirituality	Journey	Drama
Being sacrificed	What I've done to get here	Play bad people on TV
I seen the light	*Going to the end*	Get off the stage
Ain't gonna forgive him	What it took to *get to end*	Play role of redneck

*Repetition noted in italics

had been before the merger of the two tribes. References to "slitting throats," "blood baths," "*picking* people *off*," and being "hunters" were common. While metaphorical expressions of war and politics increased after the merger, there was a complete lack of any metaphorical expressions representing survival as a tribe. As one contestant argued, "People who came here to make bosom *buddies* should have gone to summer camp."

As the show reached the final stage in which the jury of fellow contestants was being formed, the remaining Tagi members also began to use the secondary metaphors of behavior as a journey and drama. They often used these metaphors to justify their behavior to themselves and others.

One of the final two contestants reflected the drama metaphor when she argued, as cited earlier, "We're not evil, we just *play* bad people on TV." The other final contestant displayed the journey metaphor when he argued, "I hope you appreciate what I've done to *get here*." Again, metaphors of drama and journey were used in an effort to deflect judgments about the ethicality of their behavior.

The Pagong tribe after the merger.

In the second stage of the game the metaphors displayed by the members of the remaining Pagong tribe also changed (see Table 5). Initially, the Pagong members looked forward to the merger with anticipation and used expressions that reflected the survival as tribe metaphor, referring to the merger as a "new beginning." One Pagong member even equated the newly merged tribe to a "a banquet of stories and excitement." These examples illustrate that members of the former Pagong tribe embraced the belief that the merged tribes were a "new tribe."

However, within a few days, the Pagong's metaphoric expressions began to change dramatically. One Pagong member summed up the changing metaphoric orientation when she said, "We came in like 'maybe we can all be *friends*,' and they came in like '*smash them*.'" Another said, "Pagong was *fun*. Now we moved into the new neighborhood, the *nasty neighborhood*." Some of the Pagong members expressed a need to move away from the tribal metaphor. At this point, the Pagong tribe members began to display the root metaphors of survival as war. However, unlike the Tagi, most of the war metaphors used by the Pagong tribe reflected a victim mentality rather than one of aggression. The Pagong members' rhetoric primarily was that of the hunted, including phrases like "sitting duck" and" "I'm the last of my kind."

While many metaphorical expressions about being the victims of war were displayed by the Pagong at this stage in the game, they also used this perspective to describe the behavior of the other tribe. The Pagong members viewed the Tagi negatively, seeing them not only as hunters, but cannibals. They made many predictions that the Tagi would "*eat* each other."

As in the first stage of the game, the Pagong continued to display some evidence of the survival as an equation metaphor, relying primarily on the use of game metaphors. However, the expressions now were used to express their dissatisfaction with the "moves" of the other team. One Pagong member said "Fear-motivated, self-preservation is the worst *game* to *play*." It was clear that the calculation of rewards and losses for the Pagong tribe members now incorporated more than task contributions. The votes on the jury would be used to judge the merits of other partic-

TABLE 5.
Pagong Tribe's Metaphoric Usage after Merger of Tribes
(abbreviated quotations)*

ROOT METAPHORS

War	*Equation*	*Politics*	*Tribe*
Eating each other	That's the *game*	Bond with women	Like a banquet
Who *eats* who	Worst *game*	Have to cut them loose	Maybe we can be friends
Start *eating* each other	Rich doesn't need it		Paranoia, irritation
Smash them	Deserves this vote		Be here or be gone
Pick people *off*	Based on merits		
Pick off one by one	Don't see him doing much		
Last of my kind	Least want to play with		
Wipe them out			
Sitting duck			
Bulls eye			
Snap kitten's neck			
Bust plan up, kill them all			
Get rid of him, everyone else is cake			
Strong-armed			
Under the radar (2)			
Double agent (2)			
Played both sides of fence			
Who scrambles on top of who			

SECONDARY METAPHORS

Spirituality	*Journey*	*Drama*
Displayed ethics	Ticket *home*	
	Needs to go *home*	
	Left emotional baggage	
	New beginning	

*Repetition noted in italics

ipants including perceptions of how ethically they had played the game—adding the normative dimension of the tribe metaphor to the rational equation metaphor.

Some Final Thoughts on the Efficacy of Root Metaphors

The final five contestants of the game all were originally members of the Tagi tribe. Therefore, one could argue that the metaphoric conceptualizations of the Tagi tribe were superior in helping them to address the mixed-motive decisions necessitated by the game. Why were the Tagi tribe members ultimately more successful than the Pagong at remaining in the game?

First, focusing on the root metaphor of survival as equation rather than survival as tribe in the early stages of the game allowed the Tagi members to retain an emotional distance from one another. This made the switch to the root metaphors of politics and war much easier. The Tagi tribe did not need to struggle with questions of friendship, and both metaphors allowed them to justify their actions without much concern for what others might deem as ethical or unethical. By focusing on the creation of alliances rather than friendships, it was also much easier to begin to incorporate metaphors of war allowing for an autonomous orientation when only members of their own political alliance remained. In other words, a focus on sub-group affiliation (alliance) based on need for power, rather than tribal affiliation led to the natural behaviors necessitated by a "war"—murder, hunting, and even cannibalism of one's own tribe.

On the other hand, the Pagong tribe's reliance on a tribal metaphor in the first stages of the game made it more difficult to switch to an autonomous orientation needed for a single winner in the later stages of the game. In the root metaphor of survival as tribe, affiliation is based on friendship and liking. This entails a strong normative influence where one has to continue to display behavior that the tribe has valued earlier or one will be sanctioned by one's own tribe. When individual Pagong members tried to change their behavior to match that of the Tagi, their own teammates viewed them more negatively than the Tagi displaying the same behavior. In essence, they had higher expectations and standards for members of their own tribe—because they were a "tribe." This led them to vote against one another once in the merged tribe.

In addition, many of the Pagong members rejected the need to form alliances in the earlier stages of the game, arguing that it was not a part of the game as they wanted to play it. When merged with the Tagi, they brought this norm with them, making it difficult to ally with one another now that they were a part of a larger group. If they created an alliance based on former tribal affiliation, they would become what they disdained. In the end, the failure to adapt to the requirements of the second stage of the game along with the desire to create a "new tribe" in which one would be judged by one's task and normative contributions became their downfall.

However, one might argue that while the members of the original

Pagong tribe did not win the game, they were more successful at meeting the process goals of creating relationships and friendships than the Tagi tribe members. The Pagong attempted to base their decisions on what an individual had contributed to the tribe in terms of developing relationships and providing physical comforts for the group. Therefore, even when using the root metaphor of survival as an equation, they often talked about how to "play" the game fairly and with whom they wanted to continue to play. If they entered the game with a focus on having fun experience rather than "winning," one might argue that the Pagong were successful in their own right.

This brings to light an interesting question that researchers and group members face when judging the efficacy of groups performing tasks and/or making decisions: Is a group's "success" measured by the group's outcome or by its process? The study of communication competence argues that one must be both effective and appropriate to be successful. However, while groups might strive to meet both goals of an optimal outcome and optimal process, in a less than ideal world groups often have to sacrifice the optimization of one goal to achieve the other.

An examination of the metaphoric conceptual system of the members of the Tagi tribe clearly demonstrated that they had a strong task orientation, and therefore, focused on the outcome of winning while choosing to sacrifice the relational dimension of their group to achieve it. Put simply, they defined an appropriate process as doing whatever it takes as an individual to win. Alternatively, the metaphorical constructs of the members of the Pagong tribe reveal that they chose to focus more on the relational processes of the group and ultimately sacrificed winning the game in order to play the game in a way that they felt was appropriate. One might argue that they redefined the outcome of the game as feeling that one had done one's best and had contributed to the success of their tribe. Based on theses differing perspectives, one could conclude that both tribes achieved success as they defined it.

The conflict for these two groups and any others faced with making difficult decisions lies in the clash of metaphorical systems that may be antithetical to one another. If all group members have the same or very similar orientations, the process will be seen as appropriate and the outcome will be deemed fair. However, when some group members focus on the outcome and others on the process, or similarly when some group members have an autonomous orientation while others stress affiliation, differences between the paradigms will create conflict within the group that can be devastating and hinder the group's ability to perform as a group. In the case of the contestants of *Survivor*, the clash of the metaphorical systems of the two original tribes prohibited them from ever becoming a single group when the two tribes were merged.

References

Choi, Y. B. (1993). *Paradigms and conventions: Uncertainty, decision making, and entrepreneurship.* Ann Arbor, MI: University of Michigan Press.

Cowell, C. R. (1972). Group process as metaphor. *Journal of Communication, 22,* 113–123.

Embler, W. (1966). *Metaphors and meaning.* Jacksonville, FL: Convention.

Hawakaya, S. I. (1978). *Language in thought and action* (4th Ed.). New York: Harcourt Brace Jovanowich.

Hill, R. C., & Levenhagen, M. (1995). Metaphors and mental models: Sensemaking and sensegiving in innovative and entrepreneurial activities. *Journal of Management, 21,* 1057–1074.

Ivie, R. L. (1987). Metaphor and the rhetorical invention of the Cold War "idealists." *Communication Monographs, 54,*165–182.

Kendall, J. E., & Kendall, K. E. (1993). Metaphors and methodologies: Living beyond the systems machine. *MIS Quarterly, 17,* 149–171.

Koch, S., & Deetz, S. (1981). Metaphor analysis of social reality in organizations. *Journal of Applied Communication Research, 9,* 1–15.

Lakoff, G. & Johnson, M. (1980). *Metaphors we live by.* Chicago: University of Chicago Press.

Lissack, M. (1997). Mind your metaphors: Lessons from complexity science. *Long Range Planning, 30,* 294–298.

Martin, J. H. (1990). *A computational model of metaphor interpretation.* San Diego, CA: Harcourt Brace Jovanovich.

Mills, T. (1967). *The sociology of small groups.* Englewood Cliffs, NJ: Prentice Hall.

Owen, W. F. (1984). Interpretive themes in relational communication. *Quarterly Journal of Speech, 70,* 274–287.

Smith, K. K., & Berg, D. N. (1987). *Paradoxes of group life.* San Francisco: Jossey-Bass.

8

Survivor, Social Choice, and the Impediments to Political Rationality: Reality TV as Social Science Experiment

Ed Wingenbach

Social choice theory occupies a privileged explanatory position within much of the social sciences, particularly economics, psychology, sociology, and political science. Social choice theory argues that the outcomes of collective action may be explained in terms of the calculation of costs and benefits in pursuit of individual preferences. Despite its near hegemonic position in the leading journals of political science and economics, most of the laboratory evidence gathered over the last 40 years mitigates against the social choice explanation of collective behavior. The absence of compelling empirical evidence may arise from our inability to create sufficient incentives or impose adequate controls to test the theory. In short, though subjects appear to be driven by social pressure, ethical norms, or failure to recognize rational strategy, the problem lies not in the results but the experimental conditions. Create high enough incentives or a sufficiently focused environment, and truly rational behavior would emerge. Social scientists have neither the funds nor authority to impose such conditions. Fortunately, CBS does.

This chapter analyzes the game structure set up by the rules and incentive structure of *Survivor* and elucidates the model of behavior predicted by social choice theory. It then analyzes the actual behavior of the contestants, showing only five of the sixteen follow the rational model to any significant degree. Next, the essay categorizes the non-rational factors that motivate the behavior of the majority of contestants; these factors include personal ethics, public image, duty, and emotions. I conclude that the *Survivor* experiment demonstrates the importance of acknowledging the limits of self-interest as a predictor of behavior, integrating moral/ethical beliefs into rational analysis, and recognizing the limits of individual rational capacity.

Social Choice and the Survivor *Experiment*

Social choice theory should be viewed as a subset or application of rational choice theory. Though its roots might be traced back as far as Thomas Hobbes (1651, see particularly chapter 13), modern rational choice emerged as a systematic and identifiable approach about mid-century, most prominently in the work of Downs (1957), Arrow (1963), and Buchanan and Tullock (1962); it has come to dominate contemporary economics and political science, and is important in a number of other fields such as psychology, law, history, and sociology. Rational choice encompasses a wide range of methods, all of which attempt to explain and predict human behavior by assuming the primacy of instrumental rationality, which merely means that individuals will always choose to pursue their self-interest by the most efficient strategy available to them. Efficient here indicates that individual actors will adopt the course of action maximizing their expected utility given the information available to them at the time of the decision. Rational choice methodologies attempt to systematize the calculations of interest and efficiency to produce predictive scientific models about large-scale behavior.[1] If a theorist can identify or hypothesize the utility orderings at play in a given situation and accurately assess the strategic options open to the players, it should be possible to predict the outcome of any situation.

Social choice theory shifts the emphasis slightly, concerning itself with the formation and ordering of preferences by individuals and the problem of accurately aggregating these divergent preferences (for an overview, see Plott, 1976). Generally, social choice focuses on elections and decision making in groups. Riker's (1982) classic text reveals the profound implications of social choice for democratic politics: if more than two people are involved in a decision, and more than three alternatives exist (or individuals have the option of introducing other alternatives), then no method of aggregating the preferences of individuals produces a coherent outcome.[2] Thus, the theory both accurately explains large-scale economic behavior and undermines the possibility of meaningful democratic governance.

The ascendance of social choice is not without critics. As Green and Shapiro (1994) have shown, the theory's predictive claims are vastly overstated, the empirical evidence sketchy, and the logic often so broad as to be tautological. The flaws in social choice explanations of political behavior fall into four categories. First, social choice theory tends toward circularity. When construed broadly, the claim that all actions are rational defies falsification.[3] Second, the social scientific evidence seems not to support the theory. As Green and Shapiro (1994) show, where good data exist it tends to refute the theoretical predictions, and where the theory seems to work best, little data exist.[4] Third, laboratory tests attempting to generate and observe rational behavior have been almost completely unsuccessful. In fact, according to Hauptmann and Clements' (1999) excellent review of lab tests in economics and political science since the 1950's, the only experiment to yield genuinely rational outcomes was one using graduate students in a PhD program in economics. We might conclude that rational behavior is observed in the lab only among those already trained in rational choice theory. Fourth, it is difficult to determine motives with any certainty, and discerning instrumental rationality without a clear understanding of motive is all but hopeless. More technically, to predict rational behavior, the theorist must assume knowledge of the actors' maximum utility (perfect outcome) and their expected utility (best plausible outcome given current constraints), while assuming the actors have full information about their options. Unfortunately, transparency of motive and full information rarely characterize real human beings in complex situations.

Thus investigators must assume that all actors are: (1) utility maximizing agents, meaning they will pursue the strategy most conducive to achieving their desired end in the most profitable fashion; (2) aware of the expected utilities of the various options given the current conditions and actions (anticipated and observed) of other players; and (3) able to access and understand this information, or, in social choice parlance, possess "full information." Eliminate any of these factors and prediction or explanation become increasingly difficult. Unfortunately, people often possess conflicting motives or contrary utilities, rendering their behavior difficult to predict in terms of utility maximization. Even individuals with clear and non-contradictory preferences may not be able to judge their expected utility as accurately at the time of decision as an analyst can, nor are they usually able to anticipate or observe the actions of their competitors. Lastly, full information is almost always absent, for a variety of obvious reasons.

Given these difficulties, a rigorous experiment testing social choice predictions in an environment both controlled and easily observed would be of great significance. The first season of *Survivor* provides exactly such a test. The *Survivor* game offers: (1) a clear incentive structure for the players; (2) unambiguous rules for conduct and victory; (3) complete transparency, both for the players, who can easily observe the strategic behavior of others, and the experimenters, who have all actions on tape for future review; (4) long term observation, allowing the predictions to be tested over time and multiple iterations; (5) opportunities for learning, since failure is openly punished and competition relatively constant (thus allowing correctives for mistaken irrationality); (6) in depth interviews with the subjects discussing their choices and some access to psychological profiles; and lastly, (7) a series of regular votes along with the voters' self-reports on their voting choices. In short, *Survivor* offers the perfect test of social choice theory.

THE MODEL

I propose a relatively simple model to understand *Survivor* as an experiment, making behavioral predictions requiring only minimal rationality and obvious choices. Such a model is most likely to generate a favorable outcome for the theory, thus rendering the results difficult to dismiss should the theory fail. My underlying assumption is that all players share the same goal: they all wish to win the game. The reward for winning is ten times more lucrative than second place, and after third and fourth place the monetary rewards decline precipitously. Other than BB, every player expressed an unambiguous desire to win the first prize money.[5] Thus all the players present a clear and uncontradictory awareness of their own maximal utility.

One obvious objection to my premise must be addressed. It is conceivable that players might envision an alternative method to attain the monetary award, or even exceed it. That alternative is fame.[6] This powerful objection may be refuted in at least three ways. First, it is important to remember that the experiment occurred far before the series first aired. The subjects could not have anticipated the frenzy that built around the show. Second, even if the subjects assumed the show would be a success, winning the first prize remains the best way to maximize the return of fame. The winner would receive more publicity and thus have the best opportunity to cash in on fame, as Richard Hatch was well aware in his pre-game planning (Lance, 2000). Moreover, the longer one stays on the show, the greater the likelihood of fame. The early segments of the show are simply too crowded for any individual to make a serious impression on the audience, a factor intensified by the knowledge that the show would be edited, further reducing any player's screen time. Thus, the pursuit of fame should, as an issue of rational behavior, be indistinguishable from the pursuit of victory. Third, the subjects all signed highly restrictive contracts consigning all story rights to CBS, constraining their ability to appear publicly for a year following the series, and giving CBS veto power over any books, articles, or interviews (Lance, 2000). Thus fame was unlikely to bring any player a return even approaching first prize, and the ancillary benefits of fame were largely dependent upon playing to win.[7]

The Team Segment

The *Survivor* game is divided into two distinct segments, each entailing a slightly different strategy. In the first segment, teams of eight compete with each other in competitions requiring cooperation and skill. The losing team must vote off a member. The primary goal of all players is to win the competitions and thus avoid exposure to exile. Assuming the improbability of victory in all team competitions, as all rational players would, the primary individual goal is to avoid being voted off should the team lose. As an issue of strategy, players can only influence the votes within their team (assuming all players compete to the best of their abilities in the intertribal competitions); thus, for social choice theory, players maximize their utility in the team portion by minimizing the likelihood that they will receive votes in tribal council. An efficient pursuit of this maximal utility dictates a rational actor should adopt three obvious strategies: alliance, culling the weak, and increasing personal value.

Alliance

Each team consists of eight players, allowing a majority faction (five or more) voting with discipline to control the selection of exiles with absolute certainty. Forging a majority alliance represents the single most rational and desirable strategy during the team segment. While a five-member alliance would be optimal, a four-member alliance might suffice if only one person out of the eight is unable to see the proper strategy and chooses to "go it alone." This strategy demands a degree of exclusivity, since an eight-member alliance is of no value; moreover, the larger the alliance, the more rational it becomes to defect and create a sub-alliance.[8] The obvious rational strategy thus involves forging an alliance of five players.

The experiment provides fairly clear evidence that the rational strategy was not chosen initially by the majority of the players, that those who learned to pursue this strategy did so haphazardly, and that even the play-ers aware of the importance of alliances were largely unable to behave properly. The clearest evidence of irrationality is seen by the contrasting behavior of the two teams. The Pagong tribe was remarkably unstrategic. The tribal dynamic was characterized by a members' desire to assert their individuality, to the point that they were unable to meet even their basic needs for food and shelter, much less think strategically about voting (Burnett & Dugard, 2000). When they did act in the manner anticipated by the theory, it was for decidedly non-strategic reasons: the temporary (one vote) "feminist alliance" when Colleen, Gretchen, and Jenna unified to vote off Joel because of his chauvinistic attitude (see Table 1, vote 6).

The Tagi tribe demonstrates more of the expected behavior; with the exception of Sean and Dirk, every member of the tribe attempted to build a majority alliance at some point. Excluding the well known "final four" alliance, all of the Tagi alliances were short lived and undermined for non-strategic reasons. The first attempted alliance was between Susan, Sonja, Stacey, and Kelly, which disintegrated almost immediately due to the other members' discomfort with Stacey and Susan's concern about the weakness of Sonja (Burnett & Dugard, 2000; Lance, 2000; see Table 1,

---

TABLE 1.
Voting History

Each person receiving votes in a given week is listed in bold type, followed by the names of those voting for the person in parentheses. The person voted off is listed first and in italics.

VOTE#

1:    *Sonja* (Rudy, Susan, Sean, Dirk); **Rudy** (Sonja, Stacey, Kelly); **Stacey** (Richard)

2:    *BB* (Colleen, Gervase, Jenna, Gretchen, Joel, Ramona); **Ramona** (BB, Greg)

3:    *Stacey* (Rudy, Susan, Sean, Dirk, Kelly, Richard); **Rudy** (Stacey)

4:    *Ramona* (Colleen, Jenna, Gretchen, Joel); **Colleen** (Gervase, Ramona); **Jenna** Greg)

5:    *Dirk* (Richard, Kelly, Rudy, Susan); **Rudy** (Sean): **Susan** (Dirk)

6:    *Joel* (Colleen, Jenna, Gretchen, Greg); **Jenna** (Gervase, Joel)

7:    *Gretchen* (Richard, Kelly, Rudy, Susan); **Colleen** (Sean); **Richard** (Colleen); **Susan** (Gervase); **Jenna** (Greg); **Gervase** (Jenna); **Rudy** (Gretchen)

8:    *Greg* (Richard, Kelly, Rudy, Susan, Sean, Jenna); **Jenna** (Colleen, Gervase, Greg)

9:    *Jenna* (Richard, Rudy, Susan, Sean); **Richard** (Colleen, Gervase, Jenna); **Kelly** (Sean)

10:    *Gervase* (Richard, Kelly, Rudy, Susan, Sean); **Sean** (Colleen, Gervase)

11:    *Colleen* (Richard, Rudy, Susan, Sean); **Sean** (Colleen, Kelly)

12:    *Sean* (Richard, Kelly, Rudy, Susan); **Susan** (Sean)

13:    *Susan* (Richard, Rudy); **Richard** (Kelly, Susan)
     Goes to tie-breaker, Susan and Richard cannot vote: **Susan** (Rudy, Kelly)

14:    *Rudy* (Kelly, Richard); **Richard** (Rudy)
     Only Kelly cast an actual vote, since she was immune.

Final Vote: **Richard** (Rudy, Susan, Sean, Greg); *Kelly* (Colleen, Gervase, Jenna)

vote 1). A second attempt to forge a female alliance failed because of personality conflicts (Burnett & Dugard, 2000). Thus the data demonstrate rational behavior by six of sixteen players at best, and that among even these six rationality was neither consistent nor strategic.[9]

Culling the weak

A second obvious strategy during the team portion of the game involves ridding your team of the least valuable members. The reason should be apparent; to the extent the team avoids losing the competitions, each individual is safe from expulsion. Weakness under these circumstances may be defined by a combination of physical strength and mental resilience. The players were all aware that the competitions would be largely physical in nature and quickly learned the importance of stubborn self-discipline. Thus the rational player will vote to eliminate those people who demonstrate either physical or mental weakness.

The evidence for rationality is ambiguous, though tending toward the model's predictions. Of the six voted off during the team portion, three were among the weakest players: Sonja, Ramona, and Dirk. Each revealed an inability to function as an asset to the team in a variety of ways. The other three, however, were relatively strong players: BB was a tenacious competitor, and one of the few on his team able to provide outdoor survival skills; Stacey was not only in excellent physical condition but also proved herself mentally strong during the grub-eating challenge; and Joel was a physical standout. Nonetheless, the exile of these three can be explained based on rational reasons. BB had requested to leave and had already built the group's shelter, while his age indicated a limited value in physical challenges. Joel was the last loser of the team votes, so it would be rational to eliminate him prior to the individual portion of the game where he would be a threat to everyone.[10] Stacey, then, seems the only irrational vote. But even her situation has a rational explanation. Richard had identified her as his main threat and used his influence in the Tagi alliance to have her voted off (Lance, 2000). In short, the players generally acted rationally according to the criteria of "culling the weak." The fact that a strong argument could be made for the expulsion of Gervase, Colleen, Rudy, and Sean, all of whom were weak players, does not particularly undermine the rationality of the choices that were made.

Increasing personal value

Social choice theory presumes not mere rationality but *strategic* rationality. People are strategically rational when they assume others to be rational and modify their own choice of strategies to account for the likely rational strategies of others. In this case, the strategic thinking need not be complex. If each player understands that the weakest is likely to be voted off the island, rational strategy dictates making oneself as valuable as possible. The physically strong need to perform well in physical competitions, the less strong might provide survival benefits or construct housing, and so on. The more indispensable players become to the team, the less likely they are to receive votes. Richard's fish spearing ability is the best example of this strategy; as the only reliable source of food, no one could afford to risk his loss.

Given the obviousness of this strategy, it would be odd indeed to find it rare. Yet an examination of the players' actions reveals that only five of the sixteen followed this course. In Tagi, Richard (fishing), Susan, and Stacey (daily hard work around the camp) attempted to prove their value, while the rest were indifferent at best. Dirk and Sean might have been expected to act this way, since they were the youngest and strongest and would be valuable in the competitions. But they quickly proved ineffective in that arena (or no more valuable than the others) and made no attempt to compensate. In Pagong, the numbers were even lower. Only BB and Gretchen worked hard on a consistent basis, making the lives of the others appreciably better.

THE INDIVIDUAL SEGMENT

Once the teams merge, rational strategy shifts dramatically. Each player has two related goals: survive to the final two and remain popular with the seven who don't make it, since they will decide who receives the grand prize. A secondary goal is to win the immunity competitions, though relying upon winning all the competitions is obviously irrational given the variety of skills tested and intentionally random elements introduced into the competitions. A minimally rational actor would pursue three strategies: alliance, culling the strong, and controlling perception.

Alliance

As with the team portion of the game, membership in a majority alliance allows a player to gain relative safety, at least until the number of players becomes very small. The best case scenario (as seen in *Survivor: The Australian Outback*) would be to create a five person alliance, allowing complete control of the voting. While no group managed such a feat, the final four alliance did manage to maintain itself for a short period. Even a four-person alliance is a valuable tool, since the last four players win far more money and fame than any others. Though an alliance won't guarantee a win, it does insure the best *chance* to win; therefore, it is rational to both form an alliance and stay in it as long as possible.

The evidence for rationality in this aspect of the game is stronger than the team segment, but still represents a minority position. Most of the players *recognized* the need for an alliance once they saw the final four group in action; however, they seemed unable or unwilling to follow the rational course, even when faced with obvious costs. Thus what we see in the team segment is not ignorance of rationality but its lack of primacy. Some examples illustrate the point vividly. The Pagong tribe knew even before the merge that an alliance existed among the Tagi players and that they would need to counter it.[11] Yet even after seeing the alliance in action they failed to act while they still might do so effectively. Eventually some members attempted a desperation alliance (Colleen and Jenna; see Table 1, vote 9), but it was far too little, and far too late. Only Greg seemed to understand the need for an alliance, but he waited too long to work to build one, thus demonstrating only marginal rationality (Lance, 2000). Even the final four alliance was subject to irrationality. After the first three votes Kelly began to feel guilt and left the alliance, endangering her own survival (in fact, only her improbable streak of victories in the last five immunity challenges kept her on the island). The experiment reveals that even under the best circumstances (high incentives for rationality, clear modeling of rational behavior, opportunities for direct observation of the strategic actions of others) only Rich, Rudy, and Sue acted as social choice theory predicts, and Rudy's actions were, as I show below, only rational in appearance.

Culling the strong

This strategy inverts the team segment. Since the immunity challenges become individual competitions, rational players will do their best to expel those players most likely to win them, increasing the remaining players' prospects of victory. The final four alliance did make their decisions this way, though Kelly found this behavior so objectionable that she defected from the alliance. The other players' choices were non-rational at best, primarily a result of emotional entanglements and resentment.[12] The players knew the rational strategy and saw it operating to their detriment. Social choice theory dictates that rational behavior will be learned under such conditions. Yet in *Survivor* the opposite occurs: rational behavior decreases based on emotional and moral considerations.

Control perception

The last aspect of a rational strategy concentrates on the final vote. Should a person make it to the final two, they need to have done everything possible to ingratiate themselves with the seven jury members. Given the obvious fact that the final vote is the aggrieved players only opportunity to take revenge, it is best to avoid offense. A rational player will want to be liked and respected, seen as a kind, fair, honest, and friendly person. This strategy is dependent on the pursuit of the first two strategies, as it does a player no good to be popular without an alliance to protect them (Gretchen or Colleen are good examples; each would likely have won had they made it to the final two, which insured they would be expelled by the alliance).

In the *Survivor* experiment, none of the three rational players makes even a minimal attempt to follow this strategy. Rudy is cantankerous and lazy, Rich arrogant and petty, and Susan obnoxious and mean. Were the players ranked based on popularity, it is likely these three would finish last. The oddest aspect of this failure lies in the fact that pursuing a strategy of popularity costs the players nothing at all and its value is easily perceived: as Rich states at the start of the game, good players must control how they are seen by the others (Lance, 2000). Despite knowing this, the three most rational actors still act irrationally in this area.

Actual Motives versus Rational Predictions: Variation Explained

As a test designed to induce rational behavior, *Survivor* fails miserably. Of the sixteen players only five act in a consistently rational manner, using the most generous criteria: Rich, Rudy, Susan, Stacey, and Sonja. Even these five are not consistently rational and do not act in the most optimal manner when they are acting rationally. As for the other eleven, their actions pose a puzzle for social choice theory. In this section, I divide the players into six categories of motive: ethics, image, duty, emotion, unclear, and rational. I explain the meaning of each term and explain which players fit in each category. The value of this exercise lies in its demonstration of the importance of non-rational motives in human behavior, motives generally dismissed by social choice theorists as either illusory, strategic, or responses to incomplete information. The *Survivor* experiment shows that these less predictable and often non-rational motives dictate human behavior even under conditions ideally constructed to produce rational actions.

ETHICS (9 PLAYERS)

Ethics in this usage indicates not the presence of a coherently developed moral code derived from first principles but rather a minimally developed sense of one's own identity and conscience, whether it be consistent and explicable or merely anecdotal and shallow. Despite my less rigorous usage, ethics as a category of motive usefully describes a dominant mode of behavior among the contestants. Many of them claimed to want to win, but only in the "right way," expressing the desire to behave according to the dictates of their conscience or "moral code." The best way to express the conception of ethics most prominent in *Survivor* involves a culturally common notion of "individualism." Contestants motivated by ethics conceive of themselves as defined by their own standards of behavior, and are unwilling to sacrifice their core identity in order to win the game. They tend to value consistency of action over strategic benefit and positive self-conception over material reward. Social choice theory generally dismisses such concerns as secondary to the pursuit of tangible interests. Thus, the importance of ethics in the decision making of the players undermines the authority of the theory's predictive value.

Gretchen exhibits the most consistently ethical behavior. She refuses Joel's offer of an alliance out of principle, refuses to vote strategically, and acts altruistically, even when doing so benefits her direct competitors. She sums up her position by saying, "I wouldn't feel right about myself winning the million dollars if I had to change my behavior to do it" (Burnett & Dugard, 2000, p. 91).

BB also reveals a stringent ethical standard. He values hard work and merit over everything else. Once he realizes that his values and standards are not reflected by the other players and winning will require a change in his behavior, he requests his teammates vote him off (Burnett & Dugard, 2000).

Greg follows an ethics of radical individualism. He sees himself as a nonconformist unwilling to submit to manipulation or compromise. He associates idiosyncratic individuality with honor, and refuses to compromise, even in the interest of building allies. "I've acted honorably the whole time and have nothing to be ashamed of" (Burnett & Dugard, 2000, p. 144).

Dirk's evangelical Christianity provides an inflexible moral code, and his self-conception as a fundamentally generous person leads him to judge the rational strategy "mean-spirited," and thus unworthy of his allegiance (Burnett & Dugard, 2000, p. 97).

Gervase reflects a less consciously articulated version of Greg's individualism. In his case, the impulse to ethical consistency comes from pride: "So I didn't win the million dollars. So what? The important thing is that I played the game Gervase's way. I can go home and hold my head up, knowing I didn't change one bit" (Burnett & Dugard, 2000, p. 181).

Sean is an interesting case. His ethical code demonstrates an attachment to procedural justice. He wants to do the right thing and seems to feel that the only way to avoid injustice is to follow an unbiased method of voting. Hence his attachment to the "alphabet strategy," which allows him to claim that he has treated everyone fairly, despite the deep antipathy it generates among the very people to whom he wants to be fair.

Collen and Jenna both articulate similar approaches. Each seems to value their own integrity, demonstrating an unwillingness to violate their notions of proper treatment of others. Even their attempt to form a belated alliance is half-hearted; they recognize the rationality of this approach but are unable to pursue the strategy with any consistency. Collen's comment captures their positions nicely: "I just want to leave with my integrity intact" (Burnett & Dugard, 2000, p. 147).[13]

Kelly might not seem an obvious candidate for this category, given her membership in the final four alliance. Nevertheless, her actions and words place her here. It is important to note that she was not a major player in the alliance, and she was not required to vote against someone she liked until the merge. But Kelly leaves the alliance less than half way through the individual segment, and expressed concerns about its morality even earlier. Her choice to leave the alliance because of the toll it took on her conscience would have cost her place in the final four had she not won the immunity challenges, and she knew it. Thus, at the most decisive stage, Kelly sacrificed rational strategy to the demands of ethics.

IMAGE (4 PLAYERS)

The players in this category tended to value control of their public perception among the other players or the television viewers over their desire to win. It is important to distinguish this motive from the rational strategy of controlling perception. These players were not motivated to control how they were seen in order to win; rather, they wished to be seen as a certain kind of person for reasons extraneous to the competition.

Joel seems most motivated by his need to be the dominant male figure in his tribe. He consistently challenges the authority and competence of the other men and belittles the women. In discussions of tribal life or competition strategy he always asserts leadership, even when others were clearly better informed. And he was aware (or should have been!) of the effects of this behavior on the others. As Burnett points out in his analysis of the show, this was not at all a rational strategy: "But Joel was so wrapped up in achieving alpha male status that he wasn't paying attention. Being alpha male wasn't necessarily a good thing" (Burnett & Dugard, 2000, p.41).

Gretchen and Jenna both demonstrate a deep concern about the example they set for their children. Both appear to place this concern over any considerations of strategy, explicitly invoking their children in defense of their ineffective game strategy (Burnett & Dugard, 2000).

Gervase fits here as well as the ethical category simply because his ethic seemed to be one of image. He was deeply concerned with being seen as "authentic" and "real," thus refusing to act any differently than he might at home.

DUTY (3 PLAYERS)

The players in this category see themselves as obligated to fulfill a higher purpose and restricted by their moral duties. Though they want to win the game, the parameters of duty restrict their choices. They will not take any action that is inconsistent with their higher purpose.

Rudy's absolute loyalty to his teammates, once declared, and absolute adherence to his word, once given, make his behavior easy to explain. In fact, he was so committed to this unfashionable approach to life that he expected to be voted off the island early, and chose not to pursue any serious strategy (he didn't even bother to learn the names of many of the players) (Burnett & Dugard, 2000). Though Rudy made it the final four and was part of the alliance, this choice cannot be attributed to a rational strategy. Rudy simply decided that Rich was the best leader,[14] declared his loyalty to him, and did what he was told. The fact that he chose the right person to follow does not indicate rationality, merely good judgment of leadership skills honed by experience in the military.

BB appears driven by a different form of duty, his commitment to the Protestant work ethic and merit based reward. His commitment to merit and work clearly hurt him among his teammates, annoying them to no end. Were his approach merely personal, he might have worked hard and shut up. But he also felt a duty to "whip the others into shape." It was their resistance to his idea of duty that led to his expulsion.

Dirk also annoyed his fellow players with his consistent witness for his Christian beliefs. Though there were other Christians on the island, only Dirk saw his religion as the primary guide for his and others' behavior. As a result, he was reluctant to engage in the strategy and deception needed to win and unwilling to tone down his evangelism, which caused considerable anger.

EMOTION (2 PLAYERS)

The two players in this category were motivated primarily by a desire for friendship and interpersonal satisfaction (negative or positive), to a degree that undermined their prospects for victory.

Susan was a member of the alliance, but her actions were governed by her desire to be friends with Kelly, and then her desire for vengeance once she felt betrayed by Kelly. Initially, Susan had planned to take Kelly with her to the final two, even though she recognized that would hurt her self-interest (Kelly was more popular, and thus likely to win more votes from the jury): "So, yeah, if I don't vote Kelly off I'm making a $900,000 mistake. But I don't mind. I'd sacrifice that money in the name of friendship" (Burnett & Dugard, 2000, p. 177). Later, once hurt and betrayed, she actively tried to expel Kelly, ending any chance Susan had to make it to the final two since she knew Rudy and Rich would stick together. In both cases, her behavior was less rational than it at first appeared.

Kelly also seems driven by emotional need, at least if her psychological profile is accurate. According to the producers, Kelly's decision to turn on Sue seemed motivated by a desire for "maternal rebellion" (Burnett & Dugard, 2000, p. 217). This makes sense, given Kelly's apparent need to publicly affirm her independence. Only anger could explain her action, since voting against Susan both reduced her chances of survival to the final two and cost her a vote if she did.

UNCLEAR (2 PLAYERS)

Sonja was not on the island long enough to permit any certain claims, though it is possible she would fall into the rational camp (she was part of the first brief alliance of Tagi women).

Ramona lasted longer than Sonja, but was sick for the early part of the game and never seemed to act on her own. The best that can be said of her is that she made no attempt to build any alliances nor did she attempt to avoid conflict; thus, she does not fall into the rational camp. Without more data it is impossible to place her more precisely.

RATIONAL (4 PLAYERS)

These players pursued a generally rational course, despite some errors, and were motivated in both action and word by a desire for victory within the game. Some of them are also in other categories, but they meet a minimal criterion for rational behavior. These players are: **Stacey, Susan, Rich, Rudy**.

If the players are forced into a single dominant category, assigning each a primary motive, the various motives may be ranked and evaluated. Under this admittedly simplified but more parsimonious approach, we can see that the players break down as follows:

1. Ethics (6): Gretchen, BB, Greg, Sean, Collen, Jenna
2. Duty (2): Rudy, Dirk
3. Image (2): Gervase, Joel
4. Emotional (2): Kelly, Susan
5. Rational (2): Stacey, Rich
6. Unclear (2): Sonja, Ramona

Conclusions

The *Survivor* experiment proves, with unusual clarity for social science, the paucity of meaningful strategic rationality in human behavior. Under the most generous interpretation, only five players acted rationally. Standard social choice rationalizations cannot sufficiently explain this failure, since the conditions of the experiment were ideal and opportunities for social learning expansive. The players were obviously intelligent, the incentive structure clear, strategic behavior observable, and consequences for irrationality high. Despite this, the social and political actions of the players demonstrate the priority of non-rational factors in human decision making. Thus the *Survivor* experiment may be considered a conclusive demonstration of the weakness of social choice theory for predictions of collective behavior.

Beyond the evident refutation of social choice, two other conclusions emerge. First, the players' actions revealed the priority of moral beliefs over rational self-interest. This inference is of striking importance to the social choice debate. The rejection of moral beliefs as a primary motive for behavior is a central assumption allowing social choice to predict outcomes on a large scale. Behavioral predictions within the theory work only if individuals consistently place their own evident self-interest ahead of moral motives, since only rational self-interest may be operationalized unambiguously for large population. Moral beliefs, on the other hand, are less predictable, both because the codes themselves are often inconsistent or vague and because a person's particular moral orientation might differ between word and deed. If complex moral concerns drive even a significant minority of people, social choice theory cannot predict behavior accurately. Social choice theorists are not, of course, oblivious to the presence of moral doctrines in peoples' lives. They merely claim that these codes either give way in the face of the clear dictates of self interest or, more commonly, that moral codes simply represent *ex post facto* justifications of strategically rational behavior. The *Survivor* experiment refutes this claim. Many of the players articulate moral doctrines clearly at odds with their self-identified material interest. That the players follow their moral codes to the detriment of their interest shows that they are not engaging in after the fact rationalization. That the players sabotage their prospects for victory, and do so with a full understanding of the consequences, proves the independence of morality from self-interest. This is not to say that the players are irrational. They do choose to follow the most efficient means to achieve their ends; however, for those whose ends are moral or ethical, social choice cannot make predictive claims. The *Survivor* experiment shows that a substantial portion of the sample, the six motivated primarily by ethics and the two motivated primarily by duty, follow moral rather than self-interested strategies.

Second, social choice theory tends to identify either emotional confusion, lack of intelligence, or lack of opportunity for social learning as the explanations for the failure of the model to predict accurately. The *Survivor* experiment refutes these assertions, showing that normative concerns are the largest barrier to strategic rationality. Only two of the players seem motivated by emotional concerns, though these two did show how emotional confusion undermines strategic rationality. The point is that emotions were only a small barrier to strategic rationality. Moreover, many of the players least likely to follow the dictates of the rational model were also the most conventionally intelligent (Sean, Colleen, BB, Gretchen). In fact, many of the players who acted least strategically understood the "proper" strategy quite well, and articulated that understanding in interviews. Lastly, the duration of the experiment offered multiple opportunities for social learning. It is evident that the barriers to strategic rationality are not intellectual, emotional, or iterative, but normative.

One last anecdote confirms this claim. At one point during the team segment, Sean, Greg, and Gervase did form a voting alliance. Their purpose, however, was not strategic or self-interested. Their goal was to act cooperatively in order to "change the moral tone" of the game and help the players "regain their ethical senses" (Burnett & Dugard, 2000, p. 139). This incident reveals the unpredictability of rational behavior where motives are more complex than simple utility maximization, defined as material interest. The position that human behavior is motivated at least substantially by moral rather then simple self-interested concerns is one social choice theorists have been at pains to disprove, since it renders their theory useful for only a small range of social phenomena. *Survivor* provides a substantial service if it helps chasten social choice theory and return it to its proper arena.

Endnotes

1. The best known example is probably Olson's *The Logic of Collective Action* (1965), though Becker's *The Economic Approach to Human Behavior* (1975) is more wide (and perhaps over) reaching. An excellent overview of rational choice can be found in Elster's *Rational Choice* (1986).

2. Consider the standard example (originally discussed in Arrow, 1963). Three voters (1, 2, 3) must choose between three options (a, b, c). If the voters rank the options as follows: (1) a>b>c (2) b>c>a (3) c>a>b, then the outcome of voting over paired options will be a cycle: a>b>c>a>b>c. The only way to end this cycle is to impose an arbitrary limit or change the rules. In either case, the outcome reflects not the "will of the voters" but the dictatorial decision of the rule maker. More importantly, rational actors can induce a cycle by offering alternatives they do not really support, thus preventing a true aggregation. In short, open elections can never reveal the preferences of the voters if the voters are rational actors.

3. Altruism is the most common example. Rational choice approaches tend to explain altruism as either the sophisticated exercise of strategic self-interest or the manifestation of self-interest as a group expression (the selfish gene theory in biology). What it cannot be is genuinely other directed and/or ethical behavior involving real sacrifice, since such behavior is not instrumentally rational. In short, no behavior escapes rational explanation.

4. For example, we know that it is irrational for any particular individual to vote, yet citizens do so. On the other hand, "in the study of congress, evidence concerning legislator's beliefs, motives, and strategic options is thin, and rational choice interpretations proliferate" (Green & Shapiro, 1994, p. 196).

5. Even BB is not an exception; despite his independent wealth, he also wants to win, simply because he is a competitive individual who sees no point in playing for any other reason.

6. This possibility was raised by Anne Caldwell and Johnny Goldfinger when the initial version of this paper was presented at the Western Political Science Association 2001 Annual Meeting in Las Vegas, NV. I thank them for their suggestions.

7. It is important to note that this argument applies only to the first series. After its success, fame becomes a realistic strategy for all players. In succeeding series, we should anticipate a bifurcated approach for some players. In the first (team) portion of the game, they should play to win, indistinguishable from those motivated by the million-dollar prize. Once they reach the second (individual) portion of the game, those interested in fame will constrain their behavior, sacrificing the most efficient internal strategy if pursuing it might hurt their "star" viability after the game. This theory explains the decision of Colby in *Survivor: The Australian Outback* to follow his agreement to "go to the end" with Tina, knowing it would cost him $900,000. Since we now see Colby's real motive was an acting

career, it made sense to be seen as a "man of character." Had he reneged on his deal with Tina, his post-game reputation would have resembled Hatch's.

8. For example, in a seven-member alliance, the rational strategy is to forge a smaller four-member sub-alliance. This allows the members to control the alliance without exposing themselves to betrayal, as other potential secret alliances are the same size as they or smaller. Moreover, once the single non-alliance member is ejected, the four-member sub-alliance now controls the rest of the votes. Thus, the optimal number for the initial alliance is five, followed by six and four. Seven or more cannot function and three or less cannot win with certainty.

9. The exceptions seem to be Richard and Stacey, both of whom pursue a majority alliance with a single-mindedness that almost resulted in ostracism. This danger might lead some to argue that alliance is *not* the most rational strategy to pursue under such conditions; however, all this danger shows is the need to pursue rational strategy with more tact than Stacey musters. Richard's success came not from abandoning the rational strategy but from modifying his abrasive pursuit of that strategy following the first vote.

10. I count Joel's expulsion as rational despite the fact that he was voted off for reasons unrelated to performance (his insulting attitude toward women). The fact that the team portion was over makes his vote less meaningful as a test of rationality.

11. Joel discussed with Gretchen the need for a block voting alliance on day 18, prior to his expulsion by the team. He was attempting to convince her to enlist the others in a strategy for the individual segment much like that outlined above. Gretchen refused, insisting that she wanted to "vote her conscience" (Lance, 2000, p. 77). The alliance idea among Pagong ended there.

12. Gervase provides an excellent example, when he acknowledges the importance of strategy while explaining that emotional connections make it hard to vote people off for the right reasons (Lance, 2000).

13. Says Jenna, "I couldn't have done ruthless. I can't even lie" (Lance, 2000, p.171). Whether true or not, her self-conception prevented her from acting in the necessarily deceptive ways required of rational strategy.

14. "If we'd all just shut up and let him lead we'd be OK" (Burnett & Dugard, 2000, p. 44).

References

Arrow, K. (1963). *Social choice and individual values.* New York: Wiley.

Axelrod, R. (1984). *The evolution of cooperation.* New York: Basic Books.

Becker, G. S. (1976). *The economic approach to human behavior.* Chicago: University of Chicago Press.

Bohman, J. (1989). Participating in enlightenment: Habermas's cognitivist interpretation of democracy. In M. Dascal & O. Gruengard (Eds.), *Knowledge and politics* (pp. 264–289). Boulder, CO: Westview Press.

Brams, S. (1976). *Paradoxes in politics: An introduction to the non-obvious in political science.* New York: Free Press.

Buchanan, J., & Tullock, G. (1982). *The calculus of consent.* Ann Arbor: University of Michigan Press.

Burnett, M., & Dugard, M. (2000). *Survivor: The ultimate game.* New York: TV Books.

Downs, A. (1957). *An economic theory of democracy.* New York: Harper and Row.

Dryzek, J. (1992). How far is it from Virginia and Rochester to Frankfurt? Public choice as critical theory. *British Journal of Political Science, 22,* 397–417.

Elster, J. (1986). The market and the forum: three varieties of political theory. In J. Elster & A. Hylland (Eds.), *Foundations of social choice theory* (pp 103–132). Cambridge: Cambridge University Press.

Elster, J. (1983). *Sour grapes.* Cambridge: Cambridge University Press.

Frohlich, N. & Oppenheimer, J. (1978). *Modern political economy.* Englewood Cliffs, NJ: Prentice-Hall.

Goodin, R. (1986). Laundering preferences. In J. Elster & A. Hylland (Eds.), *Foundations of social choice theory* (pp 75–102). Cambridge: Cambridge University Press.

Green, D. & Shapiro, I. (1994). *Pathologies of rational choice theory: A critique of applications in political science.* New Haven: Yale University Press.

Hauptmann, E. (1996). *Putting choice before democracy.* Albany, NY: SUNY Press.

Hauptmann, E. & Clements, P. (1999). *The reasonable and the rational capacities in political analysis.* Paper presented at the Midwestern Political Science Association Annual Meeting, Chicago, IL.

Hobbes, T. (1994). *Leviathan* (E. Curley, Ed.). Indianapolis, IN: Hackett Publishing Company. (Original work published in 1651)

Lance, P. (2000). *The stingray: Lethal tactics of the sole survivor.* Portland, OR: Shadow Lawn Press.

Monroe, K. (Ed.) (1991). *The economic approach to politics: A critical reassessment of the theory of rational action.* New York: HarperCollins.

Olson, M. (1965). *The logic of collective action.* Cambridge, MA: Harvard University Press.

Plott, C. (1976). Axiomatic social choice theory: An overview and interpretation. *American Journal of Political Science, 20,* 511–596.

Radcliff, B. & Wingenbach, E. (2000). Preference aggregation, functional pathologies, and democracy: A social choice defense of participatory democracy. *Journal of Politics, 62,* 977–998.

Riker, W. & Brams, S. (1973). The paradox of vote trading. *American Political Science Review, 67,* 1235–47.

Riker, W. (1982). *Liberalism against populism.* San Francisco: W.H. Freeman.

III

LESSONS BEYOND
THE LENS

9

Mutual Metaphors of *Survivor* and Office Politics: Images of Work in Popular *Survivor* Criticism

Jennifer Thackaberry

Before the first episode of *Survivor* premiered in May 2000, viewers had no ready context for what to expect from the show. Some wondered if *Survivor* would be like "*Gilligan's Island* meets *Lord of the Flies*" (e.g., Petrozzello, 2000), where contestants would be abandoned to the whims of their fellow castaways. As often happens with any new performance, text, or social practice, many different metaphors were applied to *Survivor* in the struggle to discern what the show was going to be about. Journalists experimented with adolescent group metaphors like high school, summer camp, and gang wars. One television critic imagined *Survivor* as "a cross between a frat party, a Club Med vacation, and a Girl Scout camp out" (Thompson, in Farhi & de Morales, 2000, p. A 01). While many of these metaphors eventually fell by the wayside, one adult group metaphor gained traction throughout the first season; namely, *Survivor* as the workplace, with the behavior on the show mirroring everyday "office politics."

When the series ended in August 2000, many viewers and commentators expressed disappointment with the outcome. In part due to winner Richard Hatch's occupation as a corporate trainer, many used the office politics metaphor to object that a scheming "snake" could win the million dollars (e.g., Johnson, 2000; Rosenthal, 2000; Walker, 2000a). For example, in her column on Salon.com, feature writer Janelle Brown lamented that Richard represented:

The hardened soul of the corporation, building better business by falsely encouraging everyone to get along. What he did on the island was just more of the same: building better teams that he could dominate and control and eventually screw over in his quest for the top. His win is a trophy for ladder-climbing executives everywhere. (Brown, 2000)

But statements like these went well beyond the outcome of the show and actually commented on life in contemporary corporate America. Some viewers, like one Pittsburgh fan, took the outcome of *Survivor* as "proof" that "endings like these [happen] every day in corporate America" where "we watch firsthand the undeserving and pitiless walk away smelling like a rose every day of our lives" (quoted in L. Johnson, 2000, p. B1).

This chapter begins with *Survivor's* end in asking how a simple television show could evoke so much anger and resentment about something it seemingly had nothing to do with—the everyday workplace that was thousands of miles away. It also asks what we might learn from these discussions about perceptions of the exercise of power in the contemporary workplace. To address these questions, this chapter explores mediated conversations about "*Survivor* as office politics," particularly those that used the show to comment on life in contemporary corporate America.

The chapter is organized as follows. First, the producers' deliberate planting of the office politics metaphor is described, and then the office politics metaphor is discussed from an organizational communication perspective. Next, the chapter analyzes media coverage of the show that linked *Survivor* with the workplace and office politics. The first part of the analysis explores why it may have been entertaining for viewers to imagine *Survivor* as a caricature of the seamy side of the workplace. Part I of the analysis discusses four such resemblances between *Survivor* and the workplace that helped to evoke an initial media dependency relationship of play (DeFleur & Ball-Rokeach, 1989).

Part II of the analysis explores an intriguing reversal of the metaphor that occurred later in the summer. For some, the metaphor of *Survivor* as office politics was so compelling that they began to talk and write about what might be learned about *actual* office politics in the workplace by watching the show. Because these comments were predictably cynical, opposing voices also joined in to defend the workplace and the people in it. Part II of the analysis, then, illuminates four key debates about the "real" workplace that emerged during the first season. This reversal also suggests that by mid-summer the viewer media dependency relationship had shifted from one of play to a more serious one of understanding (DeFleur & Ball-Rokeach, 1989). To the extent that viewers and commentators used *Survivor* to debate the reality of work in a serious way, these themes are worth paying attention to for what they reveal about people's feelings about work in the contemporary age. The conclusion explores the implications of these modern day discussions about the expression of power in the workplace.

A Deliberate Metaphor

The metaphor of *Survivor* as office politics was deliberately planted by producer Mark Burnett well in advance of the show's debut. Plugging the first *Survivor* series on talk shows and in media interviews, Burnett promised that viewers would see "the best and worst of office politics" on display (Perigard, 2000a, p. 1; Ostrow, 2000b, p. B-01). Indeed, Burnett was so sure of the purity of his little microcosm that he promised that the show would be "like office politics, cubed" (*CNN talkback live*, 2000; Voyeur TV hits it big, 2000).

In order to foster viewer identification with the show, the producers had cast a diverse set of contestants where occupation was an important element of diversity. Then, CBS identified contestants by occupation in press releases (e.g., CBS names sixteen, 2000) and on screen each time an individual contestant spoke to the camera. But the producers had also cast contestants *across* levels in the social and occupational hierarchy, lumping the haves and the have-nots, the powerful and the powerless together in order to incite conflict. For example, in a CBS television interview with producer Mark Burnett, anchor Jane Clayson probed, "So you'd like to put a middle-aged steelworker up against a 20-something actress from Los Angeles and see how they go together," to which Burnett replied, "Yeah, and then some" (*Early Show*, 2000a). In interviews shortly after the show premiered, Burnett encouraged the self-resemblance frame with statements like, "most of us could see ourselves at some the point in there, in the way that we try to get promoted at work" (e.g., *CNN talkback live*, 2000).

THE OFFICE POLITICS METAPHOR

Metaphors can be helpful for understanding unfamiliar situations, practices, or texts in terms of familiar ones (Putnam, Phillips, & Chapman, 1996), because they provide ready sets of vocabularies and help to define relationships among elements. The phrase "office politics" is itself a metaphor that directs our attention toward the agonistic, seamy side of life in the workplace: where individuals work through competing personal loyalties (Morgan, 1997), and where individuals and groups compete for scarce resource (Lazega, 1992; Vande Berg & Trujillo, 1989), all against the backdrop of a rationally functioning bureaucracy. Because the office politics metaphor suggests that organizations may not actually be cooperative entities where people pursue common goals (Vande Berg & Trujillo, 1989), the office politics metaphor may be a "taboo" topic in the everyday workplace (Morgan, 1997). But such taboos have consequences. For example, if it is perceived as impolite to call attention to personal gains that stem from ostensibly "organizational" decisions, then it becomes "extremely difficult for organizational members to deal with this crucially important aspect of organizational reality" (Morgan, 1997, p. 209).

Its status as a taboo topic notwithstanding, the office politics metaphor calls attention to organizations as created entities, or "arenas" (Vande Berg and Trujillo, 1989) that may (unintentionally) prefigure "political" behavior. As Morgan (1997) puts it, the political metaphor allows us to talk about the organization as a system that "more or less ensures the kind of competitive struggle on which organizational politics thrives" (p. 168). Organizational communication scholars have argued more recently that *discursive* elements of organizational culture can also constrain possibilities for action and agency (see, for example, Deetz, 1992; Mumby, 1987, 2001).

A metaphor gains traction

Following the producers' suggestions, viewers and commentators found it compelling to view the original *Survivor* series as a microcosm of the workplace, and the action on the show as mirroring office politics. In the months after the show premiered, and well into fall 2000, journalists, academics, television critics, talk show hosts, career columnists, workplace consultants, fans, and even detractors of the show reiterated the comparison in print, on television and radio, and in postings on the Internet. Sociologists commented that the producers had created a "replica of the American workplace" (e.g., Kilroy, 2000), and talk show hosts proclaimed that the show had "elements of real world corporate life" (e.g., Thompson, 2000). Trying to account for the show's popularity, journalists argued that viewers were hooked because the show was "more like surviving the corporate jungle than the wilds of Malaysia" (Powell, 2000a, p. 6). Young, urban professionals were said to relate to "the cutthroat alliances and backstabbing that mirrored office politics" (Powell, 2000b, p. 1). In other words, the workplace—the *known*—was being invoked as the way to understand the *new unknown*—this new kind of show—which didn't necessarily have anything to do with work.

At first blush it seems odd that *Survivor* would be likened to the workplace. Its pseudo-reality in other respects notwithstanding, *Survivor* did not even feign to depict a workplace. Indeed, the "real" workplace on the island—the production camp—was carefully hidden from viewers. But by promoting *Survivor* as a microcosm of the *political* workplace, the producers tapped into an image of the workplace rarely depicted on prime time television (Vande Berg & Trujillo, 1989). As Vande Berg and Trujillo (1989) explain, televisual representations of the workplace usually draw attention to the political actions of individual characters, rather than depicting organizations as political arenas per se. Rather than attribute events and outcomes to systemic (structural or discursive) sources, viewers are usually encouraged to "blame single 'bad' individuals for organizational problems" (p. 263).

Survivor, on the other hand, showcased a political arena where even *innocent* bystanders (and not just crafty individuals) were forced to play along, which may have resonated with the workplace experiences of many viewers and commentators. Given the typically taboo topic of office politics, talking about *Survivor* may have offered people a new opportunity to talk about "real" office politics. The mediated conversations examined in this chapter offer an unusual glimpse at salient themes in those conversations.

A metaphor reverses direction

While the producers succeeded in promoting *Survivor* as a microcosm of the political workplace, they could not have predicted how far viewers and commentators would run with the metaphor. As discussed in the introduction to the volume, *Survivor* was a runaway hit in its first season, which resulted in an explosion of media coverage. Print, radio, and television news reports announced the premiere, reported on the ratings, and hyped the finale. Anchors and guests on television talk shows (such as CBS's own *Early Show*) discussed the show, its contestants, its unfolding events, and its outcome. Episode synopses on the Internet provided a blow-by-blow of events while poking fun at the show, its contestants, and certain CBS figures. Print, radio and television commentaries explored the show's appeal to viewers and the phenomenon of reality television in general. Other kinds of commentaries and opinion pieces drew broader cultural implications from the show's popularity.

One subset of this media coverage discussed *Survivor*'s relevance to the real workplace. Journalists and talk show hosts invited workplace experts such as consultants, headhunters, and popular management authors to glean *Survivor* lessons for the office. Career columnists devoted space to navigating *Survivor*-style office politics. Non-expert viewers also made passing comments about office politics when summarizing *Survivor* episodes on the Internet, and when discussing *Survivor* in interviews and commentaries. For example, one career column portrayed a man using *Survivor* to make sense of his own firing with, "my mistake was not understanding that I was in a survival game ... I was the nice one and I got cut for it" (Salhani, 2000).

Collectively, these commentators weighed in on what viewers might learn *about work* by watching *Survivor*. For example, one review of Burnett and Dugard's (2000) book likened the show to "a martini-lunch-less parable of corporate life" (Stark, 2000). And, a career columnist for a San Francisco newspaper proclaimed *Survivor* to be "the most educational workplace-related television show since *Roller Derby*" (Murphy, 2000a, p. F2). News reports also made reference to "chats around the water cooler at work (e.g., Farhi & deMorales, 2000; Haga, 2000), suggesting that *Survivor* was uniting coworkers in a common cultural topic of conversation. In other words, in addition to the workplace being used as a metaphor to understand this new kind of reality show, *Survivor* was now being used as a metaphor to understand work itself. *Survivor* and office politics had become mutual metaphors for one another.

LIMITATIONS OF A METAPHOR

Metaphors are double-edged swords insofar as they illuminate certain features of a phenomenon but also draw attention away from other aspects of it (Putnam, et. al., 1996). If adopted wholesale, particularly for work organizations, metaphors can limit the possibilities for understanding and action (Deetz, 1996), and can actually reproduce undesired or unhealthy states of affairs (Deetz & Mumby, 1985). Even some academics who contested the "reality" of *Survivor* early on were content to settle on glib characterizations of the show as "merely" office politics (e.g., Blonsky & Desnoes, 2000; Kloer, 2000; Rothstein, 2000), as if that were not also a particular way of making meaning about work. It is worth exploring these kinds of everyday, commonsensical characterizations for what they reveal about meanings for work in the contemporary age (Cheney & Carroll, 1997).

As mentioned above and in the introduction to the volume, the first season of *Survivor* was extremely popular among younger viewers. Given the mass media's role in shaping young people's anticipatory socialization for work (Clair, 1996; Jablin, 2001), if young people attend to these workplace related interpretations, it may affect their expectations about work, and their perceived possibilities for understanding and action in the workplace. Also, to the extent that older viewers come to see *Survivor* as an isomorphic representation of the workplace, then this is also a conversation worth critiquing.

Tracking mutual metaphors

The remainder of the chapter explores meanings surrounding these "mutual" metaphors. In the methods section, I explain how I assembled a database of mediated conversations about this otherwise taboo topic. The term office politics can mean different things to different people, and these meanings may change over time. Thus, in the analysis, I explore operative meanings for the term as present in popular criticism. I examine how work was used metaphorically to understand *Survivor,* and how *Survivor* became a metaphor for understanding real office politics at work. Along the way I draw implications for what these conversations reveal about meanings for work in the contemporary age.

Research Methods

In order to explore meanings for these mutual metaphors—*Survivor* as the workplace, and the workplace as *Survivor*—I conducted a systematic search for domestic media coverage where commentators were explicitly making this connection. As noted above, these included experts who were called upon by the media to comment about office politics, self-nominated experts who volunteered their own commentaries, and non-expert viewers who made offhand comments about office politics in the stream of other conversations about *Survivor.*

For the time period January 2000 through March 2001, I searched full text popular press databases for instances where "*Survivor*" was paired with "workplace" or "office politics." (After trying numerous synonyms, I found that these were the most efficient and effective key terms to use.) For example, I searched Lexis Nexis U.S. News for news, commentaries, and reviews in newspapers and magazines; I searched Lexis Nexis broadcast transcripts for news and commentaries on radio and television, including talk shows; and I searched Wilson Abstracts for news and commentary in additional popular periodicals. I also collected news stories about *Survivor* from select Internet sites that covered the show on a regular basis, such as Salon.com and Slate.com, and from fan sites such as Survivorsucks.com. I also conducted a broader Internet search using search engines such as google.com and yahoo.com, to identify instances where non-experts were making connections between *Survivor* and the workplace, even if only in passing.

All told, I collected over 150 documents with over 25,000 lines of text. I organized the data using the computer program NUDIST, and I categorized the documents according to the subject being discussed. For example, there was talk about CBS, talk about the game show itself, talk about specific characters and their behavior on the show, talk about viewer interest in the show, talk about reality television, talk about metaphors for the show (including office politics), and talk about the workplace. After collecting this near approximation of all "workplace-related" media coverage of *Survivor*, I narrowed to focus to the latter two categories, namely conversations where people were explicitly making claims about *Survivor* as being like work, and where people were explicitly making claims about the workplace as being like *Survivor*. I then used the constant comparative method to identify and code meanings that emerged for both metaphors.

Unlike other chapters in this volume, this chapter does not necessarily analyze the action that took place among the contestants on the show. Rather, it analyzes mediated, workplace related commentary evoked by the show. Admittedly, this method assembles these "conversations" about *Survivor* and work in a more coherent way than any of the interlocutors probably experienced them. Nevertheless, assembling these publicly available comments helps us to explore public sense-making about an otherwise taboo topic. In Part I, I move quickly through four resemblances between *Survivor* and the workplace that helped viewers to see this new kind of reality show as something familiar. Then, in Part II, I summarize key debates about "real life" office politics that were evoked by the show.

Part I: Work as a Metaphor for Understanding Survivor

In the buildup to the premiere, there was a certain amount of anxiety about what to expect from the first season of *Survivor*. After the first few episodes aired, reviewers and commentators seemed to breathe a collective sigh of relief that the show was about "mere" office politics, at least in comparison to other draconian, *Lord of the Flies* possibilities evoked by its concept. Appendix A summarizes the lighthearted, humorous, and playful references to office politics that reflect this sense of relief about the "harmless" show. Note that these comments acknowledge that office politics is a distasteful and inevitable fact of work life, but they do not seek to change that state of affairs.

In this context, the media dependency relationship between the show and its viewers was one of play (DeFleur & Ball-Rokeach, 1989). In other words, at this point people were watching *Survivor* for enjoyment, and felt free to "play" with the resemblances they saw between the show and work. These resemblances included cooperation coupled with competition, disparity in workplace rewards, intra- and inter-group relations, and sudden and binding corporate layoffs. Each of these resemblances is elaborated below, with examples.

COOPERATION AND COMPETITION

First, viewers recognized the show's formulaic struggle between cooperation and competition as a familiar theme from work. One San Diego writer, for example, noted, "if isolating a bunch of people in a pressurized setting, and asking them to alternately cooperate and engage in cutthroat competitions, doesn't resemble work, then I don't know what does" (Kinsman, 2000, p. C1). Similarly, in a playful column that asked, "How do we love *Survivor*? Let us count the ways," Kloer (2000) quoted one expert as saying, "what's most compelling is the conflict between the need to work collaboratively and at the same time compete as individuals" (p. 1).

DISPARITIES IN WORKPLACE REWARDS

Second, to many, *Survivor* mirrored disparities between those who work and those who reap rewards in contemporary corporate life. For instance, early in the first season, workplace writer Dave Murphy (2000) proposed, "think of it this way: fifteen people are pushing themselves to the limits of human endurance for mere peanuts, just so that one greedy soul can walk away a millionaire. Now does it remind you of work?" (p. F2) Later in the summer, National Public Radio opened a story about *Survivor* with a similarly provocative question:

> Sixteen people, all working like mindless drones, and only one person walks away with a big wad of cash—sound familiar? Sure. It's the plot of the hit TV show, *Survivor*, but it could also describe many offices around the country. (Brand, 2000)

These attention-getters were obvious exaggerations, but they do rely on the reader/listener to supply the industrial age premise of the many working for the benefit of the few.

Intra- and Inter-Group Relations

Third, the show's tribal council mirrored, for many, relations within groups in organizations. Noting a resemblance between *Survivor* and contemporary workplace teams, for example, a San Diego career columnist noted, "I liked the democracy of the tribal council, though sometimes the motivations of the voters were suspect in the way they targeted people for departure" (Kinsman, 2000, p. C1). Also, in an early episode summary posted on Salon.com, contestant Richard Hatch's behavior was framed in terms of his occupation as "corporate trainer" as follows: "On the Tagi beach, tubby Richard, a 38-year-old corporate trainer, sits on a tree branch and tries to tell everyone how to process decision making [while] the others ignore him" (Millman, Stark, & Wyman, 2000). Here the discourse of Richard's occupation is being invoked to parody his behavior: the corporate trainer is trying to get everyone "to process," but his apparent "office-like" behavior seems out of place in this remote island setting.

Survivor also resembled, for some, conflicts *between* groups in the occupational hierarchy. In the same episode summary described above, Sue's appeal to the group to vote for her instead of for Richard is summarized as, "give the money to the truck driver, not the corporate guy" (Millman, 2000). Sue's "reward-the-underdog" plea can only be understood in light of the *intergroup* tensions in the real corporate context, where amorphously identified "corporate guys" presumably have more power and money than truck drivers.

Corporate Layoffs

Viewers also recognized sudden and binding corporate layoffs in the way ousted *Survivor* contestants were immediately banished from the tribal council, "not unlike an office firing in which the employee is given the bad news and marched out the door" (Powell, 2000a, p. 6). Two months into the show, workplace writer Gary Namie drew the same parallel while chatting with Bryant Gumbel on CBS's own *Early Show*. Namie noted that host Jeff Probst acts as "the personnel department":

> When he snuffs out the torch, that's called the ... exit parade. It's the little shoebox and security escorting you out the door in the end. And banishment and all. (*Early Show*, 2000c)

In sum, viewers found the producers' intentional *Survivor*-as-the-workplace metaphor compelling because the show resembled familiar workplace experiences: tensions between competition and cooperation, disparities in workplace rewards, subtleties of intra- and intergroup relationships, and sudden and binding corporate layoffs. This playful framing also helped to allay people's fears about what to expect from this potentially draconian show. Once viewers began to see *Survivor* as merely everyday office politics "in wet bathing suits" (McGrory, 2000), the show became less threatening, more predictable, and helped to establish a play media dependency relationship (DeFleur & Ball-Rokeach, 1989). The humorous references depicted in Part I worked because they simply exposed the paradoxes and absurdities of everyday work life. But for some viewers and commentators, the reality of office politics was no laughing matter. This leads to Part II of the analysis, or the sense that viewers and commentators made of the *actual* workplace through the lens of *Survivor*.

Part II: Survivor *as a Metaphor for the Workplace*

Whereas work had initially offered viewers a frame for how to "read" the show, by mid to late summer, the comparison between *Survivor* and the workplace began to run in the other direction. Workplace experts in particular were encouraging readers, viewers, and listeners to glean the action on the show for lessons to be learned for work. Pulling together the threads of these conversations offers us a rare opportunity to glimpse serious discussions about an otherwise taboo topic.

In contrast to the more playful uses of the metaphor described above, *Survivor's* apparent depiction of "real" office politics evoked outrage from some viewers, but this outrage was aimed at the *real* office politics they had experienced. Some of the statements in this section are much more serious and emotional than those in Part I, as they express feelings of pain, futility, unfairness, and betrayal. These more sobering uses of the term "office politics" are summarized in Appendix B. (It may be the case that some of these instances of "outrage" in Appendix B are also meant to be humorous tongue in cheek, but the point is to separate the obviously trivial, as in Appendix A, from even the potentially serious.)

When viewers began to watch *Survivor* for lessons to be learned about work, the media dependency relationship shifted from one of play to one of "understanding" self and other. As DeFleur and Ball-Rokeach (1989) explain, in a media dependency relationship based on social understanding, individuals use the media to learn about and "interpret people, cultures, and events" (p. 306). Similarly, to rely upon media for self-understanding means to "expand or maintain individuals' capacities to interpret their own beliefs, behavior, self-concepts, or personalities" (DeFleur & Ball-Rokeach, 1989, p. 306).

Unlike in Part I, where comments about *Survivor's* resemblances to work remained relatively uncontested (mainly because they were intended to be humorous), the "real" office politics called to mind by the show sparked a national dialogue about what people might learn about work by watching *Survivor*. For some, the behavior on the show and its outcome *proved* certain hunches about the contemporary workplace. But other discordant voices tried to weaken the strength of the metaphor by either advancing an alternate view of the workplace, or by arguing how the workplace is actually *unlike* the show. Thus, Part II identifies four main topics of debate about the contemporary workplace that were evoked by the show's first season: 1) competing individual motivations for work, 2) the necessity of communication skills for the workplace, 3) authenticity of workplace relationships, and 4) motivations of managers who espouse teamwork. The general topics are briefly summarized here, and the details of the various positions are elaborated separately below.

First, *Survivor* evoked discussions about competing individual motivations for work, particularly *greed and the ruthless pursuit of power*, on the one hand, versus an individual's *concern for the collective* on the other. Second, mainly due to winner Richard Hatch's occupation as a corporate trainer, the show elicited comments about the necessity of communication skills for the workplace. These discussions pointed to a perceived continuum of communication skills: *certain skills are necessary* for survival in the workplace, but if they are "too good" they can become *tools for manipulation*.

Third, *Survivor* sparked discussions about the authenticity of interpersonal and group relationships at work, revealing concerns about whether workplace relationships are *authentic for their own sake*, on the one hand, or actually *shallow, quickly perishable means to individual ends*, on the other. Fourth, Richard Hatch's occupation as a "corporate trainer," and therefore his perceived alignment with management, also generated a discussion about the contemporary management of corporate organizations. This part of the conversation reflects a *deep mistrust* of the contemporary *managerial rhetoric of teams*, a cynical thread that was answered by a *backlash from actual corporate trainers* who argued for the legitimacy of helping group members to achieve mutually agreed upon goals.

As each topic of debate is elaborated below, examples are provided from both cynical and optimistic voices to illustrate the key points of tension. The point of the analysis is not necessarily to "count" how many times people argued a given perspective, but rather to explore the available sentiments about actual office politics that were evoked by the show (at least those that were expressed publicly). The quotes provided are not the *only* instances of those arguments, but rather, they are representative enough to stand for those particular motifs in the conversation.

INDIVIDUAL MOTIVATIONS FOR WORK

First, *Survivor* sparked a debate about differences in individual motivation in the workplace. Some argued that *Survivor* proved that people are inherently greedy, while others maintained that it is possible to show concern for the collective and still succeed in the contemporary workplace. In June 2000, an interviewer on *CNN's Talkback Live* challenged Burnett's concept for the show by arguing "in a real situation ... they would all work together to survive" (*CNN talkback live*, 2000). Burnett replied:

> I think it's a bit naive to think that everyone would work together ... I mean, think of yourself at your job at CNN. You have to get ahead and get promoted. You're not always trying to think of the group or CNN; you're thinking of yourself, if you'd be honest. (*CNN talkback live*, 2000).

Here Burnett turned the conversation around to the interviewer's own workplace to advance his point that individuals are inherently greedy. For those who aligned with this perspective, *Survivor* represented the "frenetic pursuit of riches" in the contemporary workplace (Buccino, 2000, p. 3L). Thinking of the team is nice in theory, these people argued, but "when one member has a personal agenda that is greater than the organization's, what is to stop that person from going beyond?" (Girard, 2000).

Coupled with discussions of greed were the inevitable ruthless *tactics* employed by greedy people. For example, contestant behavior on *Survivor* was said to have "all the earmarks of a ruthless climb up the corporate ladder" (Thompson, 2000). Again, producer Mark Burnett pushed for this interpretation, arguing to CNN's Larry King that viewers were watching to see what unfolded in the workplace everyday; namely, how "people want to get ahead and will do whatever it takes." To this King glibly replied, "they'll eat rat to be vice president of sales." Burnett's earnest response was "they probably would" (*CNN Larry King Live*, 2000).

Advocates of the greed perspective argued that the contemporary workplace actually necessitates strategic, Machiavellian behavior. Richard Hatch's "cold-blooded plotting" was said to mirror the "survival-of-the-cunning ethos of contemporary society" (Sibley, 2000, p. A16). Whereas other players were identified as "naive, chaotic, and reluctant to compete" (Gilbert, 2000, p. C16), many cited winner Richard Hatch's victory as proof that "to be successful in American life, you almost have to be Machiavellian or at least manipulative and shrewd and crafty" (Levin, quoted in Thompson, 2000). In fact, some so completely identified *Survivor* as the workplace that they took the outcome of the show as *proof* that "ruthlessness is rewarded" in today's workplace and "loyalty is for losers" (Buccino, 2000, p. 3L; Ostrow, 2000a, p, A-20). By the end of the season, Brown (2000) confirmed "so the conniving, manipulative, nudist corporate trainer won the show. Score one for good old ruthless American capitalism, zero for the frailty of human emotion."

Reactions to the "unfair ending" included sadness, disappointment, and outrage, because for some it reflected what "happens every day in corporate America" where "we watch firsthand the undeserving and pitiless walk away smelling like a rose every day of our lives" (viewer cited in L. Johnson, 2000, p. B1). These voices were not only disappointed with the outcome of the show, but they also lamented how the contemporary workplace fails to keep Machiavellian greed in check and fails to reward those who advance the collectivity in good faith.

The fact that Richard, the winner, was awarded the million dollars not by the producers but by his *teammates* was particularly difficult for some viewers to take. One *Newsweek* reader complained that "watching the prize awarded to that smirking, arrogant Machiavellian antihero by the very people he despised and manipulated was a bitter pill." She added, "I don't think there'll be many high-fives around the water cooler today" (Letters, 2000, p. 16). Others felt that the final jury's decision represented a frustrating hegemonic power trap. For example, Brown (2000) argued "the decision by Sean, Sue, Rudy and Greg to reward the corporate trainer, the master of manipulation, with a million bucks says a lot about the way Americans feel the need to pay obeisance to those with power."

Altogether, these cynical voices read *Survivor* as proof that individuals are greedy, organizations are designed for the most malicious to succeed, and attempts to show concern for the collective are doomed to fail. Additionally, according to this view, organizational members not only have to worry about the Machiavellians, but they also have to worry about others in the workplace who will be steamrolled by them as well.

Corporate karma

Opposing voices in the dialogue took issue with these cynical views concerning individual motivations and peer effectiveness in the workplace. While the CNN interviewer resisted Burnett's glib statements about the motivations of the people on her production team, very few voices argued that collectivity is actually *rewarded* in the contemporary workplace. Instead, workplace experts espoused an apparent "corporate karma" theory of organizational justice. As one management consultant explained, "if you are drawing alliances to keep people out, it draws bad blood, 'corporate karma' so to speak" (Bast, quoted in Girion, 2000, p. 1). In this view, Machiavellian "terrorists" may achieve some short-term gains but they "can't survive for the long haul [because] eventually [their behavior] comes back to get them" (headhunter Lenarsky, quoted in Girion, 2000, p. 1). As Joyner (2000) put it, "every corporate crocodile eventually gets his comeuppance" (p. 1F). Thus, the opposing voices took the long view, implicitly acknowledging that some may achieve advantage in the short run, but insisting that organizations are designed so that such tactics will not last forever.

Some opposing voices also challenged the notion that the workplace necessitates greedy behavior. They did so in part by pointing out that the task on *Survivor* was structured so as to allow the most scheming Machiavellian individual to win. As Girard (2000) noted, contestants on *Survivor* "never really have to see each other again," whereas in real office politics there is no time limit: "you need to keep your word more regularly because you have to see these people again" (Medved, on *Hannity & Colmes*, 2000). Thus while ruthlessness may work in a short-lived game, "it's usually not going to be the basis of a lifetime career" (leadership author Axelrod, quoted in Joyner, 2000, p. 1F). Similarly, C. Johnson (2000) conceded, "to be fair, the focus of *Survivor* was never about creating harmony in the workplace. Rather, the point was to outlast the competition for financial gain" (p. E01). In other words, while shrewdness may have allowed one person to win this particular game, a *Survivor* is "in the end … by himself" (workplace writer Clark, quoted in Powell, 2000a, p. 6). But as one headhunter argued, "that's not what any corporation is about" (Challenger, in *Your world*, 2000).

In sum, several viewers took Hatch's strategic behavior as a blueprint for success, and lamented the futility of loyalty and teamwork in the contemporary workplace. But opposing voices in this dialogue resisted this interpretation. They did not necessarily dispute the notion that selfish people get ahead in the workplace. Instead, they argued that a kind of corporate karma checks organizational terrorists, and that in the long run these organizational sole survivors do not succeed. They also challenged the view that organizations necessitate Machiavellian behavior by pointing out how the workplace is actually unlike a game with one solitary winner.

Communication Skills

A second debate provoked by *Survivor* concerned communication skills for work. Discussants generally agreed that there were certain necessary communication skills for the workplace, namely "getting along" and "forming alliances." But some also registered suspicions about communication skills that are "too good" such that they allow some (particularly those in power) to manipulate others beyond awareness.

The first necessary communication skill discussed was the *ability to get along* with others at work. On an early *Survivor* website, CBS quoted stress specialist Gene Ondrusek as saying, "research overwhelmingly confirms that success *in the workaday jungle* [italics added] depends more on your interpersonal skills and ability to get along with people than your technical competence." Thus the skill of getting along was included as part of the original workplace frame for the show. Viewers and commentators agreed. Workplace writer Murphy (2000a), for example, argued that *Survivor* demonstrated that "the most important workplace skill was, is and always will be the ability to get along with people. If you don't have that skill, any success you have will be only temporary" (p. F2). In some cases getting along meant avoiding detection. For example, in a mid-summer discussion on CBS's *Early Show*, for example, workplace writer Gary Namie predicted that contestant Colleen would make it to the final four precisely because she stayed out of sight. Here he chatted with host Bryant Gumbel and another guest:

> NAMIE: What I'm seeing all the time [in the workplace] is the survival of the meek.
> GUMBEL: What would that say? Just fly below the radar screen—
> CRAWFORD: You bet. This is the– this is the game of politics, Bryant.
> GUMBEL: —offend no one, get along with everybody.
> NAMIE: Isn't that how the workplace is? That's the workplace. (*Early Show*, 2000c)

Others defined getting along as a more strategic skill. One CEO of a headhunting firm opined that the key to winner Richard Hatch's success was that "he read people very well. He understood what it was that would cause people to turn off ... to not want to pick him. He didn't get in their way" (Challenger, on *Neil Cavuto*, 2000). In this context, getting along meant determining which behaviors might turn others against oneself, and avoiding them (Blonsky & Desnoes, 2000, p. B04).

Besides "getting along," those looking for workplace lessons on *Survivor* identified the need to *form alliances*, and even to lead them, as another necessary workplace skill. For example, arguing that Richard "understood the power of alliances and used them to his benefit," Stafford (2000) lectured to her readers, "that, fellow workers, is a template for the career path of many highly successful business leaders" (p. C1). Those who may not like this system are cautioned, "fact is, many do work for Richardesque leaders. And if they don't, there's probably a wannabe waiting in the wings. Cynical? Yes. Real world? You betcha" (Stafford, 2000, p. C1).

Frequently, being able to build alliances was regarded as more important than having technical skills. Many agreed that the failure to form alliances explained why otherwise competent people failed at work (e.g., Columbia Consultancy, 2000). Stafford (2000), for instance, noted that "individual talent and nice people are prized in the workplace but [they] rarely get anywhere without successful, strategic alliances" (p. C1). *Survivor* finalist Kelly Wigglesworth, who won the final five challenges but not the million dollars, was often cited as someone who exemplified the lesson that "performance alone doesn't ensure success" (Columbia Consultancy, 2000). In contrast, Richard was described as "Machiavellian, arrogant and, above all, determined," yet, according to Kinsman (2000), "he turned out to be a true leader. Not the kind of leader most of us would like, but [one who] organized an alliance that devoured victims at will [and was] voted King" [p. C1]. To this he added, "sounds a little too close to the corporate world, doesn't it?" (Kinsman, 2000, p. C1).

Tools for manipulation

While some celebrated getting along and forming alliances as vital skills, others regarded them as skills possessed by only a few in the workplace (mainly those in power) that enabled them to manipulate others. Richard was said to have an advantage as a corporate trainer. He was said to have "read, if not written, the manual on corporate survival" (Salhani, 2000), and therefore "had the skills needed in today's working world in order to succeed." As C. Johnson (2000) explained, "Rich, the corporate trainer, knew about human relationships within a corporation, knew how to get people to do things and applied his skills from the corporate world to the game" (p. B1). "Apparently," some argued, "his corporate training counted" (Ostrow, 2000a, p. A-20).

For some, Hatch's occupation as a corporate trainer also meant that he shared these secrets with selected others. The day after the finale of the first season, for example, the usual panel of guests was assembled on CBS's *Early Show* to talk about Richard Hatch's victory from the evening before. The conversation turned to Hatch's occupation as corporate trainer, and to the "management retreats" that consultants like Richard might organize. Radio personality Michael Feldman, chatting with the other guests, took Hatch's victory to mean "those retreats are actually for some purpose. They actually can change ... what happens in the workplace," and "that's the price we pay" (*Early Show*, 2000d). Feldman's add-on remark, "that's the price *we* pay," suggests a perception about corporate retreats as places where some organizational members learn tools for manipulating the others. Also apparent is the belief that such skills would go unnoticed by those being acted upon, and would remain out of reach for many.

To summarize, the second theme of dialogue evoked by *Survivor* offered a rare glimpse about opinions about communication skills for the political workplace. While some voices in this conversation argued that skills like laying low and forming alliances were essential for "survival" in the workplace, others advocated the *strategic use* of these skills to "read" people and to actively lead alliances. These discussions also revealed perceptions about communication skills as a double edged sword: on the one hand, they are perceived as "necessary" to get along, but they are also cause for suspicion because some members may be "so good" at them that they might use them instrumentally for personal gain.

Authenticity of Relationships Formed at Work

Discussions about alliance building, as described above, sparked a third *Survivor*-informed debate about the workplace. Specifically, *Survivor* gave viewers a chance to express concerns about relational authenticity in the workplace, where some many be using others for their own success and then "abandoning alliances and relationships afterwards" (Barnett, on Thompson, 2000). For some, the term office politics *meant* inauthenticity. Synonyms included "currying favor" (Anonymous, 2000), being "sycophantic" (O'Hara, 2000), and forming "expedient" relationships (Barnett, on Thompson, 2000). C. Johnson (2000), for example, took from Hatch's behavior "a kind of model of what happens in the business world every day ... the smiling handshake, the I'm your friend up until the time I don't need you anymore" (p. B1).

In the parlance of office politics, an individual may not only be a "sycophant," but he or she might also be a "duplicitous backstabber." Recall the earlier references to "young, urban professionals" who were captivated by the show and its "cutthroat" alliances that ended in "backstabbing" (Powell, 2000b, p. 1.). These were particular *kinds* of alliances—cutthroat ones— and relationships with particular kinds of endings—namely *backstabbing*.

In promoting the office politics metaphor, even producer Mark Burnett mentioned backstabbing, as in "very few people rise up in organizations ... by being 100 percent on the straight and narrow path ... some us will talk behind others' backs at times or do a bit of back stabbing" (quoted in Zurawik, 2000, p. 1A). The implication is that to try to form meaningful relationships at work means to potentially set oneself up for betrayal.

Also relevant to relational authenticity was the issue of *group* alliances. Some noted that the flip side of the "necessary" skill of forming alliances was that groups of people were actively ganging up on others at work. When Hatch persuaded his fellow castaways to vote survivalist Gretchen off the island, for example, Powell, (2000a) called it "another day on a deserted South Seas island" that might as well also be "another day at the office" (p. 6). Unfortunately for the workplace, one consequence of picking off others who are perceived as threatening is that "the best and the brightest are driven out" (Namie, on the *Early Show*, 2000c).

Silent response

While we might have expected others to weigh in against these cynical views about relational authenticity at work, not many voices rose to defend the idea that relationships formed at work can actually be *authentic*. This is surprising in an age when the workplace is quickly becoming one of the most important places for young people to meet friends and life partners as they work longer hours and postpone domestic arrangements. It may be the case, however, that relationships are viewed as "office politics" only when relational expectations are *violated*. In other words, to many people it may not seem like engaging in "office politics" if they feel safe among a group of friends at work. Also, conversations about workplace authenticity may have been driven by what people watched on the show, and not by positive experiences that may have stood in contrast to what was depicted.

However, as with the theory of "corporate karma" described above, some opposing voices questioned the *viability* of expedient relationships in the corporate context. They did so in part by challenging the assumption that the workplace resembles *Survivor*. Girard (2000), for example, argued that *Survivor* was "not true to work" precisely because it was only a game "based on greed [that entailed] kicking out the most likable team players and ganging up on those who are more capable to get rid of them." Others questioned the authenticity of strategic "oustings," with statements like, "no doubt workplace relations can get pretty prickly, but we know of no one who wants an office in which employees get to vote to expel their least-liked co-worker" (*Survivor* won't, 2000).

In sum, discussions about getting along and forming alliances as necessary skills for the workplace provoked concerns that workplace relationships may be expedient or inauthentic. While opposing voices countering those assertions were relatively absent, some tried to undermine the conclusions of the cynics simply by arguing that *Survivor* was not an adequate representation of the workplace.

MANAGEMENT MOTIVES

Fourth, and finally, *Survivor* ignited a generally cynical discussion about contemporary corporate management, particularly motivations for espousing the value of teamwork. This debate arose in a two-step process. First, Richard Hatch's behavior on the show provoked criticisms about corporate trainers in general. Second, because corporate trainers were viewed as extensions of management (for example, as "water-bearers for the management fad of the month club" [Stafford, 2000]), observations about Hatch's ruthless and Machiavellian behavior were transformed into a general indictment of management motives, including the "real" reasons for espousing the importance of teamwork.

Suspicions about consultants

First, Richard Hatch's competitive, manipulative, and strategic behavior modeled, for some, what all consultants are "really like." Hatch's occupation as corporate trainer was often conflated with "consultant," and so the two terms were used interchangeably to describe his occupation. On a mid-summer broadcast of CBS's own *Early Show*, workplace writer Gary Namie noted argued that Richard was a "classic consultant" because he "came in, day one [and] sat on his butt" and then started "maneuvering everybody." While he continued to "lobby for his position" he had succeeded in "turning everybody against each other" (*Early Show*, 2000c). Similarly, Walker (2000a), argued:

> If a consultant has any skill at all, it's in cleverly positioning himself as invaluable without actually contributing anything of value, stating obvious things as though they are insights, and projecting leaderly qualities while subtly pointing a finger of blame every chance he gets. In a nutshell, extol the virtues of working together and always make sure somebody else gets whacked. (Walker, 2000a)

These kinds of statements indicted consultants as providing little value to the organization (and as actually making things worse) while deflecting blame when things go wrong. Walker (2000b), for one, took Richard

Hatch's win as proof of consultants' selfish maneuvers. Later in the season, he found it "curious" that, despite a rhetoric of "true team-ness" in the consulting business, Richard Hatch now stood out as "the most conniving, backstabbing, and dishonest person in the cast" (Walker, 2000b).

Affiliation with management

But it was the corporate trainer/consultant's connection with *management* in many people's minds that caused the action on *Survivor* to register suspicion against contemporary management per se. First, corporate training itself was painted as a tool that management uses to manipulate employees. For example, C. Johnson (2000) explained, "Hatch is a *manager-for-hire*, one of the legions of consultants who march into businesses and preside over role-playing exercises to build 'team spirit'" (p. E01). However, the imputed motive for building such team spirit was to "sooth [employees] into submission for the Good of the Corporation" (Brown, 2000). Early in the season Millman (2000) worried that the show "gets at some larger truth about our corporate society, where total loyalty and teamwork is demanded but seldom rewarded."

Because Hatch was allied with management, when he actually won the top prize, some viewers took it as evidence that management is inherently corrupt. *USA Today* noted that "the fact that Rich is a 'corporate trainer' supports some of the worst suspicions about business leadership," adding, "heaven help the employees of his clients" (Tribal politics, 2000, p. 13A). One viewer demanded, "is this what we have come to expect from executives running our corporations?" (Salhani, 2000). As noted in the introduction to this chapter, Janelle Brown (2000) took Richard's victory as evidence of the "hardened soul of the corporation" that tries to build better businesses by "falsely encouraging everyone to get along." In sum, while Hatch's occupation and his victory became lightning rods for discussing the worst elements of office politics (greed, individual skill in manipulating others, inauthenticity in relationships, etc.), by this point in the conversation his behavior was being used to indict broader management authenticity in general.

Consultant backlash

Actual consultants and corporate trainers rose to defend themselves and their industries in light of these negative comments. Many of them took Richard Hatch himself to task for his behavior on the show, accusing him of "giving corporate trainers a bad name" (Joyner, 2000, p. 1F). Aiming her remarks directly at Hatch, for example, Joyner (2000) scolded:

> Your Mack-the-Knife tendencies haven't done much to advance the
> trainer credo of togetherness, teamwork and tolerance. In fact many of
> your corporate training peers are wondering: With corporate trainers
> like you, who needs enemies? (p. 1F)

These voices in the conversation tried to promote corporate trainers
as caring, concerned helpers who "can help a group of people work together
to achieve a specific goal" (training spokesperson Galagan, cited in Joyner,
2000). Some tried to distance organizational life from what was happening on *Survivor* with arguments like, "I don't think a company would want
to pay [a corporate trainer who was] simply trying to help the individual
reach his own goal" (Turknett, quoted in Joyner, 2000). In sum, Richard's
occupation, coupled with his success, engendered suspicion for consultants
in general, and also for management motives by association. But teamwork practitioners jumped in to attack Hatch directly, defend their own
reputations, and to argue for the salience of group goals.

Conclusion and Implications

As a new kind of reality show, *Survivor* depicted an arena where
individuals were forced to sort through conflicting personal and group
loyalties. To help foster viewer identification with the show, the producers urged viewers to read *Survivor* as a "microcosm of the workplace."
Indeed, Part I of the analysis showed how viewers and commentators
were relieved to find that *Survivor* was "merely" a mirror of familiar office
politics, in contrast to other draconian possibilities evoked by the concept for the show. Past media depictions had not necessarily presented
workplaces as political arenas in which office politics were compulsory for
everyone. Thus, it was fun to play with *Survivor* resemblances to the workplace. Viewers found familiar themes of cooperation versus competition,
disparities in workplace rewards, subtleties of intra- and inter-group
dynamics, and sudden and binding corporate layoffs.

However, by offering viewers and commentators an opportunity to
talk about an otherwise "taboo" topic, the show also elicited more serious discussions about the workplace that may have been looking for a
ready outlet. As shown in Part II of the analysis, *Survivor* evoked some
very contemporary concerns about the expression of power in the workplace, particularly those relating to relational authenticity among individuals, groups, and teams. Some of the darker concerns included the
destructive force of individual greed in the workplace, the potentially

manipulative side of communication skills, fears about inauthenticity in increasingly vital workplace relationships, and cynicism about the motivations behind the popular managerial rhetoric of teamwork. Often, the more cynical voices were countered by optimistic voices, who either provided proof for their counter-assertions, or who simply tried to weaken the strength of the metaphor by pointing out how the workplace is unlike a sole-survivor game with a time limit and a cash prize. Nevertheless, the haste with which many drew conclusions about the workplace based on what they saw on *Survivor* may indicate a disturbing sense of resignation about power in the workplace that is clearly at odds with contemporary ideologies of empowerment, teamwork and workplace democracy.

These conversations are especially important to pay attention to for their potential to impact organizational socialization for work. As noted above, young people were the show's largest demographic in its first season. This is an impressionable group who may be in the early stages of organizational socialization, or even anticipatory organizational socialization. As Clair (1996) and others argue, discourses about work reflect, but also help to reinforce, meanings about work, particularly in anticipatory socialization (see also Jablin, 2001). Were young people to tune in to these overwhelmingly cynical messages about work as eagerly as they were tuning in to *Survivor*, they may be encouraged to adopt a cynical attitude about the workplace before they have a chance to imagine and fight for alternate possibilities.

Now that a few seasons of *Survivor* have aired, the producers' preferred metaphor of *Survivor* as the workplace has largely dried up. *Survivor* has become its own context. In other words, when viewers watch *Survivor*, they now know what to expect, and they need to rely less on metaphors to understand the show. Moreover, in comparison to the first season, where contestants were quixotic about the kind of community they were creating on the island, contestants in succeeding series have been less apologetic about their own strategic behaviors. Many have been more overt about their individual goals: winning the million dollars, making it to the final four, surviving long enough to be in the jury, not being the first person voted out, etc. Now, contestants and viewers alike unabashedly characterize the show as a game that regrettably, but unavoidably, necessitates having to make undesirable choices in one's climb to the top.

On the other hand, the media dependency relationship of understanding continues, along with "serious" discussions about *Survivor* workplace lessons. However, these appear more in the career advice industry per se, and less in the mainstream popular press. Nevertheless, the analysis in this chapter urges us to take these *Survivor* lessons with a grain of salt, and to consider the fitness of the *Survivor* metaphor before we draw cynical conclusions about particular workplaces based on the action on a game show. It also urges us to search for the structural, discursive, or even macro conditions that might engender such "political" behavior in any context.

There is some good news in the fact that viewers and commentators can find relevant "lessons" for work in a television show that ostensibly has nothing to do with work. For example, as educators, we can use popular programs like *Survivor* precisely to initiate critical conversations about "real" office politics. We can use the show as an allegory to help students to see and critique structural and discursive conditions in the workplace that may engender the disturbing realities discussed in these conversations. We can encourage students to imagine, and push for, alternate ways to "play the game" in order to help them to achieve different outcomes in their own work lives.

Appendix A: Office Politics
as "Harmless" Activity

- I couldn't see why it is the summer's smash. It looked to me like *office politics in wet bathing suits.* (McGrory, 2000)
- Even the conflict on the show is familiar, *as familiar as office politics.* (Blonsky & Desnoes, 2000)
- So it isn't the brutal truth that is shown, but something more like *office politics with an exotic setting and bizarre comrades.* (Rothstein, 2000, p. 11)
- Even more harrowing, they gather for a "tribal council" at the end of every episode and vote to boot somebody from the island. The last person to survive the physical challenges and the Darwinian selection takes home the cash. This isn't just survival– it's *office politics played by people who haven't showered for weeks.* (Peyser, 2000, p. 52)
- The weekly, hour-long dose of personal interaction among stressed opportunists—distilled from hours of intrusive camera work and prodding by off-camera handlers—*eventually felt like painless office politics,* just the thing for casual summer prime-time diversion. (Green, 2000, p. A1)
- Millions had tuned in for the developing drama to watch *the backstabbing dynamics of American office politics* played out on the beaches of Pulau Tiga island in Malaysia. (Rutenberg, 2000, p. 1I)
- [I don't] see why audiences enjoy watching *conflicts that amount to little more than office politics,* something they get enough of in real life. (A producer of a reality-show satire film, quoted in Clark, 2001, p. 1)
- Last year, 16 unknowns caught lightning in a bottle with *their island version of office politics.* (Hinds, 2001, p. 1)

Appendix B: Office Politics
as "Serious" Business

- [*Survivor*] will teach you about people, *office politics and working relationships,* crucial lessons if you want to be a *workplace manager or a survivor.* (Murphy, 2000b)
- Internecine battles on the island *mirrored office politics.* (A summer of shifting, 2000)
- *Office politics all over America,* Michael. People watch that *Survivor,* they watch that tribal council, they watch people being banished. They have layoffs, they have *office cooler politics.* Isn't that reality for people? (Former Secretary of Labor Robert Reich on *CNN Crossfire,* 2000)
- To some the island intrigues called up memories of high school. *The more mature saw office politics.* (Wyman, 2000)
- The appeal of the show is rooted in how the island's dynamic—people working together and yet against each other—*parallels office politics.* (Rosenthal, 2000, p. 32)
- Guest: You're really dealing with people having to learn how or know how to form alliances and yet get rid of people who are threats to them. Osgood: *Sounds like office politics, doesn't it.* (Osgood file, 2000)
- I was the nice one and I got cut for it. The show *reminded me of office politics in many corporations and firms* across America. I decided not to play the game and I lost. (Downsized executive, quoted in Salhani, 2000)
- *Survivor* was *about our collective lives at the office,* where we competitively jockey for position, try not to get passed over or killed off. (Buccino, 2000, p. 3L)
- Now why would we need a TV reality show when this kind of realism is happening in our offices 14 hours a day?... Leave it to the television networks to package our worst workplace nightmares and call it entertainment. It's *office politics with a dash of sand in your underwear.* (Anonymous, 2000)
- All the political maneuvering and game-playing that go on during *Survivor* are *but a mirror image of the office politics* that just about everyone experiences day after day in their workplaces. The motto of *Survivor*—"outwit, outplay, outlast"—would be *apropos for just about any office.* (Burrough, 2001, p. EC1)

References

Blonsky, M., & Desnoes, E. (2000, July 30). "Real" has appeal but it's not reality: What we see in voyeur TV. *The Washington Post,* p. B04.

Brand, M. (2000, August 23). CBS series *Survivor* could be a blueprint for behavior in many offices. [*Morning edition* broadcast]. Washington, DC: National Public Radio Transcripts.

Brown, J. (2000, August 24). *Anyone but Richard! The smug bastard's win is a trophy for ladder-climbing executives everywhere*. Retrieved January 25, 2001 from the World Wide Web: http://www.salon.com.

Buccino, D.L. (2000 September 10). *Survivor* recalls life at the office. *The Baltimore Sun*, p. 3L.

Burnett, M., & Dugard, M. (2000). *Survivor: The ultimate game*. New York: TV Books.

Burrough D. J. (2001 February 4). Office politics mirror popular TV program. *The Arizona Republic*, p. EC1.

CBS names 16 who'll compete for $1 Million on summer series Survivor [wire report]. (2000, March 13). Los Angeles: City News Service.

Cheney, G., & Carroll, C. (1997). The person as object in and around organizations. *Communication Research, 24,* 593–600.

CIO Confidential [career column]. (2000, September 15). *CIO Magazine*. Retrieved January 25, 2001 from the World Wide Web: http://www.cio.com.

Clair, R.P. (1996). The political nature of the colloquialism "a real job": Implications for organizational socialization. *Communication Monographs, 63,* 249–267.

Clark, J. (2001 Jan 19). Reality under the gun in "series 7." *Los Angeles Times*, p. 1.

CNN crossfire [television broadcast]. (2000, August 23). New York: CNN News Transcripts.

CNN Larry King live [television broadcast]. (2000, June 27). New York: CNN News Transcripts.

CNN talkback live [television broadcast]. (2000, June 02). New York: CNN News Transcripts.

Deetz, S.A. (1992). *Democracy in an age of corporate colonization*. Albany: SUNY Press.

Deetz, S.A. (1986). Metaphors and the discursive production and reproduction of organization. In L. Thayer (Ed.), *Organization <—> Communication* (pp. 168–182). Norwood, NJ: Ablex.

Deetz, S.A., & Mumby, D.K. (1985). Metaphors, information, and power. In B. Ruben (Ed.), *Information and behavior* (vol. 1, pp. 369–386). New Brunswick, NJ: Transaction.

DeFleur, M., & Ball-Rokeach, S. (1989). *Theories of mass communication* (5th ed.). New York: Longman.

Early show [television broadcast]. (2000a, January 11). New York: CBS News Transcripts.

Early show [television broadcast]. (2000b, May 31). New York: CBS News Transcripts.

Early show [television broadcast]. (2000c, July 27). New York: CBS News Transcripts.

Early show [television broadcast]. (2000d, August 24). New York: CBS News Transcripts.

Eisenberg, E. (1984). Ambiguity as strategy in organizational communication. *Communication Monographs, 51,* 227–242.

Farhi, P., & de Morales, L. (2000, June 21). Television's '*Survivor*' instinct: Novelty and marketing pay off for CBS's unlikely hit. *The Washington Post*, p. A01.

Feran, T. (2001, May 31). Castaways for $1 million; New CBS series dangles wealth at end of primal experience. *The Plain Dealer*, p. 1E.

Gilbert, M. (2000, August 25). Scheming Hatch knew how to play the game. *The Boston Globe*, p. C16.

Girard, K. (2000, November 13). *Survivor vs. politics at work*. Retrieved January 25, 2001 from the World Wide Web: http://www.bellaonline.com.

Girion, L. (2000 August 25). Island survival tactics might not put winner in good stead at work. *Los Angeles Times*, p. 1.

Green, K. (2000, August 24). And then there was one: Consultant edges former seal as *Survivor* and local fans react. *The San Diego Union-Tribune*, p. A-1.

Haga, C. (2000, August 23). As *Survivor* pares down to one, viewers pile up by millions. *Minneapolis Star Tribune*, p. 1A.

Hale, S. (2001, March 4). Workers who survive layoffs often share certain traits. *Los Angeles Times*, p. 1.

Hannity & Colmes [television broadcast] (2000, August 24). New York: Fox News Network Transcripts.

Hinds, J. (2001, January 27). Survival of the fittest: *Survivor II* and *Friends* square off in fierce battle for ratings Thursday night. *The Montreal Gazette*, p. 1.

Improving schools a delicate process [editorial] (2000, June 30). *Chicago Sun-Times*, p.39.

Jablin, F. (2001). Organizational entry, assimilation, and disengagement/exit. In F. Jablin, & L.L Putnam (Eds.), *The new handbook of organizational communication* (2nd ed.) (pp. 732–818). Thousand Oaks: Sage.

Johnson, C. (2000, August 25). A rat-eat-rat world; *Survivor* winner used corporate savvy. *The Washington Post*, p. E01.

Johnson L.A. (2000, August 28). The snake and the rat: Analysis finds immorality under the skin of *Survivor*. *Pittsburgh Post-Gazette*, p. B1.

Joyner, T. (2000, August 26). *Survivor* voted out by corporate trainers. *The Atlanta Journal and Constitution*, p. 1F.

Kilroy, M. (2000, August 10). *Survivor* shows reality bites. *Online 49er*. Retrieved January 25, 2001 from the World Wide Web: http://www.cslb.edu.

Kinsman, M. (2000, August 28). Surviving at work—now that's a test. *The San Diego Union-Tribune*, p. C-1.

Kloer, P. (2000, August 23) *Survivor* passion hits height tonight. *The Atlanta Journal and Constitution*, p. A1.

Lazega, E. (1992). *The micropolitics of knowledge: Communication and indirect control in workgroups*. New York: Aldine de Gruyter.

Letters. (2000, September 18). *Newsweek*, p. 16.

Levin, G. (2000, May 31). Unnatural selection. *USA Today*, p. 1D.

Levin, B. (2000, July 10). Sorry pal, get off the island. *Maclean's*, 44.

MacDonald, B, (2000, August 27). *Survivor* sends wrong message. *The Toronto Sun*, p. 3.

McGrory M. (2000, July 23). Surviving Reality. *The Washington Post*, p. B01.

Millman, J. (2000, June 1). *They've booted Mrs. Howell!* [episode summary]. Retrieved January 25, 2001 from the World Wide Web: http://www.salon.com.

Millman, J., Stark, J., & Wyman, B. (2000, June 28). *Survivor complete* [episode summaries]. Retrieved January 25, 2001 from the World Wide Web: http://www.salon.com.

Morgan, G. (1997). *Images of organization* (2nd ed.). Thousand Oaks, CA: Sage.

Mumby, D.K. (1987). The political function of narrative in organizations. *Communication Monographs, 54*, 113–127.

Mumby, D.K. (2001). Power and politics. In F. Jablin, & L.L Putnam (Eds.), *The new handbook of organizational communication* (2nd ed.) (pp. 585–623). Thousand Oaks: Sage.

Murphy, D. (2000, July 5). CBS' *Survivor* a lot like life at the office. *Milwaukee Journal Sentinel*, p. 3Q.

National Magazine [television broadcast]. (2000, August 22). Toronto: CBC News Transcripts.

O'Brien, V. (2000, August 31). *Organization politics: Winning the alliance game.* Retrieved January 25, 2001 from the World Wide Web: http://www.columbi-aconsultant.com/v12_aug00.html.

O'Hara, J. (2000, September 4). Last man standing. *Maclean's*, 62.

Osgood File [radio broadcast]. (2000, August 24). New York: CBS News Transcripts.

Ostrow, J. (2000a, August 24). Ruthlessness proves to be its own reward. *The Denver Post*, p. A-20.

Ostrow, J. (2000b, May 27). *Survivor* castaway took TV show "too seriously." *The Denver Post*, p. B-01.

Perigard, M.A. (2000a, May 31). *Survivor* pushes reality TV to the limits tonight. *The Boston Herald*, p. 1.

Perigard, M.A. (2000b, August 23). Survival of the fittest: Take a tip from the tribal council to win at office politics. *The Boston Herald*, p. 37.

Petrozzello, D. (2000, June 7). *Survivor's* snakes and rats give CBS some bite. *New York Daily News*, p. 38.

Peyser, M. (2000, August 28). *Survivor* Tsunami. *Newsweek*, 52.

Powell, B. (2000a, July 19). *Survivor* just a day at the office. *The Toronto Star*, p. 6.

Powell, B. (2000b, August 23). Who will survive? *The Toronto Star*, p. 6.

Putnam, L.L., Phillips, N., & Chapman, P. (1996). Metaphors of communication and organization. In S.R. Clegg, C. Hardy, & W.J. Nord (Eds.), *Handbook of organizational studies* (pp. 375–408). London: Sage.

Rosenthal, P. (2000, August 24). Snake kills the rat, and Rich gets richer. *Chicago Sun-Times*, p. 32.

Rothstein, E. (2000, August 5). TV shows in which the real is fake and the fake is real. *The New York Times*, p. 11.

Rutenberg, J. (2000, Dec 10). Tracking hidden *Survivor* through the Outback. *The Plain Dealer*, p. 1I.

Salhani, C. (2000, August 30). *Commentary: Are TV shows a reflection of society?* United Press International. Retrieved January 25, 2001 from the World Wide Web: http://www.live365.com/isyn/20000830-39ad9702.640f.23.html.

Sibley, R. (2000, August 25). Georg Friedrich Hegel doesn't get voted off the island. *The Ottawa Citizen*, p. A16.

Spencer, C. (2000, June 3). *Survivor:* Where even your philosophy skills are on trial. *Ottawa Citizen*, p. A16.

Stafford, D. (2000, September 14). *Survivor* skills pay off at work. *The Kansas City Star*, p. C1.

Stark, M. (2000, September 14). *Survived: Producer Mark Burnett's inside analysis doesn't make the island "dramality" any more compelling than it was from the edge of the couch* [book review]. Retrieved January 25, 2001 from the World Wide Web: http://www.salon.com.

A summer of shifting *Survivor* theories. (2000, August 23). *The Toronto Star*, p. D1.

Surviving a summer fling. (2000, August 25). *St. Louis Post-Dispatch*, p. B6.

Survivor: More than you want to know about CBS's twisted island challenge [commentary]. (2000, June 16). Retrieved January 25, 2001 from the World Wide Web: http://www.salon.com.

Survivor won't, but it was fun [editorial]. (2000, August 25). *Chicago Sun-Times*, p. 37.

Thompson, A. (2000, August 24). TV show *Survivor* ends with some surprises and much discussion. In *Rivera Live* [television broadcast]. New York: CNBC News Transcripts.

Tribal politics. (2000, August 24). *USA Today*, p. 13A.

Vande Berg, L., & Trujillo, N. (1989). *Organizational life on television*. Norwood, NJ: Ablex.

Voyeur TV hits it big in America. (2000, June 09). *CNN newsstand* [news broadcast]. New York: Cable News Network Transcripts.

Walker, R. (2000a, June 1). *The most annoying person on Survivor*. Retrieved January 25, 2001 from the World Wide Web: http://www.slate.com/moneybox.

Walker, R. (2000b, July 6). *The Survivor consultant, part 2*. Retrieved January 25, 2001 from the World Wide Web: http://www.slate.com/moneybox/.

Walker, R. (2000c, August 24). *The Survivor consultant's last laugh*. Retrieved January 25, 2001 from the World Wide Web: http://www.slate.com/moneybox/.

Weber, M. (19). The theory of social and economic organization.

Weick, K.E. (1995). *Sensemaking in organizations*. Thousand Oaks: Sage.

Wyman, B. (2000, August 23). *Who's gonna win Survivor?* [commentary]. Retrieved January 25, 2001 from the World Wide Web: http://www.salon.com.

Your world with Neil Cavuto [television broadcast] [Neil Cavuto]. (2000, August 25). New York: Fox News Network Transcripts.

Zurawik, D. (2000, August 24). Millions tune in for the final episode, but the impact of "reality TV" will be felt for a long time. *The Baltimore Sun*, p. 1A.

This manuscript was presented at the National Communication Association convention in Atlanta, 2001.

10

Self-Help for Savages: The "Other" *Survivor*, Primitivism, and the Construction of American Identity

Steven S. Vrooman

Two similar ideas about *Survivor* percolate across a cultural landscape awash with wave after wave of reality television programming. An academic friend e-mailed this response to a query about the show: "I don't know anybody who watches it (or at least will admit to watching it)." And this closing riff from a short piece on the show called "Island of the Apes" appeared in *Natural History:* "And that's the secret of *Survivor's* success. Underneath it all, we are just a bunch of apes who want to know what our fellows are up to, always eager to be part of the action" (Small, 2000, p. 87).

This, then, is the underbelly of the popularity of *Survivor*, a disdain toward the primitives who would make spectacles of themselves on reality programs and a disdain toward the primitives who would subject themselves to the broadcasts of these shows. Surely this is not quite what the two academics quoted above "really" meant, but it is hard not to connect their words with the larger skeptical aura surrounding these shows and the "dark premise" of a show like *Survivor*, glossed as "evilness" by a fan in a *Time* cover story (Buia, Goehner, Harbison, Nugent, McDowell, Ressner, Cullotta, & Kanigel, 2000, p. 56). Indeed, there is another "dark premise" at the heart of our love/hate of *Survivor*, the same dark premise that has infused Western culture's fascination with the "primitive" for hundreds of years. While Montaigne's "Of Cannibals" essay in the sixteenth century made out South Americans as relatively virtuous in comparison to ossified European society, this is a mere romanticized version of a comparison Europeans have made since the beginnings of Western colonialism. Partly to justify that same colonialism, Western ideologies have not simply argued for seeing the "dark" people of the world as inferior, but have tended to defend a fascination with the very process of seeing them. They become the "Other," the continual object lesson we use to define ourselves, to figure out what we actually mean by this thing called civilization. We must watch these Others in the "wild" to make them the embodiment of all we are not, to perform the difficult task of self-definition, to pretend toward abstract virtues like civilization, morality and rationality that are easier to grasp through antimony: savagery, brutality and chaos. We have done this task in adventure stories as far back as *Robinson Crusoe*, but *Survivor* ups the cultural ante of this task. Ever since Conrad's (1910/1999) *Heart of Darkness*, we have had the nagging suspicion that, like Kurtz, too close a proximity to the darkness we are compelled to watch and objectify makes us savages as well. In *Survivor*, we are watching the savages and they are us.

The first *Survivor* introduced this formula but rather quickly devolved into a fairly basic good-versus-evil, Pagong-versus-Tagi (the two "tribes") plot. While Rich shed his corporate "conflict management" skin and became a Kurtzian "snake," others held fast to illusions of virtue and ethics that rang hollow to many at home who would have done anything to win the million bucks. But it is the second or "other" *Survivor* that is of most interest to me. Although it attracted fewer ratings, it still trumped NBC's "Must See TV." As a sequel its popularity would presumably suffer once the novelty of the show had worn off. To keep interest level up it had to offer some changes. One of those changes was to make the game harder (Burnett, 2001): a harsher environment, more difficult challenges, etc. But another and perhaps more important change was to make the cultural forces behind the game much more prevalent. *Survivor: The Australian Outback*, by virtue of its secondness, its new location, and its new media-scrutiny, had a much clearer need to establish its unique identity. So it explicitly became a story about identity formation. It altered the kind of primitivism it explored. It changed the adventure game and as such it provides an excellent insight into the ways that we use media, television and "reality" fantasies to become the people we feel the need to be. In the case of *Survivor: The Australian Outback*, we are convincing ourselves that we are not as primitive as we thought, and that, a-hem, even if we are, is that really so awfully bad? The evolving *Survivor* text is negotiating a presence for adventure in a society that feels slightly guilty about its need for it. It does this by trumping even its own New Age hokum's grip on the primitive: it casts the encounter with "the Other" as self help, a genre similarly devoted to the "dark secrets that must be brought to the surface" (Rimke, 2000, p. 67)

This essay will examine these questions by first providing a developmental account of the genre of the adventure tale and the primitivism that underlies it. It will then examine the rhetorical moves made by the show and its contestants to re-imagine both positive and negative connotations of primitivism. In the end it is the degree to which this discourse does not fit that provides the most interesting lesson of all. It is an example of how the development of genres proceeds through a double movement of acceptance and rejection. We need certain genres, but we also need them to change. We require genres like this for self-definition, but we also need to redefine the genres as we use them. *Survivor: The Australian Outback* inserts itself into this dilemma to lever(age) its own popularity.

Adventure Amongst the Primitives

The adventure narrative has had moments of staggering importance and popularity. Haggard's (1886/1998) publication of *King Solomon's Mines* marked the birth of the age of the best seller in publishing a hundred years ago. As per Said's (1993) argument that the power to narrate is a key element of colonial power, a number of critics have pointed out the congruence between the rise of the adventure narrative and the rise of the efforts at colonial expansion in the 1870s that culminated in Europe's "Scramble for Africa" (see Bristow, 1991; Dixon, 1995; McClintock, 1995; Shohat & Stam, 1996; Taves, 1993). "Adventure," Green (1991) argues, "is the energizing myth of empire" (p. xi), and Shome (1996) argues that cultural texts can "reinforce ... neo-imperial political practices" (p. 42). Certainly much of the impetus for colonization was economic (see Dirlik, 1997), but the importance of the cultural drive to legitimize these practices should not be underestimated. Kipling's (1899/2003) "white man's burden" and the French *mission civilizatrice* both provided the same self-justifying ideological cover: whites needed to bring their light of civilization and rationality to a dark and savage world.

The typical form of adventure gives us the white hunter or explorer traipsing around the jungle with some unhelpfully citified feminine love interest. Our hero, of course, has a surpassing knowledge of the area, its peoples and its languages. They search for lost mines or artifacts, lost tribes or lost brothers. Our hero tests himself in the uncivilized world, proving with action those virtues that citified life sometimes lacks, like leadership and courage, and proving with the simple fact of his whiteness the other virtues of Western civilization, like intelligence and morality. This narrative loses momentum as the century rolls forward and its ideological work become obsolescent. When India begins the wave of decolonization in 1947, it becomes increasingly hard for Americans to respond to this kind of storyline, and the films largely disappear (Cameron, 1994). But even though the larger cultural need for the tales no longer exists by the fifties, at an individual level the need for an identity-clarifying encounter with the primitive remains strong. Forty years ago, one of every thirty paperbacks sold was a *Tarzan* novel (Torgovnick, 1990). Author Edgar Rice Burroughs' explanation of his works' popularity is presented in this way:

> Tarzan's appeal, he said, is escape. Escape from "the narrow confines of the city streets," escape from "the restrictions of man-made laws, and the inhibitions that society has placed upon us. We would each like to be Tarzan. At least I would; I admit it" [Watson, 2001, p. 62].

The Tarzan story is about what Achebe (1988) has famously described as the most pernicious of the racisms in Conrad's (1910/1999) *Heart of Darkness*, the arrogant notion that Africa (or any other "primitive" setting) is merely the place where whites go to struggle over their identity. It is a place where Kurtz confronts his own primitive darkness, where Burroughs goes to abandon the velvet trappings of civilization to find its true meaning.

After the 1960s, Tarzan began to disappear. Perhaps Vietnam, as explained in *Hearts of Darkness* (Mayfield, Zaloom, Bahr, Coppola, & Hickenlooper, 1991), laid waste to the illusions that these stories were supposed to maintain. At least until the 1980s, when our actor president gave us back our illusions, hand-in-hand with Third World jingoism and "sporadic fits of military gangsterism" (McClintock, 1995, p. 392), we find, for a time, Indiana Jones in *Raiders of the Lost Ark* (Marshall & Spielberg, 1991) and Michael Douglas in *Romancing the Stone* (Douglas & Zemekis, 1984). Both heroes deconstruct the mythology even as they enact it—the quainter identity of a mythological yet preferred age. The genre becomes a nostalgic journey into an ideological past when the enemy Others were not seated in the Kremlin with their fingers on the button. But films to follow in the genre are unable to maintain the burden of deconstructive comedy. What remain are soulless and meta-nostalgic imitations like the recent *Mummy* remakes (Daniel, Jacks, & Sommers, 1999) and *Lara Croft:*

Tomb Raider (Gordon, Levin, Wilson, & West, 2001). Tarzan has had some fitful returns over the past two decades, but the films have either been guiltily deconstructive, as in *Greystoke: The Legend of Tarzan, Lord of the Apes* (Canter & Hudson, 1984), or avoidant, as is the recent Disney cartoon, which hides its racism in cool skater-dude special effects (Arnold, Buck, & Lima, 1999).

Enter *Survivor*. Theorists of genre argue that genres strategically change over time in response to (and perhaps as commentaries on) the cultural and ideological needs of a society (Beebee, 1994; Todorov, 1990). Or, as Bazerman (1994) argues, they are "important levers" in the "complex societal machine" (p. 79). Does *Survivor* show up now, as it does, because we need it, because we need to again encounter the primitive and encounter the primitive in ourselves? Westerners, especially white ones (see Dyer, 1997), have always needed this encounter with the fantasy primitive. But now we are able to watch its syncretistic-primitivism art direction (see Burnett, 2000) without a Harrison Ford wink because we need it more than ever. The primitive once gain rears up, after proliferating *National Geographic*-style channels are beamed to our satellite dishes, after the Asian economic meltdown trickled home, and after the genocide in central Africa gave news reporters increased access to Conradian references. *Survivor* gave us the formula again, and we loved it, elevating its finale to a ratings firmament double the typical top of the Nielsens. *Survivor: The Australian Outback*, however, does the more interesting work. It wants us to have our myth guilt and irony free, two things which self-help literature and discourse work hard to banish (Rimke, 2000).

Perhaps *Survivor* and reality television in general are how we find identity in Fukayama's (1992) end of history. When there is only one superpower, how does it define itself without an evil empire to compete with? Pre 9/11, "American" was insufficient for us as an identity term, given that we were no longer quite sure what it meant. Thus we went further back to the prehistory of the adventure story, its primitive form, we might say. We looked for the absent yet footprinted figure of Crusoe's primitive Friday, not as expert hunters who know and are trying to ideologically defend out place in the world, but as castaways, even to ourselves. We are no longer hunters who know the lay of the land. We are a "failed expedition" (Burnett, 2001, p. 32). *Survivor* links the version of the primitive adventure/encounter that we remember from a childhood of movies and theme parks—"The primitive was a scary place in which Americans could find themselves stranded by plane crashes or (more traditionally) shipwrecks" (Torgovnick, 1990, p. 13)—with more adult questions of existential identity crisis. Tarzan in therapy, if you will.

Survivor

Survivor opens with a bellow and a theme song that might contain words or just nonsense sounds (such distinctions are unimportant for the adventuring American). Warpaint and mud splashed on bodies, images of fire and water and predators make up the primal setting for what host Jeff Probst calls in both the Pulau Tiga show and the Outback show, "the adventure of a lifetime." There are tribes. There are Immunity Idols and Talismans. There is a Fire Spirit in the first show and Sprits of the Land in the second. The survivors eat bugs and worms and rats, which khakied Jeff Probst informs us is how the Aboriginals survived for tens of thousands of years in the Outback.

The first *Survivor* clearly gives us an encounter with the savage and the savagery within all of us. This "deserted" island in the South China Sea is close enough, by everyday American standards of geography, to those islands where the real cannibals live(d). The two tribes, later one tribe, must cannibalize their own members by voting them off. Much to-do is made of how difficult it is to have to vote someone off, especially by the seemingly naively goody-goody members of the Pagong tribe. Although this is an issue in the *Survivor: The Australian Outback*, contestant Jeff's comments to the contrary showed up not only in the first episode but in numerous promos:

> I'm looking forward to voting somebody off, because it's part of the game. And I'm here to play the game. I'm not looking to make friends. I'm not here for that. People have got to go and I look forward to walking up, writing someone's name on a card and talking about them.

By the second go around, the brutal aspects of the game itself are underemphasized in favor of depicting the harshness of the land and environment.

In the first *Survivor* there are no natives. They are completely absent from the place, and this facilitates a storyline whereby the contestants themselves become the primitives. Rich's evil genius Kurtz-power becomes the focus, and by the end of the game, the winner is decided by a jury vote of previous cast-offs that is to them, as Sean says in the finale, "Who's least objectionable." The other primitives we love to hate in the Tagi alliance are Rudy, the sexist, racist and homophobic military guy, Kelly, "the rat" who changes sides at will, and Susan, the hick whose now famous "I would let the vultures take you" speech to Kelly makes her seem a bit unhinged. Sue tells us in the first episode that "I'm a redneck and I don't know corporate world at all and corporate world ain't gonna work out here in the bush" when Rich tries to bring some negotiation skills to the Tagi team. Later, when confronted with the idea of eating rats, Sue continues to play up her stereotype: "All a rat is is a squirrel without a fuzzy tail." The producers, in editing together clips that mock her Minnesota accent, play into this game as well. These people become a sort of "Other" for us, a primitive we can feel superior to and yet also take a vicarious thrill in the idea of being them. When I talk to people about my *Survivor* research, many point out that they didn't watch after the first, and some argue that the people in the various sequels were too boring. The first show highlighted their primitivism, making them more exotic. It made our voyeurism more stimulating.

Survivor: The Australian Outback changes the terms of the adventure. It is hotter. The contestants have less food. And they are staying in a place where the Aborigines are a constant, yet invisible rhetorical presence. Aboriginals are invoked in the very first promo for the show, and their knowledge and experience is mined for a number of challenges. But just as the presence of the Australian cowboys in one episode indicates, the Aborigines, like the Native Americans, are a people displaced by colonization. They are clearly the noble savages of *Survivor*'s rhetorical architecture. Thus this second iteration of the show is left in a quandary. The multiplicity of negative and barbaric savagery given to us by the first show and the noble savagery of the Aborigines makes the contestants' status as savages all the more difficult to maintain. It is harder to watch this new set of castaways with the clearly gleeful and superior feeling we might have taken away from the first show (feelings which had to be more difficult to sustain after *Big Brother* sucked the fun out of such voyeurism). *Survivor: The Australian Outback* helps us compensate by making it a life-changing identity experience to which we have front row seats. Instead of being primitives watching primitives, we become the evolved watching evolution.

The Re-articulation

Hence the change in the plot. The show and its contestants become more "noble" the second time around. This is also, it should be said, partly a plot of necessity. In some ways, it seems that the more "primitive" castaways are voted off too early in this show. Yet, the ultimate victors, Colby and Tina, perform many of the behaviors that the Tagi alliance did to win in the first series, but in this second series, those behaviors are sanitized.

This occurs through two distinct rhetorical movements on the part of the design of the competitions and the editing of the show. First, other contestants who are voted off have their primitivism played up, whether it be the mean-spiritedness of Jeff and Jerri, the racist logic of Nick's laziness, or the Lord-of-the-Flies oddity of Mike. The second and more important move made in the show is the recuperation of what the first show coded as unethical behavior into a larger discourse of personal growth and of "earning it." This is done in a number of ways. Certain gamesmanship behaviors from Tina and Colby are reinterpreted or hidden in the emerging self-help discourse. The "good" people on the show, Rodger and Elisabeth, are shown in an entirely positive light, without a touch of the naiveté seen on the first series. Finally, other contestants who showed signs of being hated or of being savage, notably Mike and Keith, are heavily recuperated into the life-changing essence of the new message.

This shift in the rhetorical scope of the show is a result of a complex interaction between its sequel status, the particulars of the landscape, the people on the show, and the editing choices made after the fact. But at each of these levels, it would be a mistake to assume that any of this happened "naturally" or in unmediated "reality." Aside from the heavy manipulation of events involved in filming the show itself (see Hochman, 2000) and in the editing of the mass amounts of footage into seventeen hours of programming, it is unlikely that any of these contestants are unaffected by the discourse of adventure narrative that, especially for the male contestants, was such an influential part of America's child-culture.

A number of contestants are shown as primitives, especially in the beginning third of the episode. Jeff is relatively charming and funny, but his comments are very akin to the kind of nasty gibes Rich and Sue would make as they voted someone off in the first series. In episode 1, in response to Kimmi's talking, Jeff says: "I just want to grab her by the neck and shake the s*** out of her." In episode 5 Jeff gives a bottom-line interpretation of the action of the show, complete with grins and chuckles:

> I don't mean to sound evil, but it's all about kicking someone's ass.... Some of the people in the tribe are talking about how guilty they feel and how bad they feel for the other tribe and—screw it. I mean, chop their heads off, chop their legs off. This is a game and I'm ready to beat every one of them.

In case we weren't certain of his savagery, later in that episode he makes the only specific reference to cannibalism uttered in the series so far: "Chop their eyeballs out so Mike can eat them." In episode 6 he continues on this tack: "It's fun to beat them and make fun of it. It's fun to have them talking about how hungry they are and us go in and win all their food." In episode 3, Mike is shown putting on war paint saying, "I'm going to find something that's alive that I'm going to kill" as he heads out to go hunting. In episode 4 Mike kills a pig. He puts dots of blood on his cheeks as a joke, but the promos for the show showed only the blood dots, Jeff's opinion of Mike as "an idiot," and some strange laughter from Mike. Later we hear him say "I'm feeling the need to shed some blood." For a good span of three episodes, his goofy savagery was the focus of his tribe, Kucha's portion of the show.

In episode 3 Jerri is the victim of the first edit from her face to that of a spider in its web as she discusses how she'd still vote someone off, even if they developed an Outback romance. The show continues to show her nasty and negative side, with the beef jerky incident that got Kel kicked off in episode 2 to her fatal power play to insist she get paired with Colby in a challenge in episode 10. She is the spider, or, as indicated by a later attempt to align with Colby, the "devil." She is Rich but without the camp. Even after the show ended, no one seemed to believe that Jerri was anything other than what she seemed, in spite of her protests.

The place where the racist drive of primitivism comes most uncomfortably to the surface is with the character of Nick. After Gervase's proud display of his laziness and Ramona's sickness induced lethargy in the Pulau Tiga *Survivor*, there is precedent for the show to create a picture of African American laziness. In the second show, Nick is the first person to have his work ethic questioned. In a comment that Nick would challenge in his *Early Show* appearance and which the speaker would later take back in the wrap-up show, Jeff says:

> Nick is very lazy. He won't pick up anything; he won't lift anything. If you ask him to help you he'll act like he doesn't hear you.... He's done our kitchen, which is lovely. And he's built a lovely little outdoor chair and he's built a lovely little patio, but only because he doesn't want to do anything else.

This commentary is interspersed with shots of Nick sitting in a chair on this porch he's built, saying "What?" in response to what someone says to him. The racist assumptions in this comment and the degree to which the producers almost gleefully go along with the comment are extremely disquieting, especially given that it appears to be a trend. Later, at the tribal merger, all the remaining contestants are disappointed that they won't be allowed to move into the relatively posh Kucha camp, almost all of the amenities of which were built by Nick.

We hear almost nothing from Nick in these early episodes. There is no temptation to identify with him and see him as other than a primitive racial other. He is in these early episodes so little that the party of us watching the show at my house didn't even know his name until Jeff's laziness comment. Nick's next big spot in the show's edit is a shot of him eating chicken and joking "Once you go dark meat you don't ever go back." Laziness, a porch, and chicken. Words just fail. Aside from his response to Mike's accident in episode 6, his only role is in a relatively long sequence showing him moving rocks and things to prop up a travois like a hammock. In episode 10 people complain that Nick isn't fishing. In episode 9 he is shown sitting down while others build. At tribal council the host asks "Anyone here not pulling their weight?" and the camera cuts to Nick. Only in later episodes is it revealed that he got sick after the merger. Alicia, meanwhile, who is also black, but, as a muscular personal trainer cannot be lazy, becomes, in episode 5, the embodiment of attitude, as she gets into a finger-waggling fight with Kimmi over the chickens (a shot repeated over and over again in promos and in the final wrap-up show). In case we didn't get the message that she's a bossy black woman, Elisabeth tells us that "Alicia is in charge of telling people to do things. Alicia is also in charge of talking trash about people." In the end, that sounds a bit lazy after all.

These different versions of primitivism, all classical adventure story savagery, are exorcised from the show. These parts of the adventure story, which synechdochically stand in for the adventure myth and the first season show itself, become the Other to which we and the remaining adventurers define ourselves against. They are the base from which the merged Barramundi tribe evolves. Increased rhetorical work to this effect becomes evident in the show and its surrounding PR discourses once the turning point of Mike's accident occurs. Mike, the slayer of pigs and the eater of fish eyes, inhales too much smoke and passes out in the fire in episode 6. His hands are burned so badly he has to be helicoptered out. In his appearances on *The Early Show* and in the finale, he was stricken with tears as he discussed the spiritual growth his accident instigated in him. In the finale Mike tearfully addresses this with:

> What happens just—it transcends money or prizes or anything and the spiritual growth and the family growth. What happened to me was—a million bucks couldn't buy it.

Or, as Rodger sums up near the end of the fateful sixth episode, "Possibly Mike's accident might've brought some of them to the realization maybe there's other things more important even than the million dollars."

But even before his accident he was beginning to represent this shift toward a kind of self help mentality. Near the beginning of episode 6 he says:

> It's amazing how you can live off the land, eight city people.... My out-look on life has changed one hundred and eighty degrees. And I'm this kind of guy. This should be nothing for me. But I'm a changed man already after sixteen days. Very changed. And if I last another sixteen days who knows what will happen to me.

He doesn't, in fact, last. But the people who do are either caught up in or edited into that spirit.

In episode 7, after the accident and heading into the merger, Colby is clear: "I'm here for one reason, and that's to win." But he soon changes his tune. After the merge he opines that "Jerri doesn't deserve to win this" because of how's she's acted. And Tina reveals the extent to which alliances might be sacrificed for this "deserve" criterion:

> You go into a merger thinking that you're very much aligned as a team, but then as time goes by you might find out that there's people that are more deserving. I want this to be on an individual basis, and I want the good guys to win.

Eventually the Ogakor alliance is broken and Jerri is voted off. This makes the Ogakor alliance vulnerable. It was not the kind of strategic move Rich might've agreed with, but it is in line with the new discourse.

In episode 12, Colby spells out the way the encounter between the good of people like Rodger contrasts with the bads of a guy like Keith:

> Being the oldest guy still here he's got a lot more energy than any of us do. I think it comes from his heart. Because we're not playing by ourselves now. We're playing for those who are deserving to be here. Rodger and Elisabeth and Tina are all pretty deserving of being in the final three. As far as Keith goes, there's not anything memorable or outstanding that has kept him in the game.

This comment indicates the further strength of the rhetorical shift. Keith is not deserving not because he's a bad guy, but because he hasn't done anything extraordinary. Colby is apparently unaware or he is skeptical about what is eventually revealed as Keith's change of heart.

At this time, however, questions of "deserve" are still secondary to questions of winning. Rodger and Elisabeth are too much a threat in the final two, when their goodness and popularity would presumably lead them to ultimate victory. So they are eliminated over Keith and Amber. Of course, as a sop to the new discourse, Tina asks Rodger who needed the money the most, allowing Rodger to sacrifice himself and determine the order the two are eliminated by. Cold comfort, I'm sure.

Yet the elimination of these two well-loved people seems to provide some kind of turning point for Colby at least:

> The biggest struggle I deal with in the final few tribal councils is whether I want to sit beside someone who almost guarantees me the million bucks or whether I want to sit beside someone who if I don't win the million bucks I'd still feel good about the other person winning. I don't even have the answer to that. I did yesterday, but it changed this morning and it'll change again tonight. (episode 12)

In episode 13, on the way to vote off Elisabeth (both of Colby's speeches are certainly included in the episodes to create some suspense regarding the upcoming vote), Colby concretizes his dilemma:

> It comes down to two things, strategy or co-empathy. On the one hand you've got the "Who deserves it? Who's a good, who's a righteous person? Who needs that money?" On the other hand you have strategy. How can I get there? How can I put that money in my pocket?

The final show, where Colby picks Tina to go into the final two with him instead of Keith, a decision which basically cost him a million dollars, is the one where this decision is most fully used to recuperate the *Survivor* experience into a kind of romanticized self-help primitivism. The final three are given the equipment for making "idols": wood, feathers, beads, paint, etc. They are instructed to make them while thinking of what the land has given to them. Then they are to "offer" them up to the land by tossing them in the river. On the way to the river, they pass by the torches of all the other survivors who'd been eliminated. Soaring and overwrought flute music accompanies an almost painfully overlong segment that shows those contestants laughing or crying or struggling. As Rimke (2000) notes, suffering is a key part of the self-help healing process. When they finally get to the river, Jeff Probst tells them:

> One of the things I've gathered from chatting with you guys for 41 days is that this has been a life-changing experience for the three of you. Part of that growth comes from examining the past. That was the purpose of the walk you just took.

These three contestants embody this new ideal, even though Keith is the only one to embrace the ideology specifically. As he says during one of his frequent loner trips to commune with the land in the last shows, "When we had a chance to work on the idols, it was an all-day process, so we had a lot of reflection time.... It was a healing process—it helped put closure to everything." Colby speaks of how the game has changed for him, and obviously his choice of Tina in the end indicates that to some extent it had. But is he making decisions based on this notion of "deserving," as he seems to indicate? Tina, in the last episode, indicates that she has changed and the game has changed for her, but for her the change was that she became more "strategic." As she says after Keith is voted off:

> What it boils down to is did I come here for 42 days to starve, to live in the type of environment I've lived in, to make those type of sacrifices to give somebody like Elisabeth a million dollars, or did I come here to play this game and me to win a million dollars.

This is not the "kindler, gentler" game that she after the show indicated that she wanted to play.

The closer one looks at the final show, filled with what first *Survivor* winner Rich Hatch (2001) calls "countless moments of nauseating reflection" (p. 31), the more hollow this discourse seems. We remember Colby's earlier assessment of Keith as "a bozo" when he tells Tina, "He got us where we needed to be and he didn't win a million dollars; that's the best part about it." He tells the camera "I don't think Keith earned the right to sit in the position of one of the final two in this game." But now it simply appears that the New Age veneer that Rich sees as claptrap really is a kind of dodge to position the game in a different sort of way, as a different kind of experience. The contestants on *Survivor: The Australian Outback* were supposed to be more attractive (Burnett, 2001), and Burnett seems to indicate that *Survivor: The Australian Outback's* status as sequel meant that the land had to be more of a character and a challenge in this iteration. Both of these things impede our ability to see these contestants as base primitives we can watch and judge.

But in the end, the game still remains the same, as Probst intones at the beginning of each successive show. Colby and Tina express emotions not entirely dissimilar to those expressed by Sue in the first show. Yet, Keith, as the terminal runner up, works hard to create what Rich (Hatch, 2001) evaluates as a "moronic attitude" (p. 31):

> The time that I've spent here has been a cleansing process. In the last five days I've realized this really is not about the money and it shouldn't be. You should walk away from this with something that is more valuable than just money. And I will. And I don't think I have the opportu-

nity to win the money. I don't think I'll be at that level. I mean, I'm close, but I don't think I'll be in the last two. And it's totally fine with me. I'm totally enriched by everything I've gained from this experience. I feel really great about it. I feel very content.

He seems to protest a bit much here, given that Colby is willing to give up a million bucks just so Keith won't be able to take home the $100,000 for second place. I'm not sure I believe any one of the last four sentences Keith utters here, much less all of them as a whole.

Conclusion

So many of us watched the first *Survivor*. We had a vicarious adventure. As creator Mark Burnett (2001) has written, as we watched we imagined ourselves on the island. We imagined what we would do and if we could win. But further, "Some even realized that they were already playing the game, although in their daily lives instead of on a remote island" (p. 9). As we bought "Voted Off the Island" T-shirts or loudly proclaimed that we only watched it once and didn't understand the big deal, we crafted identities based on different degrees of primitive watching. By the time *Survivor: The Australian Outback* rolled around, simple voyeurism was not enough. Indeed, the hallmark of the adventure tale is that the adventurer must do something. If the survivors themselves remain the primitives even as they have all the fun, this leaves little discursive space for us to reclaim a Western and American identity based on an adventure we only had in our armchairs.

So the show began to be about that dilemma. Even as references to the first show were edited out of the contestants' discourse, it was clear that these were people who had watched the first show. They were spectators like ourselves who had gone the extra eight thousand miles. They were, as we watched, continuing a process of identity formation that we also began the summer of 2000. For them, as for us, the show couldn't be entirely about the money. It was about the show, the journey, and who we would be on the other side.

Adventure tales like this enable us to be the people we need ourselves to be. By the second go around, the show needed to make that process as explicit as possible. It put the underlying purpose of the dream of adventure out on the carpet and only Richard Hatch seemed to be crying foul. Of course, as this analysis has indicated, that self-help discourse did not easily fit the show, its events, or its participants' motivations. As the jury in the last tribal council asked a rather pedantic repetition of questions all focusing on the themes of guilt and deservedness, the abundance of it all looked like nothing more than a kind of meta-defensiveness about the entire process. From Tina's unfounded idea of setting up a charity foundation to her last dig at Jerri in her response to the last question, none of it seemed to quite fit.

In closing, it seems as if the issue lies not in the translation of the adventure story to a new time and medium and plot, but in the prehistoric bones of the adventure myth itself. The adventure tale must be based on a series of problematic notions about the status or various peoples and parts of the world. It is a story told to craft an identity for people like us who are uncertain. But that identity is founded upon the shifting sands of misconception and myth as well as a basic structural flaw: the adventure tale can create for us a real identity only through actions that must happen in an unreal place. This is Achebe's critique. Or, in Burnett's (2001) words:

> A *Survivor* location has to be special. It must be evocative, transporting the armchair adventurer into the realm of fantasy, making them wish they were there. Nothing about a *Survivor* location should be mundane. No suggestion of the real world is allowed. (p. 32)

Survivor: The Australian Outback's attempt to lay this on its un-ironic face merely revealed the tensions inherent in the narrative itself, tensions which have historically imploded the genre at many points since its inception and which seem to have danced a slow implosion in the other *Survivor* sequels. *Survivor: Africa* gave us the same formula, with primitives mean and lazy Lindsey, food-stealing Clarence, and goat-herder (!) Tom. But the self help doesn't stick, even after winner Ethan plays hackeysack with kids in the village where he dropped off AIDS hospital supplies as a reward (!!). As the ratings slump, the self-help angle is abandoned. *Survivor: Marquesas* gives us explicit references to a cannibal past and the castaways are given no food – the easier to consume each other. The break is clear when prayerful Vecepia's God-anointed win is allowed to simply be hypocrisy and is not recruited into a furthering of the earning-it discourse. By *Survivor: Thailand*, the show is awash with primitives, from skater Robb to an inordinate number of Texans. Their primitive contrast with snippets of Thai high culture gives us the exact formula of the first show. You can feel the Mike-Keith soliloquies edited out of tearful Jake's comments the episode he is voted off (as this chapter goes to press).

Why does this self-help pass? Perhaps its addition uncomfortably reveals the artificiality of primitivism's ideology game. Or perhaps it was a game we could no longer afford to play after 9/11. As bin Laden lurked in the caves of Tora Bora, we no longer needed anything but CNN to tell us what it meant to be an American. Or maybe it was the ratings.

As a genre, self-help rises to prominence in the 1980s, the decade when postmodern irony begins its relentless march in America. PoMo, incarnated as Indiana Jones or not, both creates the opportunity and need for self help (by crushing those grand narratives), and at the same time thwarts it (by challenging the existence of the unified subject) (cf. Lyotard, 1991). In the end, it is this deferment that continues to stoke our continued desire for it. The "other" *Survivor* stepped into a rhetorical situation that created a need for its discourse at the same time as it cannibalized it. As such, it remains a fascinating moment in the hundred-year history of the adventure story. It embodies the double movement of repulsion and desire for the Other which spawned this, the original genre of self-help literature, a hundred years ago. It underlines the furious need, both individually and politically, that Western society has had for the Other, but it also demonstrates its thunderous insufficiency.

References

Achebe, C. (1988). An image of Africa: Racism in Conrad's *Heart of Darkness*. In R. Kimbrough (Ed.), *Heart of Darkness, an authoritative text* (pp. 251–261). London: Norton.

Arnold, B. (Producer), Buck, C., & Lima, K. (Directors). (1999). *Tarzan* [Film]. Hollywood, CA: Disney.

Bazerman, C. (1994). Systems of genres and the enactment of social intentions. In A. Freedman, & P. Medaway (Eds.), *Learning and teaching genre* (pp. 79–101). Portsmouth, NH: Boynton/Cook.

Beebee, T. O. (1994). *The ideology of genre: A comparative study of generic instability.* University Park, PA: The Pennsylvania State University Press.

Bristow, J. (1991). *Empire boys: Adventures in a man's world.* London: HarperCollins.

Buia, C., Goehner, A. L., Harbison, G., Nugent, B., McDowell, J., Ressner, J., Cullotta, C. A., & Kanigel, R. (2000, June 26). We like to watch: Led by the hit *Survivor*, voyeurism has become TV's hottest genre. Why the passion for peeping? *Time, 155,* 56+.

Burnett, M. (2000). *Survivor: The ultimate game.* New York: CBS.

Burnett, M. (2001). *Survivor II: The field guide.* New York: CBS.

Cameron, K. M. (1994). *Africa on film: Beyond black and white.* New York: Continuum.

Canter, S. C. (Producer), & Hudson, H. (Director). (1984). *Greystoke: The legend of Tarzan, lord of the apes* [Film]. Hollywood, CA: Warner.

Conrad, J. (1999). *Heart of darkness.* New York: Penguin. (Original work published 1910).

Daniel, S., Jacks, J. (Producers), & Sommers, S. (Director). (1999). *The mummy* [Film]. Hollywood, CA: Universal.

Dixon, R. (1995). *Writing the colonial adventure: Race, gender and nation in Anglo-Australian popular fiction, 1875–1914.* Cambridge, UK: Cambridge University Press.

Douglas, M. (Producer), & Zemekis, R. (Director). (1984). *Romancing the stone* [Film]. Hollywood, CA: Fox.

Dyer, R. (1997). *White.* London: Routledge.

Fukayama, F. (1992). *The end of history and the last man.* New York: Free Press.

Gordon, L., Levin, L., Wilson, C. (Producers), & West, S. (Director). (2001). *Lara Croft: Tomb raider.* [Film]. Hollywood, CA: Paramount.

Green, M. (1991). *Seven types of adventure tale: An etiology of a major genre.* University Park, PA: The Pennsylvania State University Press.

Grewal, I. (1996). *Home and harem: Nation, gender, empire, and the cultures of travel.* Durham, NC: Duke.

Haggard, H. R. (1998). *King Solomon's mines.* D Butts (Ed.). Oxford, UK: Oxford University Press. (Original work published 1886).

Hatch, R. (2001, May 21). The Hatch report. *US Magazine,* p. 31.

Hochman, D. (2000, Jun. 9). Well, isle be! *Entertainment Weekly, 544,* p. 24–27.

Kipling, R. A. (2003). The white man's burden. In J. Zwick (Ed.), *Anti-Imperialism in the United States, 1898–1935.* Retrieved Jan. 15, 2003 from http://www.boondocksnet.com/ai/kipling/kipling.html. (Original work published 1899).

Lyotard, F. (1984). *The postmodern condition.* Minneapolis, MN: University of Minnesota Press.

Marshall, F. (Producer), & Spielberg, S. (Director). (1981). *Raiders of the lost ark.* [Film]. Hollywood, CA: Paramount.

Mayfield, L., Zaloom, G., (Producers), Bahr, F. Coppola, E., & Hickenlooper, G. (Directors). (1991). *Hearts of darkness: A filmmaker's apocalypse* [Film]. Hollywood, CA: Paramount.

McClintock, A. (1995). *Imperial leather: Race, gender and sexuality in the colonial contest.* New York: Routledge.

Rimke, H. M. (2000). Governing citizens through self-help literature. *Cultural Studies, 14,* 61–78.

Said, E. (1978). *Orientalism.* London: Routledge.

Said, E. (1993). *Culture and imperialism.* New York: Knopf.

Shohat, E., & Stam, R. (1994). *Unthinking Eurocentrism: Multiculturalism and the media.* New York: Routledge.

Small, M. (2000, Sep.). Island of the apes. *Natural History, 109,* 87.

Taves, B. (1993). *The romance of adventure: The genre of historical adventure movies.* Jackson, MS: University Press of Mississippi.

Todorov, T. (1990). *Genres in discourse* (C. Porter, Trans.). Cambridge, UK: Cambridge University Press.

Torgovnick, M. (1990). *Gone primitive: Savage intellects, modern lives.* Chicago: University of Chicago Press.

Watson, B. (2001, March). Tarzan the eternal. *Smithsonian,* 62+.

The author wishes to thank Tom Nakayama, Jenny Reeder, and A. Todd Jones for their help in preparing this chapter.

11

The Communication Ethics of *Survivor*

Marilyn Fuss-Reineck

What lessons in communication ethics does *Survivor* teach as contestants "Outwit, Outplay, and Outlast?" Survivors live together, share resources, cooperate/compete, and attempt to keep relationships positive enough to remain in the tribe. The combination of revealing group observations presented in an engaging format makes the *Survivor* series appealing material for group communication classes. The series' instructional effectiveness was tested when two college-level group communication courses were asked to evaluate the communication ethics in *Survivor* and *Survivor: The Australian Outback*, using the National Communication Association's (1999) Credo for Ethical Communication. This guide seeks to "apply broadly to all forms and settings of communication rather than being specific to any one setting or role" (Andersen, 2000, p. 139). Although the credo was designed as a social contract for ethical communication, it also provides an ethical standard for evaluating communication. The comparison between desired and observed communication can help students develop moral sensitivity, making NCA's Credo for Ethical Communication a potentially useful pedagogical tool.

For example, the human actions presented in reality television can be examined from such an ethical perspective. Knowledge of communication ethics assists viewers in looking beyond an action's effectiveness, to evaluations of its moral impact. Teaching ethics is essential in small group courses because students' experiences potentially impact how they work with others in society (Hess, 1995). Charron (2001) grounds communication ethics pedagogy in Rest's four steps in ethical decision-making: (1) moral sensitivity, (2) judgment, or moral reasoning; (3) motivation;

and (4) character (Rest, 1982). The first two steps are particularly perti-
nent to ethical analyses of reality television shows such as *Survivor*.
Instructors can fuel moral sensitivities that students demonstrate through
recognition of ethical dilemmas and issues. Moral reasoning potentially
develops as students examine a group over time in a complex environment and engage in dialogue about ethical issues, including sins of omission, often overlooked in ethical analysis (Jensen, 1997, Charron, 2001).
Utilizing a series such as *Survivor*, avoids overly simplistic, one-shot applications that do not lend themselves to examination of consequences and
possible alternatives. Moreover, providing tools for ethical analysis can
stimulate students' moral imaginations (Jaska & Pritchard, 1994), helping them to become critical media consumers and ultimately, ethical communicators. As demonstrated in the following sample responses, students'
analysis of *Survivor* and *Survivor: The Australian Outback* tested the didac-
tic usefulness of NCA's Credo. The students, who averaged 20 years in
age and primarily identified themselves as Christian (68 percent), were
enrolled in introductory group communication classes at a midwestern
university. The study participants fall in the 18–34 year age group, a primary CBS target for *Survivor*.[1] During fall 2000 and spring 2001, students analyzed weekly episodes of *Survivor* and *Survivor: The Australian
Outback*. Each week students watched an episode, completed an individual written analysis, and then participated in an ongoing small group discussion and written analysis. At the end of the semester, groups had a
cumulative discussion in which they were asked to evaluate the survivors'
communication ethics, using principles from the NCA Credo for Ethical
Communication as a standard. Although the principles are not numbered
in NCA's Credo, they were numbered for this analysis to facilitate discussion (see Appendix A). Group and individual analyses were examined
for evaluations of communication ethics and specific Credo principles.
Group evaluations are represented by two letters or a number they used
to identify themselves (e.g., C.M), while individual comments are marked
by a single letter (e.g., J).[2] Analysis of *Survivor* is referred to as Study 1
and analysis of *Survivor: The Australian Outback* is designated as Study 2.

     Students' evaluations of the communication ethics in both studies
demonstrated awareness of ethical issues as well as debate and critique of
actions. With guidance from the NCA Credo, students evaluated the
overall communication as unethical and gave examples of violations of
every principle. Students' evaluations are grouped into five categories of
values: truthfulness/integrity; freedom of expression; fairness; respect; and
responsibility, the values the Credo's authors ranked highest in importance
(Anderson, 2000).

Truthfulness/Integrity

The first principle of NCA's Credo for Ethical Communication states: "We believe that truthfulness, accuracy, honesty and reason are essential to the integrity of communication." Students in both Study 1 and Study 2 identified blatant lies, half-truths, and lies of omission in the service of strategy. Survivors lied to protect themselves and their alliances in order to engineer others' departures at tribal council. As one group indicated:

> In *Survivor* we noticed both tribes really didn't follow the NCA Credo for Ethical Communication. In Tagi they were two-faced and withheld the truth. For example, Kelly was honest to certain people in the beginning but then she went against that and tried to go off on her own. She also agreed to be with the alliance and then turned her back on them. She tried to be honest to herself but in the end it ended up coming back to haunt her because she wasn't really sure what to do until it was too late. Another example is Rich. Rich didn't openly lie but he worded his way around things. He is a master of words. He was more honest to Rudy but to everyone else he told him or her one thing and then did something else in order to win. In the end he even reminded everyone of how "honest" he was during the whole thing [C.M—Study 1].

Students gave kudos to the Kucha tribe in *Survivor: The Australian Outback* for maintaining group integrity at tribal council, observing, "The team never compromised the integrity of the group. They did use reason when voting for each other, they had good cause and valid points" (#7— Study 2). The successful Ogakor alliance also received praise: "When the alliance between Keith, Colby, and Tina was formed, the trio had a long-term commitment to truthfulness" (3 Cs—Study 2). Conversely, students identified numerous occasions when contestants were less than truthful:

> *Survivor: The Australian Outback* was filled with communication that undermined truthfulness, accuracy and honesty. From Day 1, players were scheming and strategizing as to how they could be the "sole survivor." That strategizing included many instances of being untruthful and untrustworthy. Colby told Jerri a blatant lie when he said he was in an alliance with her. The remaining Ogakor members omitted to tell Amber about the impending mutiny to vote Jerri off. Despite the numerous attempts to unify Ogakor and Kucha in Barramundi, the tribal lines continued to exist, and there were many occasions in which the truth was not told to various members of Kucha regarding specific members being voted off. Also, at each tribal council when members were asked specifically about certain alliances or something they had said about another person, the player either lied or didn't tell the entirety of the truth [J—Study 2].

The cumulative effects of deceptive communication took their toll when alliance members were uncertain if they could trust each other. This created a society where relationships deteriorated, people felt degraded, promises were broken, and contributions to the greater good were withheld. In some cases, people lied without guilt because they rationalized that the other deserved this treatment. "Colby, for example, used 'The end justifies the means' in rationalizing his lying to Jerri" (3C's—Study 2). Furthermore:

> There were too many strategies and schemes for the quality of communication and well being of all individuals to abound. There were too many instances of lying and people bashing that did threaten the quality of the players and their society [J—Study 2].

Freedom of Expression

NCA's Ethical Credo reflects the individual choice citizens enjoy in a democracy: "We endorse freedom of expression, diversity of perspective, and tolerance of dissent to achieve the informed and responsible decision-making fundamental to a civil society." In *Survivor*, Pagong followed this second principle more closely than Tagi, but still violated it. For instance, BB was dogmatic in his decision of where to build the shelter. He would not listen to others' perspectives or take suggestions, so Pagong members (with the exception of Gretchen) stopped trying to discuss decisions with him. After BB's departure, Pagong became more accepting of diverse viewpoints.

> In the beginning Rudy (Tagi) was very commanding and just told people what to do and didn't want to hear anyone else's opinion. Pagong was a lot more accepting of opinions except in the very beginning with BB. While he was there everyone fought a lot about where to put the shelter, about food, and about how to do things. After he left things seemed to be a lot more fun and people listened and respected each other more [C.M—Study 1, parentheses added].

In *Survivor: The Australian Outback*, Kucha's Kimmi found that her objections to eating meat caused tensions that erupted in a confrontation with Alicia. Most students viewed this quarrel as showing a lack of respect and tolerance for Kimmi's beliefs; however, others saw it as open expression of diverse perspectives. The competitive goal structure generally restrained open expression. An exception to this occurred after the merger when Barramundi tribe members were permitted to talk with their families via the Internet.

> "Freedom of expression and perspective diversity" of NCA credo was also not upheld. Kimmi and Alicia fight over chickens and no one really respects Kimmi's perspective on being a vegetarian, they get annoyed with her. Speech is restrained because survivors use what they say to manipulate people (alliances), get on people's good side (lip service) and distort the perspective of the group [I.I—Study 2].

Students' evaluations noted tensions between individual expression and the rights of the other. Rich was open about his homosexuality and didn't face direct intolerance, although ex–Pagong members voiced dissent against his nudity. Dirk's religious witnessing irritated Sue and Rudy, and their comments indicated intolerance of his frequent Bible reading. Sue's impassioned address to the jury compared Richard to a snake and Kelly to a rat. Those words, however, paled beside the venom Sue showed when she said that she wouldn't give Kelly a drink of water if she were dying of thirst in the desert. One group commented, "Sue degraded and did not show respect to anyone, especially Kelly, when they began having large conflicts with each other" (CU—Study 1) and another noted:

> Rich did this (expressed himself freely) and everyone was okay with his walking around naked but Colleen didn't like it. Sue and Rudy ripped on Dirk about his religious beliefs. Dirk was irritated that Richard talked about his homosexuality so much but didn't express it to him [7HJS—Study 1].

Students in Study 2 singled out Jerri for the intensity and number of her degrading communications. A variety of negative effects from degrading communication were noted, including injustice and diminished self-esteem.

> Jerri continually degraded Keith by picking on his cooking and Keith likewise said nasty things about Jerri, i.e., "The witch is dead..." Other instances include when Michael spoke about Kimmi not bathing, Jerri said that Kel had beef jerky, Alicia yelled at Kimmi for liking the chickens, and Colby lost his temper with Keith serving large portions [J.—Study 2].
>
> Jerri's hostile attitude and need for control created an environment that made individuals feel uncared for, misunderstood, and disrespected. Jerri's nonverbals and sarcastic attitude towards Keith were degrading. Even though he was a well-known chef, she made him feel insignificant [I.I—Study 2].

Fairness

Several NCA Credo principles relate to fairness, most notably the claim that: "We are committed to the courageous expression of personal convictions in pursuit of fairness and justice." Students analyzing *Survivor* did not give examples of violations or applications of principle number seven. One possibility for this absence is that *Survivor* contestants were, for the most part, pursing strategic advantage rather than fairness. Another explanation is that degrading communication kept expressions of personal convictions to a minimum. One example of the courageous expressions of personal convictions comes from Episode 8, when Sean declared that he was ethically against any kind of alliance. In response, Rich commented, "I consider myself ethical and moral. But it sounds like pure stupidity." Students who analyzed *Survivor: The Australian Outback*, however, provided examples of "courageous expressions." Maralyn and Kimmi stood up to their tribes and expressed convictions about basic values that left them standing alone. Rodger sacrificed a position in the final four because he thought the money should go to the person who needed it most.

> The only bright stars in this night of unethical behavior were when Maralyn tried to get a group apology for Kel, when Tina was honest and up front with Elisabeth about voting her off, and when Rodger decided to step out first and go before Elisabeth.... Kimmi was courageous enough to hold her value of being a vegetarian, even when there was a chance for her to be kicked off because of what she believed [I.I—Study 2].

NCA's Credo also states, "We advocate sharing information, opinions, and feelings when facing significant choices while also respecting privacy and confidentiality." People need information in order to make knowledgeable decisions and to construct persuasive arguments for their positions. Tribes both followed and ignored this principle. Sharing took place in large group tasks, such as building shelter and creating a distress signal. However, some thoughts and feelings were only verbalized in smaller groupings or to the camera. Within the smaller units, people acknowledged differences but put joint goals ahead of disagreements. The secret Tagi alliance controlled tribal council decisions, revealing its existence through voting patterns (Study 1).

> It seemed that the "hidden" agendas really came into light when the tribes merged into one and formed Rattana. The alliance was evident to the "Pagong" members when "Pagong" members got kicked off at tribal council [C.M.—Study 1].

Survivors monitored information that they shared because they didn't want tribal council votes to go against them. The voting strategy for tribal council became a closely guarded secret among alliance members, or between the alliances within the alliance. In spite of this context, a couple of tribal council decisions did follow principle eight (Study 2). Kucha members talked with each other about some decisions and strategies. Tina discussed the vote that eliminated Rodger with him before it took place.

> Information was not treated ethically as it was filtered for manipulative reasons or kept secret. For example, when tribes merged, the animosity between Keith and Jerri was downplayed [I.I—Study 2].
>
> In our opinion, the most significant choice that can be made in the game of *Survivor* is who to vote off in tribal council. When the Barramundi tribe was facing the decision to vote off Jerri, once again the members of the group did not express the ideas written in the Credo. During this decision, the Ogakor alliance did not share any information to two of the members in their alliance. . In accordance with the Credo, the Ogakor alliances should have discussed their reasoning (behind why Jerri was about to be voted off) with all of the group members [Detail—Study 2].

The credo also states: "access to communication resources and opportunities is necessary to fulfill human potential and contribute to the well-being of families, communities, and society." Students' evaluations in both Study 1 and 2 viewed communication resources existing mainly outside the tribes (Internet communication and family members). The competitive game structure may influence this interpretation. Students acknowledged the importance some individuals placed on meeting social needs within the tribe.

> Communication from home and resources from families helped them personally to continue with the game. Jenna was affected greatly because she didn't get something. Kelly began to bond with the members of ex–Pagong, because of the social needs she had [7HJS—Study 1].

Respect

The NCA Credo advocates the creation of "communication climates of caring and mutual understanding that respect the unique needs and characteristics of individual communicator." The competitive goal structure in *Survivor* influenced people to jump to conclusions and distrust, rather than respect each other. Students were more likely to provide examples of breaches rather than of positive applications of this principle. Both Tagi and Pagong evaluated and responded to messages without respect and understanding of communicators.

> The Ogakor tribe didn't try to strive to understand and respect Kel's stance before looking through his bag for beef jerky. They didn't believe him, even though they had no evidence ... Communication was not clear because people read into messages or manipulated messages [I.I—Study 2].
>
> Due to the nature of the game, this was hard to instill in *Survivor* as everyone was to be viewed as "the enemy." A specific opposition to this code was displayed after Colby became upset with Keith for serving the large portions and Colby began evaluating Keith's every statement and intention. Another example was found in the paranoia many experienced when they would see people in groups, possibly discussing who was the next to go [J.—Study 2].

Overall, Pagong, the more relationship-oriented tribe, came across as generally caring, understanding, and respectful. Students expressed suspicion about Kelly's friendly actions to Pagong after the merger. Tagi's Sue, Rich and Rudy violated principle number five. Rich admitted that trying to maintain thumbs on all these people's personalities that he cared little about was wearing on him. Rudy bluntly said, "I'll probably never see these people again. That's the way I want it." On the other hand:

> Colleen—is concerned for others and at least attempting to keep her morals ... Colleen is a truly nice person and even stated how she could not be mean. She said, "Play fair. Be nice" [CU—Study 1].
>
> Pagong used it because of their relational skills. Kelly used it when the two tribes met ... she may have used it to her benefit because she knew everyone's personal background [SHJS—Study 1].

Elisabeth and Tina promoted "caring and mutual understanding" while Jerri did not. When environmental and emotional conditions worsened in Barramundi, survivors drew together for support. Students primarily mentioned women's actions in their analysis of this principle.

> This was displayed in many conversations involving Elisabeth and Tina. Both of these women filled social-emotional roles in the *Survivor* tribes and they were able to promote caring understanding. In the instance when Elisabeth and Tina gave Colby flowers for his Pontiac Aztec, they were genuine in the gift and promoted a climate of caring. Jerri was the most obvious about opposing this ethic as she had no qualms about not respecting other's needs or being uncaring towards them [J.—Study 2].

Responsibility

The NCA Credo states: "We accept responsibility for the short- and long-term consequences for our own communication and expect the same of others." The tribal council, as well as the final jury vote, kept people accountable for their behaviors. However, survivors did not always accept responsibility for their actions and expressed surprise when the vote went against them.

> Rich was so strategic, had the goal in mind. Sue and Kelly were in it for the long term, but when the groups emerged, Kelly changed her mind and Sue didn't take that too well. Some of the members were using immediate actions (winning the game). Kelly wasn't ready to take the consequences of being in the alliance [SHJS—Study 1].
>
> In the beginning Ramona became sick and was unable to help the group out, then, as she became better, she tried to merge back into the group. BUT, the moral was, too little too late. They expected her to accept responsibility, and the consequences [CU—Study 1].

Students saw Colby's choice to bring Tina into the final two as ethical, because it was based on his promise to her and not on his own short-term self-interest. However, students noted that the choice might have long-term positive consequences.

> Especially near the end, the Barramundi tribe accepted responsibility for the choices they made. They made sure to communicate thoroughly and base their votes on that communication. Colby chose to bring Tina into the final two, knowing that his chance of winning would be significantly impaired. He chose to do this, based on their previous communication, rather than on what would help him win [#7—Study 2].
>
> This principle is especially evident when the two tribes merged into Barramundi. All members of this group expressed how they were afraid of being mean while voting off other people. They were hesitant to be honest because they all knew that the people they voted off would later be voting for the winner. This is definitely the only aspect of the Credo that was followed by all cast members of *Survivor 2* [Detail—Study 2].

Conclusions

Students agreed that communication in both *Survivor* series was generally unethical, but disagreed in their views of the game's ethics and of individual actions within it. Views expressed included: (1) *Survivor* is not an ethical game, and one must play by its rules to succeed; (2) *Survivor* is a "game," and constitutes a special context for judging the ethical quality of actions; and (3) *Survivor* is not an ethical game, but one can choose how to act.

Students who advocated for the first view argued that *Survivor* is a competitive game and one must communicate unethically (operate within the framework rules) in order to succeed. Choosing to participate in the game is an ethical decision.

> In the game of *Survivor*, the theme of the game is Outwit, Outplay, and Outlast. By its very nature, then, *Survivor* entails unethical communication to achieve one's individual goals. In fact, to win, one must systematically break almost every guideline of the NCA Credo for Ethical Communication. Perhaps the only ethical principle that could eventually be followed by everyone is accepting short/long term responsibility of his or her communication [Fab Four—Study 2].

The second perspective argues that games such as *Survivor* constitute a special context. Actions can range from ethical to unethical, but are ultimately interpreted as part of a game.

> In the *Survivor 2* Finale, each jury member was given the opportunity to ask Tina and Colby a final question. Rodger's question dealt specifically with ethics and morality. Rodger posed this question, "Have you played the game as ethically as you could have?" Both Tina and Colby's responses stated that yes; they were as ethical as they could have been within the context of the game. A game such as *Survivor* poses special exceptions, influences and twists on what is considered ethical. However, the NCA gives some universal ethical principles that are fundamental "whenever people communicate." There are many cases in which *Survivor* coincided with these ethics and even more that they opposed. If a formal conclusion is to be made, according to the NCA's standards, the communication tactics used on *Survivor* were as a whole, unethical. However, abiding to the nature and purpose of the game, one must be able to recognize that communication on *Survivor* was in a different context and poses a different perspective [J—Study 2].

Survivor is not an ethical game in the third view, but individuals can choose whether they act ethically or unethically. Ethical behavior is evaluated according to principles that apply across contexts.

> In one word, *Survivor* is *NOT* an ethical game. Most of the action of the group is centered on an "everyone for him/herself" attitude. This is clear in how big strategy is. For example, both Maralyn and Tina were

involved in backstabbing their friends for the sake of strategy. Maralyn did not agree with voting off Kel, yet she did go with the crowd. Tina was friends with Maralyn, yet she voted her off for the sake of strategy. This shows selfish tactics of the survivors and violated ethical trust [I.I.].

Individuals make choices in all of these perspectives. In the first view individuals choose whether to participate in a competitive game and whether or not they will strive to win. The cost of winning may be too high for some individuals, who may change strategy or suffer conscience pangs, as did Kelly.

Individuals choose to act more or less ethically in the second view. However, they redefine what constitutes ethical behavior in a competitive game context. Tina, for example, reflected upon her actions at the final tribal council. She admitted that she didn't tell Amber that it was her time to go and regretting opening Kel's bag when he was accused of eating beef jerky. However, she placed actions within the context of the game. "When you play backgammon you know you have to cover that man. There was nothing personal. It was a strategy and that's all there is."

Individuals choose to act ethically or unethically in the third view. Actions are judged according to principles that promote justice, etc. Principles are universal, so actions are ethical or unethical across contexts. Rodger's decision to leave first because Elisabeth needed the money for her mother's hospital bills exemplifies this view.

The three views that emerged may represent different levels of moral reasoning. The third view, for example, shares characteristics with Kolberg's post-conventional thinking (Jaska & Pritchard, 1994). Other comparisons can be made to reasoning from consequences, rules, and virtues. Benne (1988) describes egoism (self-enhancement), heteronomy (loyalty to the group), autonomy (reasoning from a universal base), and theonomy (striving to follow God's will). The search for truth/search for virtue differs between European and Asian cultures (Hofstede & Bond in Lustig & Koester, 2003). Future research needs to examine whether the views that emerged in the *Survivor* studies surface in other samples, to explore reasoning behind the views, and to make comparisons with stages and levels others have identified.

A recommendation based upon this research is to provide the NCA Credo for Ethical Communication to students early and often. Students in Study 1 received the NCA Credo for their final discussion. Students in Study 2 received it four times, beginning with episode 8. Students in Study 2 provided more examples of Credo principles and greater detail in explanations. The Credo repetition provides one explanation for the differences.

Negative applications (violations) of the NCA Credo were identified with greater frequency than positive applications in the *Survivor* studies. Jensen (1997) suggests that our attention is naturally drawn to negative occurrences, but that the Ethical Quality Scale can aid us in also seeing positive examples. Instead of asking whether an action is ethical or unethical, the seven point EQ scale asks *how* ethical it is, extracting a "degree of ethical quality" (p.7). Instructors can ask students to evaluate the degree of ethical quality of NCA Credo principles.

Students' applications of the NCA Credo for Ethical Communication to the *Survivor* series suggest that the Credo and the series are useful pedagogical tools. The NCA Credo's use can stimulate students' "moral imaginations" and help them develop moral sensitivity and reasoning. Instructors can and need to help their students mature ethically as well as intellectually.

> As the mass media are an important source of meanings for many people, they contribute to our understanding of human dignity and respect for life. When their images and messages rob people of their dignity, we do not remain unaffected.... They disclose what life is worth and how human dignity is valued or devalued [Traber, 1997, p. 341].

The importance of stimulating our students to critically reflect upon media messages may be the most valuable lesson we can gleam from *Survivor*.

Appendix A: NCA Credo for Ethical Communication

Questions of right and wrong arise whenever people communicate. Moreover, ethical communication is fundamental to responsible thinking, decision-making, and the development of relationships and communities within and across contexts, cultures, channels, and media. Ethical communication enhances human worth and dignity by fostering truthfulness, fairness, responsibility, personal integrity, and respect for self and others. We believe that unethical communication threatens the quality of all communication and consequently the well-being of individuals and the society in which we live.

Therefore we, the members of the National Communication Association, endorse and are committed to practicing the following principles of ethical communication:

1. We believe that truthfulness, accuracy, honesty, and reason are essential to the integrity of communication.[3]

2. We endorse freedom of expression, diversity of perspective, and tolerance of dissent to achieve the informed and responsible decision-making fundamental to a civil society.

3. We strive to understand and respect other communicators before evaluating and responding to their messages.

4. We believe that access to communication resources and opportunities is necessary to fulfill human potential and contribute to the well-being of families, communities, and society.

5. We promote communication climates of caring and mutual understanding that respect the unique needs and characteristics of individual communicators.

6. We condemn communication that degrades individuals and humanity through distortion, intolerance, intimidation, coercion, hatred, and violence.

7. We are committed to the courageous expression of personal convictions in pursuit of fairness and justice.

8. We advocate sharing information, opinions, and feelings when facing significant choices while also respecting privacy and confidentiality.

9. We accept responsibility for the short- and long-term consequences for our own communication and expect the same of others.

Endnotes

1. CBS's strategy was successful, as unprecedented numbers of 18–34 age viewers watched the show. *Survivor*'s third episode outdrew the other 5 networks combined in this demographic group (Grover, 2000). By the 12th episode, 975 percent more 18–34 age viewers watched *Survivor* than watched during the same night and time period the previous year, the largest gain for any age group (TV: News, 2000).

2. *Informed consent.* Students were informed about the study and asked for written permission to use their work in analysis and publication. They were also asked for permission to identify groups and individuals by group name and/or initials. They were assured that withholding permission would not affect their grade in the course.

3. The principles are not numbered in the NCA Credo for Ethical communication. The numbers were added for ease of identification in this study.

References

Andersen, K. E. (2000). Developments in communication ethics: The ethics commission, code of professional responsibilities, credo for ethical communication. *Journal of the Association for Communication Administration, 29,* 131–144.

Benne, R. (1988). *Ordinary saints.* Philadelphia: Fortress Press.

Charron, L. (2001, November). *Connecting communication theory, ethics, and the profession.* Paper presented at the annual convention of the National Communication Association, Atlanta, GA.

Grover, R. (2000, June 20). For CBS, *Survivor* is a strategy—and a fountain of youth. *BusinessWeek Online.* Retrieved January 24, 2003, from http://www.businessweek.com/bwdaily/dnflash/june2000/nf00620c.htm

Hess, J. (1995, November). *Life in the intersection of social science, rhetoric, and philosophy: Teaching ethics in small group communication.* Paper presented at the annual convention of the Speech Communication Association, San Antonio, TX.

Jaska, J., & Pritchard, M. S. (1994). *Communication ethics: Methods of analysis.* Belmont, CA: Wadsworth.

Jensen, J. V. (1997). *Ethical issues in the communication process.* Mahwah, N.J.: Lawrence Erlbaum.

Lustig, M. W., & Koester, J. (2003). *Intercultural competence: Interpersonal communication across cultures.* New York: Longman.

National Communication Association. (1999). *Credo for ethical communication.* Retrieved December 4, 2001, from http://natcom.org/policies/External/EthnicalComm.htm

Rest, J. (1982). A psychologist's look at the teaching of ethics. *The Hastings Center Report, 12,* 29–36.

Survivor. (n.d.). Retrieved December 7, 2001, from http://www.cbs.com/primetime/Survivor

Survivor: The Australian Outback (n.d.). Retrieved December 7, 2001, from http://www.cbs.com/primetime/survivor2/polls/index.html

Traber, M. (1997). Conclusion: An ethics of communication worthy of human beings. In Christians, C., & Traber, M. (Eds.) *Communication ethics and universal values* (pp. 327–343). Thousand Oaks, CA: Sage.

TV news: News daily. (2000, August 17). *Survivor* breaks new records. Retrieved January 24, 2003, from http://tv.zap2it.com/news/tvnewsdaily.html?10907

12

Traveling the Terrain of Screened Realities: Our Reality, Our Television

Marcy R. Chvasta
and
Deanna L. Fassett

"Like a Virgin" (Operative Word Being "Like")

I have been trying to watch Murder in Small Town X, *but only with marginal success. After seeing five episodes, I am pretty sure I hate this show (which is strange given my predilection toward novels like* The Bone Collector *and shows like* The X-Files*). But I am something of a reality-TV virgin, and I feel as though I am missing out. I have no "survivor stories," no office cooler reflections on what has happened in last night's episode, no means to pontificate on who should be voted off the island. And so, each week, I find myself planted in front of my television set, trying desperately to enjoy a show that I am coming to hate, pointing out to the television that Kristen is socially repulsive and should be sent off to be murdered (of course, her peers keep trying, but Kristen returns each time, ever more vengeful and brewing with heinousness). Sadly, no one around my office cooler has actually seen this show, so perhaps I have made a poor choice. I suck at this game.*

In this chapter, we weave narratives of our own experiences with (reality) television with theories of truth and falsity, and liveness and mediation. In particular, we incorporate the philosophies of Jacques Der-

rida (1972/1982) and the media theories of John Ellis (1992) and Pierre
Lévy (1998) to highlight the ways our perception of electronic screens
and their content have an impact our perception of the world around us.
Take note that one of us is an avid viewer of reality television. The other
is trying to become one. In either case, we learn and shape our realities
in part from experiencing reality television. Central to our endeavors here
is our desire to tease out the onto-epistemological complexities of what
constitutes "reality" in contemporary Western mediated society. We invite
our readers to explore the narrative and philosophical voices of this essay
as they would any other virtual text—as a foil for their own careful
reflection and theorizing.

Diegetic and Non-Diegetic Elements
(and What They Can Mean for You)

Diegetic and non-diegetic elements are essential to any television
show—or movie, or story, or play, or song, or painting, for that matter.
Briefly, diegesis is the story being told (*what* is being conveyed); anything
else you perceive is non-diegetic, or narration (*how* the story is conveyed—
e.g., the use of multiple cameras, the manipulation of lighting and sound).
For instance, many of us know the story of *The Wizard of Oz*, but not too
many of us take note of the elements that carry the story along and perhaps enhance it. Changing the film from black and white to color when
Dorothy opens her door to Oz is but one example of the deployment of
non-diegetic elements. Sure, the movie could have been made only in
black and white, but would it have been as spectacular? Probably not.

An important difference between early television and today's reality
programming is that the programming of the mid-twentieth century was
low on non-diegetic elements. Broadcasting companies and local television stations did not have the money, the means, or the vision to film
shows in ways beyond the theatrical tradition. Moreover, the actors and
the photographers did not have the technological savvy to downplay the
non-diegetic elements the way professionals do today. As Baughman
(1992) notes, television viewers of the late 1940s "could often see the
microphone boom" bobbing in and out of the screen during live broadcasts (p. 41). Moments such as that may well have had the power to remind
the viewers that the action on screen was not "real."

In contrast, unscripted shows of recent years are highly produced;
every attempt is made to make the audience forget that a narrator exists.
Non-diegetic elements (such as editing) are made as transparent as pos-

sible. Networks and producers want us to believe in the reality of reality-television. Given the ratings (e.g., see Carter, 2001; Littleton, 2001), it seems that we do. But we are smarter than that. Even if we do not pay much attention to the constructed-ness of reality TV, we know it is there, just like we know that professional wrestling is "staged." We are attracted to reality programming for what it represents: the drama of the human condition, to put it a bit loftily. Even if events did not transpire the way they seem on the screen, reality programming shows us the way things *could have* transpired. It displays the potential of human beings to be certain ways in various contexts. We witness others being alternately kind, cruel, strong, sorry, and sweet. We project ourselves into their situations and decide whether we would behave similarly.

Although we can perceive fictional programming is the same way, we cannot be assured that "actual" people would behave as the characters do. Reality shows are filled with people who are held accountable for their actions—both on the show and when they return to their "real" lives. We delight in their accountability; we demand it. Hopefully, and arguably frequently, we learn from the participants' mistakes.

"I Am So Glad I Am Not You": Lessons by Negation

Every Tuesday night, fighting the urge to do anything else, I sit down on the couch to watch Murder in Small Town X. *Each week, two "investigators" (i.e., contestants) are sent out into the town to look for a murder clue; one comes back with a clue and the other is dispatched in a gruesome but ambiguous way. Interestingly creepy, I thought. But now, after five or six episodes, I think I hate watching it. But then, why do I keep watching? Mainly because I hate Kristen so much I hope she will die in the next episode. Kristen has managed to enrage every member of the show since the first episode. They keep voting her "off the island" in a sense, sending her out to slaughter, but she keeps coming back, much to their disdain. And my own. I wonder if Kristen's repeated good luck is a nasty ploy on the part of Fox to perpetuate the contentious element of the show. In watching the first episode, I found myself wondering who these people were and how they got to be on the show. Later though, I just wondered what sort of person would subject her/himself to this scrutiny. And then I began to wonder what sort of person I was to be scrutinizing. I wonder if I care. Nevertheless, each week I wish her murder... What does this say about me?*

Ironically enough, reality television frequently forces me to differentiate between the world on the screen and the world around me. When I watch reality television, I learn lessons by negation. Whether the show is Murder in

Small Town X, or The Real World, *or (especially)* Cops, *I find myself trying to interact with the screen, belting: "Good grief! How stupid are you? You are so not-me! I am so glad I'm not you!" Rather than easily identifying with the people (as networks invite us to with messages like, "Look! People just like you are on TV! You could be too!"), I am encouraged by reality television to distance myself from the bodies on the screen. I find fault in nearly everything they do. I perceive them as subjects of severe criticism and objects of ridicule. I learn how not-to-be when I watch reality television. But I also cringe, seeing myself in the people projected. Could it be that Kristen annoys me so because I see a tiny bit of myself in her?*

In *Margins of Philosophy*, Derrida (1972/1982) introduces his thoughts on *differánce*. Drawing from the work of Ferdinand de Saussure, *differánce* is designated by Derrida as "the movement according to which language, or any code, any system of referral in general, is constituted 'historically' as a weave of differences" (p. 12). Signifiers (such as "reality" and "television") at once differ from and defer to other signifiers (such as "truth" and "falsity"). This simultaneous difference and deferral constitute meaning for us; despite this simultaneity, however, we tend to focus only on difference (e.g., "Reality is true because it most certainly is not false."). We often do not recognize that every signifier is constituted by a multiplicity of signifiers that are constituted by a multiplicity of others—that any sign not only differs from others, but also defers to (points toward and depends upon) others. For example, over time, "reality" has come to be associated with "truth," and "television" with "falsity." What we often forget, however, is that we can only understand "reality" in relation to "television," and "truth" in relation to "falsity." Later in this chapter, we will further explore these relationships. For now, it is important to note that phenomena that appear to be oppositional—or, mutually exclusive—are actually interconnected, interdependent, and co-constitutive. Rather than focusing solely on the differences between phenomena (including the ways in which we perceive ourselves and others), we should also take not of the connection between phenomena and how that connection is vital to our understanding of the world around us.

"Reality Television": Neither Oxymoronic Nor Redundant

Something need not be true to be truthful. Sixteenth century Shakespearean classics like *Othello* and *The Taming of the Shrew* spoke to the people of the time and they continue to speak to twenty-first century audiences (although they are often re-contextualized for modern audiences as in the cases of *Moonlighting* and *Ten Things I Hate about You*). Fictionalized accounts of "authentic" historical events—ranging from ocean liner (*Titanic*) to moon rocket (*Apollo 13*) catastrophes, and from the reigns of Joan of Arc to Bill Clinton-esque presidents (*Primary Colors*)—attract audiences generation after generation. Is truth as important as garnering empathy? And, what is the relationship between "truth" and "reality" television?

When "truth" and "falsity" are respectively connected to "reality" and "television," one perceives "reality-TV" to be an oxymoron. In other words, television, as a fictional, contrived world, could not, by its very nature, be real. Such a perception, however, is problematic, primarily because the relationship between "truth" and "falsity" is not as tidy as one might think. Derrida has spent several decades highlighting the ways in which Western thought has been fueled by metaphysical binary mechanisms (such as truth-falsity)—all of which are structured in terms of the binary presence-absence. Binaries of any kind (e.g., presence-absence, truth-falsity, good-bad), as Derrida (1972/1982) explains, are "never the face-to-face of two terms, but a hierarchy and an order of subordination" (p. 329). Derrida names this order of subordination "logocentrism." Quite simply, within logocentric discourse, "presence" renders something good, "absence" renders something bad. Furthermore, for our purposes here, it is important to note that in logocentric discourse, presence is equated with truth; absence is equated with falsity. Thus, in Western (mediated and capitalist) societies, anything that is not associated with presence (truth) has the potential to be looked upon poorly.

For many years, media theorists such as Ellis (1992) have argued that television has the power to create presence in ways other media cannot. That is, when we watch television in the comfort of our own homes, night after night, week after week, we get a sense of immediacy. The images on the screen are right there with us, time and again. The action feels as if it is happening in the present, right here and now. It feels as though we are watching "the real" unfold, that we are co-present with the bodies projected on the screen. We find comfort in the seeming presence as it creates a sense of reality, of truth. It allows us to believe that we know the difference between what is real and what is not, what is true and what is not. Yet, as Derrida (1972/1982) would argue, the relationship between presence-absence and truth-falsity has always been more complicated than most like to acknowledge.

Designating "reality" and "television" as oppositional also implies a clear difference between "live" and "mediated." As Philip Auslander (1996) argues in his essay "Liveness: Performance and the Anxiety of Simulation," such a distinction is not only simplistic but also detrimental to our understanding of the world within which we live. There is no "live" without "mediated"; in this age of mediation, there is no "reality" without "television." Each of the significations has no meaning without the other; each of the signified exists only in relation to the other. Evidence of such complex relationships can be found in early television's live broadcasts or contemporary projections of "live" events such as music concerts on MTV. Reality-television and liveness-mediation are murky pairings that either can hinder or fruitfully complicate our perception of the world around us.

When I was a child, growing up in the 1970s, I really, really, really wanted to be the Bionic Woman. Who could blame me? I saw Jamie Sommers as stronger and smarter than any male foe she faced. I watched her jump enormous heights, pulverize metal with her bare hands, and hear the tiniest of sounds. I saw her do it all in wondrous slow motion. I projected myself into the screen every week. I re-enacted her adventures daily. When I was the Bionic Woman, I was stronger and smarter than my brother and his friends. When I was the Bionic Woman, I moved in slow motion, faster than any other mere mortal. I was everything I was not in real life. Or, at least, I thought I was.

Fortunately for me, my experience with The Bionic Woman *helped me to become stronger and smarter than I thought I could be. Unfortunately, I did not want to be a Bionic Woman; I wanted to be* the *Bionic Woman. It was not enough to be* like *Jamie Sommers; I hoped to wake up one day as Jamie Sommers. Or, more to the point, I prayed to be able to walk, talk, and look just like Lindsay Wagner. Some might say that I was not as bright as other kids my age, for I did not really distinguish between actor and character. But I believe I knew what I was doing. I realized that any separation between actor and character would take the fun out of television viewing. Rather than cleanly differentiating between reality and television, I allowed the world on the screen to exist with the same force as the world around me. More often than not, I think I am a better person for having done (and sometimes continuing to do) so.*

In other problematic ways, "reality television" can be (and often is) seen as a redundancy. That is, as we argue above, reality and whatever we see on the screen are not mutually exclusive; one can never be separated from the other because each influences the other. Perhaps it is better to say that reality television is something in between an oxymoron and a redundancy. We could make the case that all of television is reality-based programming. Borders necessarily bleed between reality and fiction or fantasy. Anyone who has ever taken a basic fiction-writing course knows that most writers will advise you to write what you know. However, were we to interpret this advice literally, our individual and collective imaginations would wither on the vine. (Sometimes we have to write beyond what "is" and focus on what "could be.") To believe that "reality-based television" is somehow more real than, say, fictional programming is to believe in a modernist fantasy. Perhaps it is better to focus our attention on contemplating the nature of and relationship between what "is" and what "could be."

"Virtuality Television" (or, Learning from the Digital Age)

In *Becoming Virtual: Reality in the Digital Age*, digital media theorist Pierre Lévy (1998) contemplates the relationship between "the real" and its presumed counterpart "the virtual": "Consider the simple and misleading opposition between the real and the virtual. As it is currently used, the word 'virtual' is often meant to signify the absence of existence, whereas 'reality' implies a material embodiment, a tangible presence" (p. 23). As a scholar of digital media technologies (media that arguably demand perceptual adjustments), Lévy is dissatisfied with these connotations. He seeks to determine more precisely the complicated nuances of "reality." Much like the French philosophers Derrida (1972/1982), Gilles Deleuze (1968/ 1994), and Félix Guattari (1992/1995), Lévy challenges perceptions of reality that are founded in metaphysical binaries. Lévy states, "[T]he virtual, strictly defined, has little relationship to that which is false, illusory, or imaginary. *The virtual is by no means the opposite of the real*" (p. 16; emphasis added). Lévy continues, further defining the virtual in relation to the physical: "[The virtual] is a fecund and powerful mode of being that expands the process of creation, opens up the future, injects a core of meaning beneath the platitude of immediate physical presence" (p. 16). This "immediate physical presence" or "tangible presence" is what is often mistakenly construed as "reality." We agree with Lévy that "reality" is not—must not be—so easily defined.

Lévy embraces and extends Guattari's (1992/1995) "four ontological functors" (outlined in Guattari's *Chaomosis: An Ethico-Aesthetic Paradigm*): the real, the possible, the actual, and the virtual. Each of these functors—or "vectors," in Lévy's (1998) terms—operates "almost always" (p. 176) in conjunction with the others. Levy is not interested in these vectors as *stable* modes of existence. Rather, he is interested in "*the process of transformation from one mode of being to another*" (p. 16; emphasis in original). Specifically, he engages in the "study of virtualization that ascends from the real or the actual toward the virtual" (p. 16). According to Lévy, this transformation moves in the opposite direction from the transformation that always has been studied in the philosophical tradition (from the virtual or actual to the real). This is significant, for while actualization moves from problem to solution, "virtualization [moves] from a given solution to a (different) problem" (p. 27). While the real is present-oriented (in the temporal and spatial sense of the term), the virtual is future-oriented.

In the following passage, Lévy (1998) offers his reading of Deleuze's (1968/1994) distinctions (outlined in *Difference and Repetition*) between the possible and the real:

> The possible is already fully constituted, but exists in a state of limbo. It can be realized without any change occurring either in its determination or nature. It is a phantom reality, something latent. The possible is exactly like the real, the only thing missing being existence. The realization of a possible is not an act of creation in the fullest sense of the word, for creation implies the innovative production of an idea or form. The difference between the possible and the real is thus purely logical [p. 24].

This difference, however, is not often recognized in everyday life. There is a tendency to mistake the possible for the real—to concretize that which, technically, is without existence.

This is perhaps most notable in our perception of electronic images— images that *seem* real, but are not. Whether in the context of reality television or fictional series/sitcoms, we tend to be careless in our perceptual processing of images. Our carelessness results in misperceptions—stereotypes and the reification of signifiers. We have a tendency to concretize the possible. Perceiving images as *virtual* is a way to *resist* concretization. Lévy (1998), further discussing the relationship between the possible and the virtual, states:

> The virtual should, properly speaking, be compared not to the real but the actual. Unlike the possible, which is static and already constituted, the virtual is a kind of *problematic complex*, the knot of tendencies or forces that accompanies a situation, event, object, or entity, and which invokes a process of resolution: actualization [p. 24; emphasis added].

The relationship between the four vectors is transformative, the movement circular. The virtual tends toward the actual, which tends toward the possible or the real, which—for the sake of resisting reification— should be conceptualized virtually. This is not say that there is no real. Rather, *the real is more a process or an event than a thing*. It is to say that reality, like the possible, when perceived as concrete, strips away at potentiality—the essence, perhaps, of life. Lévy (1998), although not explicitly referring to potentiality as life, uses evocative language to caution against concretization:

> Only in reality do things have clearly defined limits. Virtualization, the transition to a problematic, the shift from being to question, necessarily calls into question the classical notion of identity, conceived in terms of definition, determination, exclusion, inclusion, and excluded middles. For this reason virtualization is always heterogenesis, a becoming other, an embrace of alterity. We should not confuse heterogenesis with alienation, its intimate and menacing opposite, its enemy sister, which I would characterize as reification, a reduction to the thing, to the "real" [p. 34].

For the reasons and example we offer above, reification must be recognized and questioned when faced with phenomena. We must resist our tendencies to concretize the possible and simplify the real. We must adjust our perceptual process to recognize virtuality rather than mis-perceiving reality.

As (reality) television continues to influence—even partially constitute—our everyday existence, it seems that many people seek to make clear distinctions between the real and the not-real, reality and appearance, truth and falsity. In a way, we can view these attempts as resisting the reification of media images. For example, when we see a gorgeous, rail-thin blonde woman on television—in an episode of *Friends* or *The Real World*—we may say to ourselves: "Not everyone is like that—nor should they be." Yet, we cannot help but be affected by others' perceptions of her. More often than not, audiences view media images as the possible concretized: "That blonde exists on TV and should therefore constitute our reality; I must be the rail-thin blonde." We should view this woman as "the virtual" rather than actualizing her or concretizing her possibility. To resist reification, we should look at the woman and problematize her— ask how and to what ends she might exist otherwise. We must note that our perception of her is constituted by our perception of other phenomena, as well as our understanding of the relationship between those phenomena (signs defer from and defer to other signs). We should avoid accepting simple (logocentric) relationships between signs, such as thin=reality=truth=good. The rail-thin blonde woman must be viewed as a virtual body, even though she exists in the world. Adjusting our perception to read televised images—within the context of fiction or "reality"—as virtual will enable us to have a better understanding of (the complexities of) reality.

Truth and Consequences

As I watch Murder in Small Town X, *I find I am less charitable, less willing to suspend my disbelief than I am when I watch an episode of a fictional show like* The X-Files. *Paradoxically,* Murder *seems contrived. Perhaps this is because these "real" folk are tossed into a fictional scenario, with elaborate gaming rules that most of us do not experience in "real life." Furthermore, the non-diegetic elements are too present. I am acutely aware of the cameras in ways that I am not when I watch fictional programming. As the final credits role, I wonder what I am to take away from this series. Though this series is marketed as entertainment, a little piece of reality—simulated and commodified for my own pleasure—there is so much more to it. This show, and shows like it, is teaching me about my own reality, however welcome or unwelcome the lessons.*[1] *People concerned with reality-based programming often point to the rawness, the starkness of the participants; shows are often edited to reveal what will garner the most ratings—conflict, anger, fear, jealousy. What does it mean for me, as a viewer, to see this overly aggressive, conniving aspect of their participants' lives each week?*

No doubt I come to appreciate conflict as a natural and necessary aspect of human relations, but do I understand, upon viewing, how to negotiate my own lived conflicts effectively? No doubt I come to appreciate the power of negotiation and working well together as a team, but do I understand what to do in my own life when I can't simply "vote away" a difficult family member or friend?

While reality television seems like a recent and faddish phenomenon—entertainment for viewers, and a low-cost alternative for television networks—it begins with the beginning of television. All television programming is reality-based programming. Each participant or actor is embodying a character, more or less based on her/his life. Each show emerges from a contrived setting—whether characterized by a script or gaming rules. This blurring of boundaries is crucial—reality television is neither oxymoronic nor redundant—if we consider that "We communicate with the world, with ourselves, with our past, present, and future, via television for an average of 5 to 8 hours a day. We live in television's environment" (Weimann, 2000, p. 10).

Exploring the onto-epistemic implications of reality-based programming, questioning our own widely-held assumptions about reality and fantasy, places viewers in the position of assessing and challenging "television's environment." Viewers would do well to question how any screened reality shapes them, as well as how they serve to shape those realities.

"I Suck at This Game"

I don't know what to do. Nobody is watching Murder in Small Town X—*a fact confirmed by my students, my colleagues, my family, and* Entertainment Weekly. *My students, aware that I'm writing a piece on reality television, suggest that I switch to a "more real" reality show like* Survivor *or* Big Brother. *I feel cheated. Fox promised me the next phase in reality television; they promised the show would be scary. Call me crazy, but I think the proverbial water cooler discussions are a part of these promises, and the water cooler conversation doesn't work if I have to backfill six weeks worth of episodes. It's even harder if the conversation begins, as it usually does, with the demoralizing, "So you're the person watching that show!" Then I'm demoralized and obliged to explain why I'm watching while my bemused friend, colleague, student summarily dismisses any critical comments I make about the show as attempts to mask my guilt over watching such an awful television series. I'm beginning to think Fox is running this show just for me (and my own personal edification/degradation).*

I've been in a bit of a quandary though. Tonight is the series finale— where one of the investigators will reveal the murderer and win a fabulous cash prize—but I don't know whether I'll bother to watch it. For so long, I've been watching each week, just to see if Kristen would finally die playing "the killer's game"; now that she's gone, I'm not sure I care what happens to anyone else. For what it's worth, after two months of viewing, Kristen's name is the only one I remember. I don't know the name of the town or the names of the murdered victims. The series created itself in the crux of fictional story and contrived conflict—without the interpersonal conflict, the show collapses into a relatively uncompelling narrative. In the end, I know that these people haven't died, that a crime hasn't really been committed (yes, shameless product placement is tasteless, but still not a crime), and I don't really care if someone I don't know makes money on solving this convoluted tale. Next time, maybe I'll watch Survivor.

Endnote

1. Several articles have explored how crime television (e.g., *Cops*, *America's Most Wanted*), as a precursor to our current reality-based programming, serves to reproduce disabling stereotypes of women as victims (Consalvo, 1998; Cavender, Bond-Maupin, & Jurik, 1999; Cavender & Jurik, 2000).

References

Auslander, P. (1996). Liveness: Performance and the anxiety of simulation. In E. Diamond (Ed.), *Performance and cultural politics* (pp. 196–213). London: Routledge.

Baughman, J. L. (1992). *The republic of mass culture: Journalism, filmmaking, and broadcasting in America since 1941.* Baltimore: Johns Hopkins University Press.

Carter, B. (2001, August 6). On television; Viewers flee summer re-runs, and networks grow alarmed. *The New York Times* (Late Edition). Lexis-Nexis. August 26, 2001. Keyword: reality television.

Cavender, G., Bond-Maupin, L., & Jurik, N.C. (1999). The construction of gender in reality crime TV. *Gender and Society, 13,* 643–645.

Cavender, G., & Jurik, N. (2000) Reality crime TV: Perpetuating "woman-as-victim" fears. *Gender and Society, 28,* 4–7.

Consalvo, M. (1998). Hegemony, domestic violence, and *Cops*: A critique of concordance. *Journal of Popular Film and Television, 26,* 62–71.

Derrida, J. (1982). *Margins of philosophy.* (A. Bass, Trans.). Chicago: University of Chicago Press. (Original work published 1972)

Deleueze, G. (1994). *Difference and repetition.* (P. Patton, Trans.). New York: Colombia University Press. (Original work published 1968).

Ellis, J. (1992). *Visible fictions: Cinema, television, video.* London: Routledge.

Guattari, F. (1995). *Chaosmosis: An ethico-aesthetic paradigm.* (P. Bains & J. Pefanis, Trans.). Bloomington, IN: Indiana University Press. (Original work published 1992).

Lévy, P. (1998). *Becoming virtual: Reality in the digital age.* (R. Bononno, Trans.). New York: Plenum Trade.

Littleton, C. (2001, August 8). *Fear* motivates peacock; Gen X eyes on *Brother 2. The Hollywood Reporter.* Lexis-Nexis. August 26, 2001. Keyword: reality television.

Weimann, G. (2000). *Communicating unreality: Modern media and the reconstruction of reality.* Thousand Oaks, CA: Sage.

Contributors

Sean Baker is an assistant professor in the Department of Mass Communication and Communication Studies at Towson University in Maryland. He earned his Ph.D. from the School of Communication at the University of Washington. Sean has been fascinated with reality television for years. He wrote his master's thesis on *Cops* and continues to explore the cultural meaning in reality television.

R. Thomas Boone is an assistant professor at St. John's University in Jamaica, New York, and received his Ph.D. in Social Developmental Psychology from Brandeis University. His primary research interests include the development of nonverbal emotional communication skills and their behavioral consequences. Tom has also made two appearances on CBS's *Early Show* to talk about how his research is related to *Survivor*.

Marcy R. Chvasta is an assistant professor of communication at the University of South Florida. Her specializations include performance studies, cultural studies, and media theory. One of her fundamental and frequent research questions is, what constitutes presence in a mass-mediated society? In consideration of this question, she intently watches reality television in whatever form she can find.

Deanna L. Fassett is an assistant professor of communication studies at San Jose State University. Her research interests include communication pedagogy, auto-ethnography, and the relationship between youth violence and media influence. She freely admits that she still sucks at the social game of watching reality television, and, rather than the "real people" on TV, she prefers the company of the *X-Files* fictional duo of Scully and Mulder.

Ellis Godard is an assistant professor of sociology at California State University Northridge where he teaches statistics and research methods courses. He previously served as a lecturer at the University of Virginia, Santa Clara University, and the Pacific Graduate School of Psychology; on staff for the Center for Survey Research (Charlottesville, VA) and Applied Survey Research (Watsonville, CA); and as a research consultant to nearly a dozen firms, on both coasts. His work addresses the role of information in patterns of social control, including those observed in reality shows as well as in cyberspace.

Debora Halbert is an associate professor of political science at Otterbein College in Westerville, Ohio. Her research interests primarily focus on the social implications of intellectual property law, specifically copyright and patent law. She is the author of *Intellectual Property in the Information Age: The Politics of Expanding Property Rights* and articles on the subject of copyright that have appeared in *The Information Society, The Journal for the Semiotics of Law,* and *The Journal of the Copyright Society of the USA.* She is currently working on a second book that will evaluate possible alternatives to the expansion of copyright and patent law.

Terri Toles Patkin is professor of communications at Eastern Connecticut State University in Willimantic, Connecticut. She earned her Ph.D. and M.A. in the sociology of communication from Cornell University. Her research interests include mediated interpersonal communication, persuasion, popular culture, and the construction of virtual communities.

Kathleen M. Propp is an associate professor in the Department of Communication at Western Michigan University. She received her Ph.D. from the University of Iowa. Kathy's research interests are primarily in the areas of small group and organizational communication, focusing on decision-making processes, information processing, and the impact of status and hierarchy. Her work has been published in *Human Communication Research, Small Group Research, Communication Studies, Communication Reports, Journal of Communication Studies,* and edited books.

Marilyn Fuss-Reineck is professor and chair of the Department of Communication Studies at Concordia University in St. Paul, Minnesota. She teaches a variety of traditional, continuing education, compressed video, and online courses. A frequent presenter at professional conferences, she has published in *Communication Education* and other teaching publications. She also received the Outstanding Dissertation Award from the Family Firm Institute in 1995.

April L. Roth is an instructor at James Madison University in Harrisonburg, Virginia. She holds an M.A. from Auburn University, where she wrote her thesis on *Survivor* as a pseudo-event. She has also presented her work on reality television at both regional and international conferences. April has taught courses in public speaking, leadership, and human communication, and she has performed editorial duties for the International Listening Association.

Matthew J. Smith is an assistant professor of communication at Wittenberg University in Springfield, Ohio. He completed his doctoral work at Ohio University and is the co-author of two textbooks, *Exploring Human Communication* (written with Sue DeWine and Melissa K. Gibson) and *Online Communication: Linking Technology, Identity, and Culture* (written with Andrew F. Wood). Matt was inspired to assemble the present work in the summer of 2000 when the media hype surrounding the first *Survivor* series suggested that other scholars would be viewing and critiquing the latest forms of reality television as its popular production and consumption intensified.

Jennifer Thackaberry is an assistant professor in the Department of Communication at Purdue University in West Lafayette, Indiana. She earned a Ph.D. in organizational communication at the University of Colorado. Jennifer specializes in rhetorical and critical approaches to the study of organizational communication, with particular interests in metacommunication in organizations and political metaphors for organizational communication inquiry. Her chapter on metaphors and office politics herein is part of a larger project investigating metacommunicative translations between political metaphors for organizing and everyday talk about office politics.

Steven S. Vrooman is an assistant professor in the Department of English and Communication Studies at Texas Lutheran University. He earned his Ph.D. from Arizona State University. His research interests include issues of primitivism in film and television and in "real life" rhetoric. He has also published articles on flaming and internet culture in journals like *New Media & Society*.

Ed Wingenbach is assistant professor of government at the University of Redlands in California. His work focuses on democratic theory, political ethics, Continental philosophy, and liberalism. His articles have appeared in a range of journals and books in political science, philosophy, and political theory, including the *American Journal of Political Science, Strategies,* and *International Philosophical Quarterly.*

Andrew F. Wood is an assistant professor in San Jose State University's Department of Communication Studies. He completed his doctoral work at Ohio University. His research explores the intersection of place, memory, and power in multiple contexts. Among his publications, Andy coauthored (with Matthew J. Smith) the best-selling *Online Communication: Linking Technology, Identity, and Culture* and authored *Road Trip America: A State by State Guide to Offbeat Destinations.*

Index